Viral Hero

How to build viral products, turn customers into marketers, and achieve superhuman growth

INDIGO RIVER
PUBLISHING

Viral Hero

How to build viral products, turn customers into marketers, and achieve superhuman growth

Travis Steffen

Indigo River Publishing

Indigo River Publishing
3 West Garden Street, Ste. 352
Pensacola, FL 32502
www.indigoriverpublishing.com

Editors: Hannah Fortna and Regina Cornell
Cover and book design: mycustombookcover.com

Ordering Information:
Quantity sales: Special discounts are available on quantity purchases by corporations, associations, and others. For details, contact the publisher at the address above.

Orders by US trade bookstores and wholesalers: Please contact the publisher at the address above.

Printed in the United States of America

Library of Congress Control Number: 2019941921

ISBN: 978-1-948080-95-8

First Edition

Contents

Introduction: What Is Viral Marketing?

"The only sustainable growth is viral growth."
—Peter Thiel, Zero to One

Stop Googling "How to go viral" as if there's a magic bullet. There isn't.

If you're asking this question, chances are you don't actually know how viral marketing works. Not completely anyway—but few truly do. Which is why the first thing we're going to do before we move forward is nail down an understanding of what viral marketing is.

When somebody asks, "What is viral marketing?" the first thought most people have likely has something to do with the latest and greatest thing "going viral," whether it's a hilarious cat video or the latest Kardashian ridiculousness.

While those things might make us laugh, bring us joy, or capture our attention like a train wreck, they play merely a supporting role in the game changer that is viral marketing. If you want to spread your product and grow your business at an exhilarating rate, you'll have to broaden your horizons beyond this limited definition of virality. And it all starts by asking the right questions—which is exactly what we'll do in this book.

So You're Wondering How to Go Viral

If you have a product, website, app, or business you're working on, chances are you've had this thought: *If only I could create something for my site that spreads virally . . .*

Anyone with a working brain, diligent planning, access to a bit of capital, and a data-driven approach can achieve viral growth to *some* degree. However, few actually do to a **meaningful** degree. This is mainly because most people don't truly understand the mechanics of viral marketing.

> Here are a few things that contribute to the miseducation of the masses:

- Most resources on viral marketing are actually resources on social media strategy. They steal the term *viral* to make what they do sound sexier.

- Most "viral marketing firms" are actually production companies that specialize in creating controversial or funny videos and memes that people share. This is not viral marketing. It's a marketing channel that Gabriel Weinberg and Justin Mares call "unconventional PR" in their book *Traction*. It is essentially the purposeful use of publicity stunts to get media coverage.

What Is Viral Marketing?

I created *Viral Hero* to help entrepreneurs achieve viral success the right way. But we'd better clear up a common misconception first—that the word *viral* simply describes a piece of content that spreads like wildfire.

This is false.

Take the latest funny video on YouTube for example. While the video content is an important part of viral marketing, in this case it's actually YouTube that's experiencing viral growth, **not the video itself**. The video is just the "viral media," or the thing that's being shared to spread the site or app.

Think of it this way: So you see that latest funny video on YouTube and then send it to a few friends. As this video spreads, more and more people are exposed or reexposed to YouTube's video player. YouTube then gets more users to its site, reactivates dormant traffic, and likely sucks users in via various "recommended for you" features to get people watching even more videos. So, it's not the content or media being shared that spreads virally; it's **the application that houses it**—in this case, YouTube. The media displayed in YouTube's player is just a tool to help its application spread, and it is just a single piece of a much larger viral puzzle.

Of course, on a user-generated-content site like YouTube, content creators *can* experience some added benefit themselves from taking a ride on YouTube's "viral loop," but usually, **content creators are simply using YouTube as a medium of marketing more akin to PR** and aren't experiencing viral growth themselves.

(*Note: YouTube is unique because its user-generated-content model also allows for "channels." Content creators actually* may *see user growth in the form of channel subscribers, though this is still a feature on YouTube itself.*)

Think you can answer the question "What is viral marketing?" with certainty?

Hey now, don't get cocky.

Why "Viral" Marketing?

Viral marketing gets its name from the spread of disease. If one person is infected, the people he or she touches will likely be infected as well. Those people then infect others, who then infect others, and so on. Before you know it, there's an epidemic. Content spreads in a similar way on the web, so marketers adopted the same term.

Let's try this again. What is viral marketing?

Viral marketing is the act of leveraging your own audience to pass your website or app to their friends.

In a nutshell, viral marketing is a form of direct-response marketing in which your users are the ones who pass your message on. As you get more and more users, you will have more and more people simultaneously spreading your product, so the exposure of others to your message may—in some cases—be exponential.

This is why "going viral" is such a big deal.

Why I've Written Viral Hero

As a growth engineer, I recognize the sheer power virality has for marketing success. As such, I've focused on gaining a much deeper understanding of viral marketing mechanics so I can use these lessons to build companies. I wrote *Viral Hero* to put my thoughts down on paper, poke holes in them, allow my own understanding to evolve, and help piece the puzzle together.

I've scoured books, research papers, and blogs. I've done countless case studies and built my own viral products to test what I've learned. As I've done these things, I've dissected some of the strongest, most applicable pieces of knowledge from top founders, brilliant investors, and even top virologists in medicine. From these dry, academic, and jargon-laden resources that are more likely to bore you to sleep than inspire you to succeed, I've pieced together what I like to think is a far more approachable resource.

And now that we're hopefully all on the same page about what viral marketing is, we can move forward in our discovery of everything this resource has to offer. We've got a long way to go toward mastering virality and becoming a viral hero. But don't worry—I'm going to help you get there every step of the way. Just keep on reading.

To ensure you get maximum value from *Viral Hero,* I've created the exclusive *Viral Hero* Workbook for you to fill in as you read - absolutely free. Go get your copy right now at viralhero.com/workbook.

Part 1: What Is Viral Marketing?

Chapter 1: How to Go Viral — and Why Most Products Never Do (or Should)

Before we dive into the ins and outs of viral marketing and how you can use it to grow your business, we need to lay down some foundations.

First, let's talk about three very important words: *go*, *viral*, and *more*. These words are vital to your understanding of viral success—but not to mean what you might think.

Every site has a certain viral factor. This means that there will always be an average percentage of users who will invite others to your site or app in some way. For most sites, this percentage will never reach anything insanely high. However, even limited degrees of viral growth can make other modes of marketing much more cost effective.

Some people do happen to create a crazy rocket ship of a viral growth engine, and good for them—drinks are on those people. For everyone else, unless you're creating something like a communication or collaboration tool, **you probably won't** ***go viral.*** What's more, unless you've already built enough value to keep users once you acquire them, **you probably shouldn't.**

But can you make your site *more* viral? Absolutely. You'd really be screwing the pooch if you didn't do so as soon as humanly possible. Achieving even a limited degree of virality can drastically reduce your marketing spend on a per-user basis. It can allow you to create a more sustainable, scalable growth strategy. It can help you build a more successful business.

At which point, you'll be the one buying everyone drinks.

Some Products Can't Go Viral

One major reason most people don't create viral products is because they can't. Most business models, industries, and site structures are **not inherently viral.** The creator of such a business didn't necessarily make a mistake; it's just that the nature of the business doesn't make things easy or intuitive for users.

Often, founders will give up on virality after their product doesn't instantly spread like wildfire. Many of them get frustrated and shift their focus back to more traditional linear forms of digital marketing. After all, this is easier to understand. Dollars in, dollars out. They stop researching how to go viral entirely because, since their site isn't *currently* going viral, they believe it *can't* go viral.

Sometimes they're right. Most of the time, they're just uneducated—but it's not their fault. Viral marketing mechanics at the product-architecture level are not widely taught. They're not included in any business or technical educational curriculum, so the best education happens on the job.

The Chicken and the Egg—You Need Both Simultaneously

Most founders gain their viral marketing education *after* they've created their product. After all, most people start companies because **they have an idea**, and this idea then creates itself in the founders' minds. Unless the founders have already deeply researched viral mechanics, viral-specific architecture of their product becomes an afterthought.

What typically happens next is those founders learn a bit of the higher-level theory behind what other folks mistakenly call viral marketing (which is typically content marketing or unconventional PR). They *then* try to build in "viral carriers" (methods of sharing or sending invites such as sharing buttons or referral systems) *after* they create their site or app.

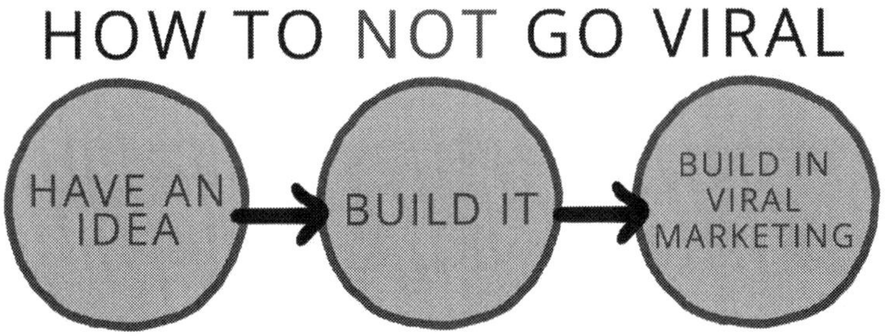

Most people don't realize their mistake until after they've created a product. However, it's not too late—when they try to make up for this mistake, their products *will* become more viral in comparison to products that don't utilize viral marketing at all, although they may never achieve the same self-driving growth engine as products with virality built in.

The Self-Driving Car of Growth

Think of cars today. There are cars you drive by hand that you must control at all times. Then there are "self-driving cars" at the forefront of technology and innovation that use things like AI and machine learning to drive passengers around automatically. Think about it:

- One of these is very hands-on, requiring the participant's constant attention.

- The other is more hands-off, with the participant subtly guiding things as needed.

True viral marketing is the self-driving car of growth. Self-driving user growth expands itself without stealing most of the growth engineer's time. Certain engines—like incentivized viral marketing—can still cost money, but it's typically far less than the pay-to-play advertising game.

As a growth engineer, your viral engine will still require you to strategically steer the ship, but if it's done correctly, your product should do the lion's share of the work for you. However, it's important to recognize that viral marketing is *not* a simple feature you can just bolt onto your product. It *must* be built deep within the core of the product. It *must* be sparked by an inherent value-driven desire your users have to invite others.

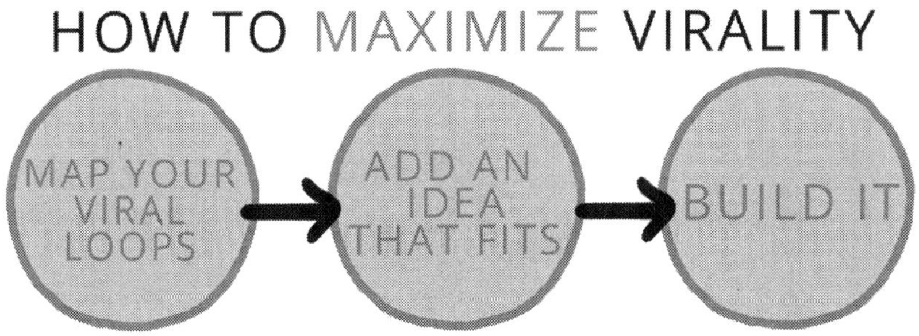

No amount of convincing users to share or bolting features or widgets onto your product will make something truly "go viral." If that's your plan, you may as well stop Googling "How to go viral" for good. It's futile.

But fear not. These actions may help make your site or app *more* viral than it was before. This can still be the difference between a massive crash-and-burn failure and a world-conquering success story.

Back to those words I mentioned at the beginning of this chapter: stop researching how to *go* viral, and shift your focus to becoming *more* viral.

Why Don't Most People Create Viral Products?
Anyone can create viral products, but few actually do. Here's why:

- **Why marketers don't do it:** Virality is something that must be engineered by people who know how to build products from the ground up.

- **Why engineers don't do it:** Most engineers can build beautiful, clean, scalable code; however, few have enough knowledge of (or interest in) how virality works. This interest is necessary for learning how to build a self-driving growth engine.

- **Why new founders don't do it:** Most new founders are so enthralled by their idea that they build it as it is in their head, without considering viral marketing. They rarely, if ever, craft simple and fundamentally sound viral architecture first and then search for ideas that fit within it.

- **Why most experienced founders don't do it:** Most experienced founders have used tactics other than viral marketing to become successful. Rather than educating themselves on a new area of marketing, they instead lean on the existing areas they've mastered.

All this is largely because the mechanics of viral marketing can be so difficult to grasp. Even most of the high-level minds out there (I'm talking top product architects and VCs) only understand about 50–60 percent of viral marketing and growth. They haven't learned how to reduce their risk or confirm that a viral engine works before investing large amounts of time or capital into it.

Basically, most VCs only understand viral marketing well enough to vet investments, and most product architects only understand viral marketing in the context of the specific products they've worked on. Even those who do understand it (this includes me) often grasp it only to a certain degree. This is largely because of factors like the complexity of the process of reporting viral growth metrics and the dramatic variability of use cases.

A good chunk of people who actually do understand the nature of viral marketing choose to all but completely ignore it. They instead focus on simpler growth engines, such as pay-per-click advertising. That said, the ease of implementation of these other forms of user acquisition has resulted in oversaturated and much more expensive growth channels. With increased competition comes higher prices, making it harder for new founders to find success with them.

Accidental Viral Growth

I know what you're thinking: *But several big-name companies* have *reached exponential virality. Was this just an accident?*

I believe so, yes. Though I doubt they'd ever admit it. All founders likely believe, or hope, their products will go viral. Does this make the successful ones geniuses? Or were they simply the lucky few?

I'm not saying these founders *aren't* brilliant, and I'm not saying they *didn't* optimize their viral loops after they witnessed users sharing their product. However, it's likely they didn't understand viral marketing on more than a rudimentary level in the beginning.

What Does All This Mean for You?

It means that armed with the right information, you can move **one step ahead** of those companies that still don't realize the power of viral marketing or don't understand how it works. After all, it's largely because viral growth is so complicated and difficult to understand that many of the few companies that do build strong viral marketing engines are later acquired for nine or ten figures.

So what do you need to know to build viral growth strategies into your product? Just keep reading.

What You Need to Build a More Viral Product

There are *tons* of variables involved in perfectly accurate viral-growth equations and predictions. To be honest, I haven't seen or created any equations that even come close to predicting completely accurate viral growth . . . yet.

But as famed statistician George E. P. Box said, "**All models are wrong; some models are useful.**"

Adding to the wonderful Mr. Box's wisdom, famed Finnish scientist Hanna Kokko compares predictive models to drawing maps. Not enough detail, and you can't successfully help travelers get where they're going. Too much detail, and those same travelers can become overwhelmed or confused.

This book will provide you with quite a bit of advice and instruction and several equations to help you both create and predict viral growth. Based on the philosophies of Box, Kokko, and myself, it stands to reason that the best way to view the formulaic approach to projecting viral growth is to shoot for just enough accuracy to help you make the best-possible decisions you can regarding which initiatives you should prioritize and how many resources you should devote to them.

Do you need exact accuracy in your models to make sound decisions? Nope. Do you need them to be reasonably accurate? Yes. This is what we're shooting for.

You'll be happy to hear that unless you're planning to pitch a strategy on going viral to a Fortune 500, **you don't need prediction equations.** You need the fundamentals. Using only those, you can start making serious progress toward a more viral product.

Here's what you need to start the process:

- A clear, engaging resource to help you understand the fundamentals

- A working knowledge of how to build your viral engine
- Tools to help you improve, systemize, and automate things along the way
- A framework to help you systematically see behavior, learn, hypothesize, continue to build your viral engine, and measure its results

So where can you find all this? Right here in this book. Sound like a plan? Okay, you're ready to begin.

Five Questions to Help Increase the Viral Nature of Your Website or App

It is important to remember **viral marketing does *not* look the same for everyone**. In fact, it often takes a very different shape for each individual product, which can make things very frustrating for the copycats out there.

To take you out of your copycat mind-set and into a place of true understanding, I've mapped out the twelve types of viral marketing, which we'll cover in the next few chapters. As we do that, keep the following five questions in mind, and pay attention to how they factor into each of the twelve viral marketing types. This will help you see how these questions will influence your own viral marketing engine too.

- **Why would my users share?**: What incentive are you offering your users to share your content with others? Is there some sort of intrinsic value of sharing? For example, will sharing make your users appear some sort of expert, somebody in-the-know, or somebody really funny?

- **What do my users get for sharing?:** Are there any extrinsic rewards that you're offering in exchange for sharing? Will users earn elevated status on your site? What about special privileges? Will they get some sort of discount, deal, or free gift?

- **What ways do I want them to share?:** Is user-sharing of this content better accomplished via a wall post on social media, a one-to-one personal email invite, an address book invite, or something different?

- **Where do I make the ask?:** Are you providing calls to action (CTAs) at the moment a user would best realize the value of sharing your content?

- **How quickly and easily does this "referral" or "invite" process occur?:** If a user follows your invite instructions, how quickly can others come to the site, become users, and start inviting others?

We'll get into all of these questions and more in greater depth as we go, but this should hopefully get you thinking about viral marketing in a clearer and more productive way, especially as it pertains to your site or app.

Don't just answer these questions in your head. Actually write your answers down in the *Viral Hero* Workbook. Don't move on until you've grabbed your free copy over at viralhero.com/workbook.

Chapter 2: Viral Marketing Engines — Foundations

Inherent Viral Marketing—How Skype and WhatsApp Used It and Got Acquired for Billions

As we begin our discussion of the twelve types of viral marketing, keep in mind that each could be a game changer for your website or product. However, the king of all types of viral marketing is **inherent viral marketing.**

So let's start there.

Inherent Viral Marketing: All Hail the King!

Few things spread faster than a well-designed value-adding viral site or app—especially when its marketing campaign adds to the user experience. Growth, at least for a little while, can be hyperbolic. Which means awesome things for your bottom line.

So everyone should use inherent viral marketing to grow, right?

Wrong.

Not every site, app, or product is inherently viral. In fact, **few are**. This isn't necessarily because you screwed up or developed poorly or because people don't like what you're providing. In fact, you may have a perfectly constructed website with a loyal, fast-growing audience that loves what you do and *still* not have an inherently viral site.

That being said, if your product *is* inherently viral, here's what that means: in a nutshell, inherent viral marketing is a form of viral marketing where people get *zero* value from your site, app, or product unless others are using it as well.

Who's Doing It Right: Skype and WhatsApp

If a product or service solves a user's problem *because* others are using it as well, **you win**. This is why inherent viral marketing is the Shangri-La of viral marketing. Few have managed to ascend to these lofty heights and return to tell the tale. But those that have often emerge with billions to show for it.

Let's use the popular VOIP and messaging app Skype as an example:

- What value do you get out of Skype when you first

download it but have no contacts? None. Skype does **absolutely nothing** for you at this point.

- The moment you send a contact request to somebody and it's accepted, you unlock a *ton* of the value Skype has to offer. You can send instant messages, place calls for free (domestically and internationally), have video calls, share screens, and more.

- But wait—what happens when you invite a second person? You then magically unlock conference call features allowing you to get *more* than two people on a call from anywhere for free.

- The more friends you add to Skype, the more value you'll get from it, and the more frequently you'll use it.

Since the core usability of Skype *only* gets unlocked when you invite others to use it with you, it's a product that should grow itself (and it did—to three hundred million users and counting).

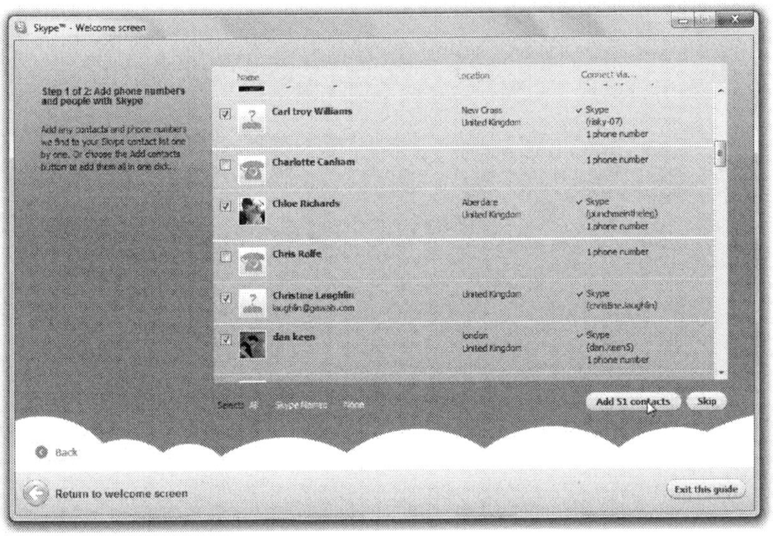

In other words, the entire value proposition of the product depends on users getting more people to use it. The more people you invite to join, the more **valuable** Skype becomes to you as a user. If you've heard the term *network effects*—or the positive effect the addition of another user of a product or service has on the value others are already getting from it—you've already been introduced to this concept.

You're then much more likely to use it regularly and maybe even unlock some of its paid features, which makes for a pretty lucrative business for Skype. (This is evidenced by Skype's being acquired by eBay for **$2.6 billion** in 2005, after only existing for two years, and then reacquired by Microsoft in 2011 for **$8.5 billion**!)

Another great example is WhatsApp. Like Skype, it's a communication tool. But instead of revolving around phone calls, WhatsApp's platform is based on the familiar UX of text messaging. But it uses the same viral mechanics as Skype.

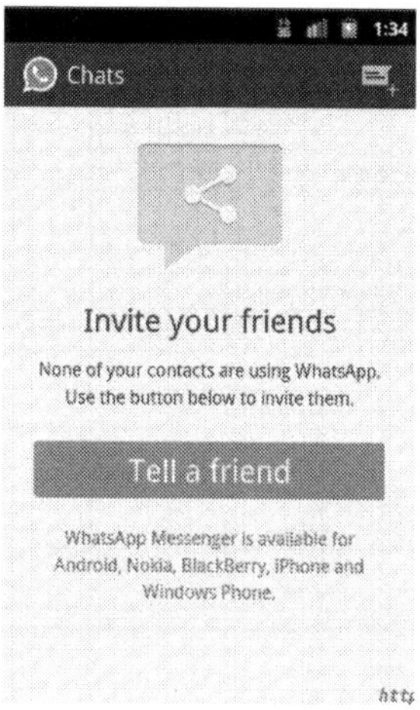

As a result, WhatsApp is another inherent viral marketing powerhouse with insane user-growth stats, which culminated in a **$19 billion acquisition** by Facebook.

So, the essence of inherent viral marketing is that **users have to share** the website or product to actually use it or to add value to their experience. Then, as the product or service starts to reach ubiquity, users essentially have no choice but to stay and continue to be active since they will actually *lose* value by leaving. That's the genius behind inherent viral marketing. It doesn't just create something cool with the hope that others will pass it on—it makes the act of inviting others **absolutely essential** to unlocking the value of the product.

How Do You Create an Inherent Viral Marketing Engine?

Okay, so now you're all set to be a billionaire. All that's left is to implement inherent viral marketing and watch the checks roll in.

Or so we'd hope.

The truth is, succeeding with inherent viral marketing is very difficult. (No one said being king was easy.) And unfortunately, if you've already built a website or app, it's most likely too late to create inherent virality. That is, unless you built in some sort of communication tool or component that only has value when used with other users—in which case you've accidentally already created an inherently viral product. Well done!

If that's not you, don't worry. You're still off to a great start by learning as much as you can about inherent viral marketing. This knowledge will provide a strong understanding of viral growth in general and help your business grow much larger as a result. In addition, it may give you some ideas for how to build future products with inherent virality in mind.

The Hard Part of Inherent Viral Marketing

Once you get the ball rolling with an inherently viral product, growth is easy. However, **getting the ball rolling is the hard part.**

Remember I mentioned how valuable an inherently viral product becomes as it approaches ubiquity? The exact opposite is true early on. There's often *very* low value for the first users of inherently viral products. It's like entering an empty room. No one likes to be the first person to a party.

However, as more people join, social proof increases drastically, and signups snowball. If you haven't heard of Metcalfe's law, it essentially states that the value of any network is proportional to the squared number of users using the network. While I personally can't speak to the accuracy of the formula, the theory is sound and applies to inherently viral products in the same way. These types of products are incredibly valuable at scale but incredibly worthless early on.

In other words, the early days of using inherent viral marketing will be the toughest you'll face. But as T. Jefferson liked to say, with great risk comes great reward.

How to Succeed Early On

There are a few things a company can do to offset the growing pains of inherent viral marketing, such as the following:

- Niche Targeting
- Brute Force
- Getting Lucky

Facebook is a great example of a company that handled this issue with grace. In its infancy, instead of existing as purely a communication tool, it was a blend of niche group communicating, self-advertising, and flirting, marketed to the college crowd one poke at a time. By confining its product to individual universities, it was easier for Facebook to grow and take advantage of niche PR (i.e., campus newspapers, blogs, and newsletters).

Of course, Facebook is also a massive example of a right place, right time, right audience, right UX perfect storm. As is the case for most viral products, **Facebook's success early on was largely accidental**.

But you don't have to narrow your focus or wait around for luck to come knocking at your door. Sheer brute force is another fine way to overcome early underuse of your inherently viral product. In other words, spend money to acquire users. After all, you won't be able to optimize your viral loop or know which subset of users is most viral unless you've got a base number of active users providing feedback and data. With a little proactive spending, you can establish a test group to pave the way for future virality.

Once you've achieved one of these approaches and survived the "viral feeding," growth can be explosive.

Viral Communication Marketing—How Apple, MailChimp, and Hootsuite Used Hotmail to Inspire Explosive Growth

Now that we've met the king of viral marketing campaigns, let's meet the rest of the court. The second type of viral marketing is called **viral communication marketing**.

Before we dig into the mechanics of viral communication marketing, let's recap. In the last section, here's what we covered:

- **Inherent Viral Marketing**—a product or service that offers zero value unless used with others and makes inviting others the key to unlocking that value.

That's the first type of viral marketing and reigns supreme as the most lucrative form. The only problem is that it is very hard to achieve.

A close second and a far easier method to implement is **viral communication marketing**.

What Viral Communication Marketing Is Not

Early on, Skype was an **exclusive two-way tool**. It was a closed system.

This means that, in order to communicate with others on Skype, both you and whoever you were communicating with had to be on Skype.

An even earlier example of a closed two-way system is the telephone. To communicate with somebody on the telephone, both parties must have (or at least have access to) telephones themselves.

On the surface, these two examples of closed systems may *seem* like they are utilizing viral communication marketing because two people are communicating. However, they lack one key component.

Viral Communication Marketing Is Inclusive

A product using viral communication marketing is not necessarily an exclusive two-way street. It's an inclusive medium. In addition to allowing two people to communicate with one another, it also touches the outside world—for example, though Skype used to require both communicators to be on Skype to have a conversation, it now lets users call outside telephone numbers not associated with the service. While this lowers the potential for explosive viral growth as the product reaches ubiquity, it can improve early growth by not forcing people to adopt the product in order to receive communication from those using it.

The key to viral communication marketing is that communication through the product must contain an **on-ramp** back to that product.

To see an example of a successful on-ramp, let's look at one of the hottest viral hits of all time.

Hotmail—the Legendary Viral Sensation

In 1995, two friends, Sabeer Bhatia and Jack Smith, came up with an idea for a free web-based email client that would eventually be called Hotmail. Their service worked like a charm, but after it exhausted a bit of traction from some niche PR on online message boards, its growth slowed.

To stay afloat, Bhatia and Smith raised a small round of venture capital from a Silicon Valley firm called Draper Fisher Jurvetson. In addition to providing some much-needed cash, this firm also had an idea that would prove imperative to Hotmail's success. Tim Draper, a partner at the firm, suggested the company include an **on-ramp** in the form of a small message at the bottom of every email sent by a Hotmail user.

The message was short and simple: "Get your free email account at Hotmail." And the last word was linked back to the site.

--
Get your free Email at Hotmail

Reflexively, Bhatia and Smith pushed back. To them, it felt like a "spammy" move. But as they began to run out of options and money, they gave in. What happened next was entirely unexpected.

In just two short years, Hotmail became far and away the world's largest email provider, boasting over thirty million members and eventually selling to Microsoft for $400 million. And it's all thanks to some brief copy and a hyperlink. (Who says financiers aren't creative?)

Viral Lessons Learned from Hotmail's Success

Hotmail is the classic example of viral communication marketing. With just one simple line of text and a link, it explained its core value proposition, solved a key need in the market at the time, and provided an easy method to learn more and sign up.

As a result, Hotmail's platform rapidly spread via user-generated communication. Users used Hotmail to send emails to other people, many of whom were not using Hotmail and were instead working with subpar emailing tools that they often had to pay for. When they received the email from a friend on Hotmail, they saw the branding below the message.

*Hmm . . . what's that? I wonder what this Hotmail thing is. Sounds cool . . . *click**

The "Get your free email account at Hotmail" on-ramp was seen **every single time** a user sent an email to somebody else. When some of those people clicked the link and became users, they suddenly became further sources of referrals with every email *they* sent.

In essence, each user became a sales rep. Each message each person sent was an endorsement. Signup rates soared. Bhatia, Smith, Draper, and everyone else involved with Hotmail high fived their way to the bank.

Where One Succeeds, Others Will Follow

Let's look at a few quick examples of companies that used Hotmail's legendary example of viral communication marketing as inspiration for their own tactics.

- Apple's iPhone-based email client includes a default signature that reads, "Sent from my iPhone," at the bottom of each user email. Sound familiar?

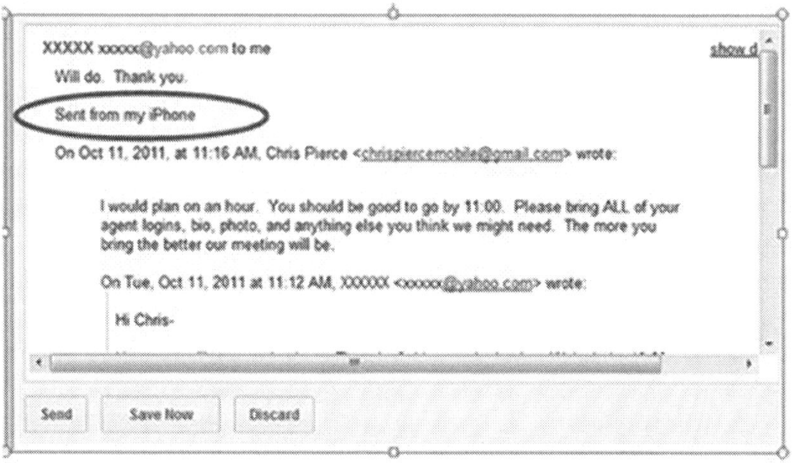

- MailChimp includes a linked graphic promoting its service at the bottom of emails sent from its free accounts. This allows MailChimp to leverage a user's own mailing list as growth engines for its product.

- Hootsuite includes a "via Hootsuite" tag next to tweets that were scheduled through its system.

Just like Hotmail, each of these three services allows you to communicate with others in various ways. Each message sent from each platform acts as a vessel that exposes the brand to others in mass quantities, many of whom become users themselves.

Starting to get the picture?

That's viral communication marketing. Think of it as network-enhanced word of mouth.

Viral Collaboration Marketing—How Dropbox, Basecamp, and Draw Something Bring Users Together

The first two types of viral marketing we've covered are incredibly powerful due largely to their high branching factor (which we'll talk more about later). However, there are still ten more types of viral marketing to get into.

Not every viral engine revolves around communication. What if you simply want to invite coworkers so you can work together to achieve a common goal?

I'm glad you asked. That's exactly what we'll cover next.

A Brief Recap

We just learned that the strength of both inherent viral marketing and viral communication marketing lies in users interacting with others while using the product so the people they share it with will become users as well. This interplay between communication and interaction with others is central to the **core value** of the product.

As we discussed, products utilizing these two types of marketing can be massive viral hits. They can become self-driving growth engines that, if executed well, can lead to giant acquisitions or IPOs. However, while many absurdly successful companies have a strong viral component, it's obvious that not every gigantic acquisition or IPO involves a product that facilitates communication between users.

In fact, most hugely viral products *don't* revolve around communication at all.

So what *do* they revolve around?

Viral Collaboration Marketing—Solve Things Together

Say you have a product that helps users solve a problem or addresses a particular pain point. Developing that product to achieve this goal has been your focus. You've finally succeeded, and your customers are satisfied. How do you know they're satisfied? Because you've surveyed your customers, and over 40 percent say they would be "incredibly disappointed if your product magically disappeared tomorrow." Not just somewhat disappointed. *Incredibly* disappointed. As a result, you've reached a major milestone and likely achieved what's called **product-market fit.** In other words, the market itself indicates demand for the solution your product provides. (Credit to Sean Ellis of GrowthHackers.com for this specific survey technique.)

Now you are ready to grow.

If your product's goal is to solve a specific problem, allowing a user to solve it on his or her own may suffice early on. But if you want to grow en masse, you're going to need more than one person using your product at a time. This can be accomplished by allowing the user to invite others to **collaborate**.

Enter **viral collaboration marketing.**

Let's explore a few examples for a better understanding of how this works.

Basecamp: When One Is Good, More Is Better

Basecamp is a simple project-management platform that allows users to get more done in a clear, simple way by effectively organizing their work. The interface is incredibly easy to navigate, and the value prop can be applied to any project anyone is working on.

People can use Basecamp by themselves to get organized on one-man projects. However, the product really shines when users add others to Basecamp to collaborate on projects.

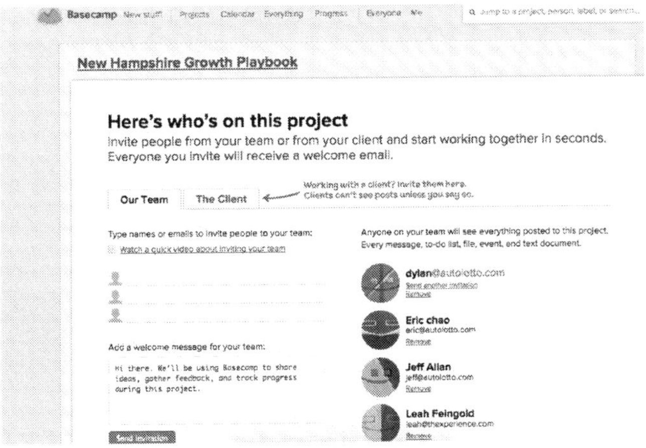

With separate user roles for teams and clients, **the value of the platform is amplified.** Users can carefully organize and manage ongoing work in a professional manner with multiple contributors to the project. Basecamp then grows virally as a result of delivering value in both a one-to-one and a one-to-many format.

Dropbox: The More We Share, the More We Have

Dropbox is a file-sharing platform that allows you to store files in the cloud to free up space on your hard drive and then access those files seamlessly across multiple devices. Users can use Dropbox individually to store and access files, but the true power behind Dropbox lies in inviting others to share and collaborate in a Dropbox folder.

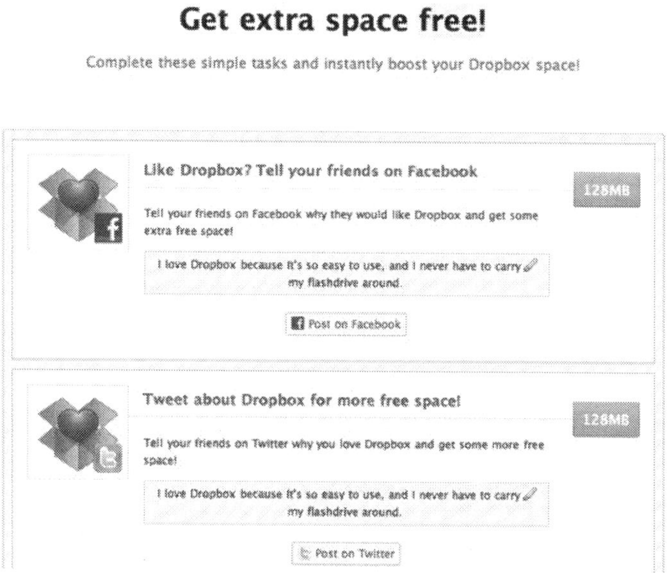
Get extra space free!
Complete these simple tasks and instantly boost your Dropbox space!
Like Dropbox? Tell your friends on Facebook
128MB
Tell your friends on Facebook why they would like Dropbox and get some extra free space!
I love Dropbox because it's so easy to use, and I never have to carry my flashdrive around.
Post on Facebook
Tweet about Dropbox for more free space!
128MB
Tell your friends on Twitter why you love Dropbox and get some more free space!
I love Dropbox because it's so easy to use, and I never have to carry my flashdrive around.
Post on Twitter

This amplifies the value of the service by saving users a ton of time and headache. Users would otherwise need to go through the painful process of trying to send files back and forth via email or some other means. With Dropbox, this is no longer necessary. Changes made by each party are reflected almost immediately on their collaborator's end.

Draw Something: Less Work, More Play

What if you don't have a B2B utility like Basecamp or Dropbox? Fear not—viral collaboration marketing doesn't need to revolve around collaborating on work. In fact, it can be utilized by any type of product that solves a problem but solves it even better when people come together. Even if that just involves sharing a laugh with friends.

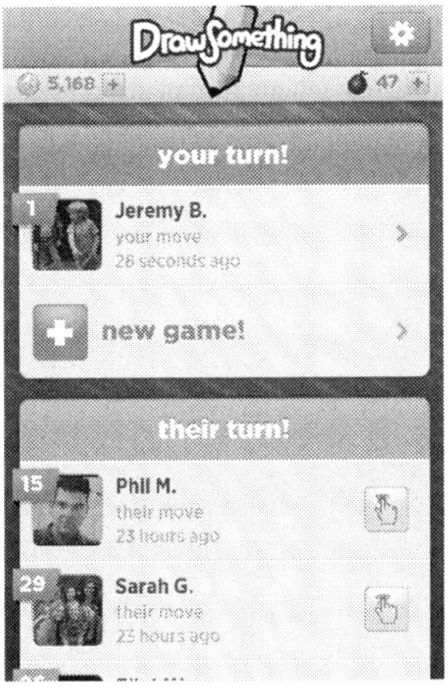

Draw Something, a Pictionary-type app developed by OMGPOP, is a game in which you guess what your friends draw on their phones in a Wheel of Fortune style. You can play with total strangers, or you can invite friends to play with you.

If these friends aren't on the app already, you can invite them from your phone's address book or via Facebook, quickly and easily. Then you can collaborate to solve puzzles and earn points.

This invite action amplifies the entertainment value of the app for you as the user. You'll be able to laugh with your friends later about the hilarious things you drew and what terrible artists they are. It's not the same value one would get from a B2B utility, but it adds value for its users nonetheless.

Viral Collaboration Marketing Is Not Inherent

It should be noted that sites or apps that leverage viral collaboration marketing are not inherently viral. This is because it's not an **absolute necessity** to invite others in order to gain value from using the product. In other words, you can use a product that implements viral collaboration marketing by yourself, without passing it on, and still get some value.

However, as with Basecamp, Dropbox, and Draw Something, the experience will be further enhanced if others get in on the fun. So the goal of any company hoping to benefit from viral communication marketing should be to make it as clear as possible that by inviting others to collaborate, users will get more from the product.

It Takes a Village to Solve a Problem

As we've discussed, viral collaboration marketing is possible when a product solves an in-demand problem in an intuitive way and others can get involved to help solve the same problem. While users can gain value from the product on their own, the value of the product is amplified when users invite others to use it too.

This shared collaboration can include the following types of users:

- Team members and coworkers
- Contractors and consultants
- Clients and customers
- Colleagues and connections
- Friends and family

Because all parties involved have a strong desire to work together to solve the problem your product addresses, your conversion rate on invites will typically be far higher than the invites sent via other forms of viral marketing.

Of course, this entire form of viral marketing hinges on the fact that you've reached **product-market fit**. That is the point at which your market indicates that your product is the preferred solution to the problem they're having. Until that time, your viral collaboration marketing campaign won't be a huge needle mover. It still may drive some growth from enthusiastic early adopters, but you should manage your expectations accordingly.

Open Viral Marketing—How Apple, Zapier, and Udemy Commanded an Army of Passionate Promoters

Next, we'll examine an often-overlooked form of viral marketing. It pretty much resurrected Apple's entire company and helped brands like Amazon and Udemy build their businesses into market leaders.

As we've seen, the basic premise of viral marketing is leveraging users to promote your product for you. If optimized well, **this viral promotion is often free**. For example, Skype effectively leverages inherent viral marketing when it requires that users invite others to the platform in order to talk.

In other cases, **viral marketing can cost some serious coin**, as we'll find out in the next chapter.

But what if there were a scenario in which **people paid *you* for the privilege of promoting your site**?

I know what you're thinking: *Wait . . . so people pay* me *for promoting my site? What poppycock! This certainly must be some sort of preposterous farce. How dare you, sir!*

I dare indeed. It's not some fantasy world. It's very real. And it's our fourth type of viral marketing.

Open Viral Marketing: The Marketplace Engine

Open viral marketing involves opening up your product to third parties, often as a distribution channel for the products they are producing.

Any viral loop, this one included, relies on the six "phases" of people:

- **Prospect**: somebody who needs the value your product provides but hasn't been exposed to your product yet.

- **Lead**: a prospect who is exposed to your product and interested enough to request more info by giving you contact details.

- **User**: a lead who, after receiving the additional info, is impressed enough to take the leap and begin using your product.

- **Acolyte**: a user who reaches an "Aha!" moment about your product's core value and has now seen enough value to stick around.

- **Advocate**: an acolyte who reaches an "Aha!" moment about your product's viral value through using your product and has now seen enough value to invite others to become users also.

- **Immune**: somebody who never needed (or no longer needs) the value your product provides, regardless of whether he or she has been exposed to your product or not.

The best part? Open viral marketing often transforms acolytes into advocates without them ever realizing it. They instead believe they're promoting a **completely different product**, either their own or another they really love. All while happily paying you to do so.

I'll use a popular example to demonstrate.

How Apple Convinced Developers to Pay to Distribute Apps on the App Store

Let's say you're a huge fan of Instagram's app for the iPhone. You want one of your photographer friends to post photos more frequently, so you share the link to Instagram's app with that friend. Your friend installs it.

But wait—you've shared a link to Instagram's app **on the App Store**. Your friend has now seen the value in this Apple product *and* become a user of it.

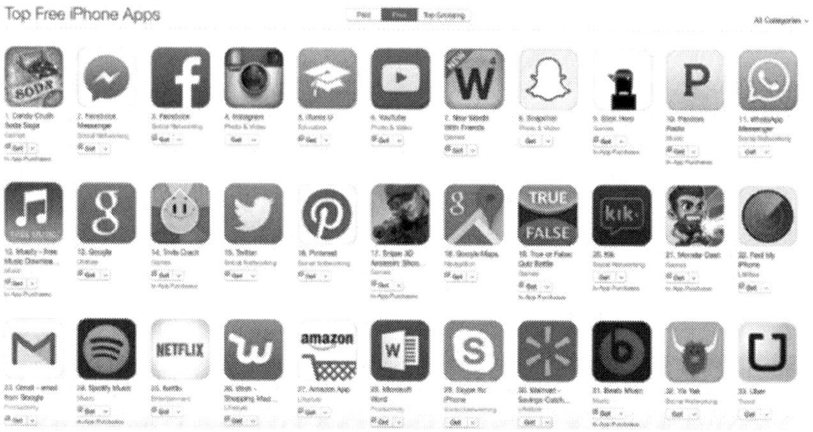

This, my friend, is **open viral marketing in action**.

The high viral value of this method provided early success to Apple as app developers continued to build tools (i.e., apps) for their various devices. Apple had so *much* success that it decided to **charge developers an annual fee** for a developer account. Since nearly all these developers could make more than ninety-nine dollars per year (the cost of a developer account), they were more than happy to buy in.

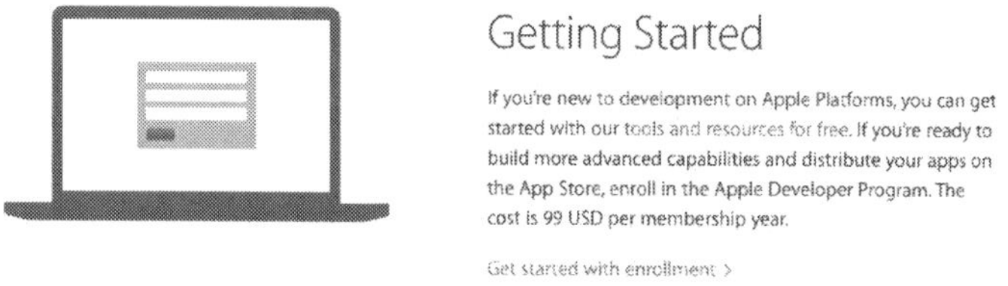

Getting Started
If you're new to development on Apple Platforms, you can get started with our tools and resources for free. If you're ready to build more advanced capabilities and distribute your apps on the App Store, enroll in the Apple Developer Program. The cost is 99 USD per membership year.
Get started with enrollment >

This financial investment had the double effect of ensuring content creators felt invested enough to promote their apps in order to offset their operational costs—which is just another way of saying they were enthusiastically paying to promote Apple's services.

These app developers work hard to promote the App Store by promoting their own apps because they have a **direct financial interest in**

doing so. As a bonus, great app developers **leverage viral marketing themselves** from within their own apps—which places millions of smaller viral loops within Apple's larger viral loop.

Here's how open viral marketing works in a nutshell:

- Developers pay Apple for the right to distribute apps on Apple's platform.
- Those people actively promote Apple's App Store by promoting their own apps.
- Many of those apps have their own viral loops, which increases the power of Apple's larger viral loop.
- Apple also makes a commission on every paid app purchase and in-app purchase.

Simply put, Apple's App Store and iTunes products are two of the most pure and profound examples of open viral marketing in history.

But there are other effective examples that have helped brands command the marketplace.

Viral-Success Story: YouTube

YouTube is a great example of open viral marketing. Content creators often have a direct or indirect financial interest in promoting their own video content. In doing so, they spread the YouTube brand in the process of spreading their own videos.

People who see the media YouTube users create are then exposed to YouTube (i.e., prospects transitioning to leads). A few of them then want to create videos themselves and sign up (i.e., leads transitioning to users).

Like Apple, YouTube has become so popular as a discovery engine that users often *pay* YouTube to promote their videos *on* YouTube (i.e., YouTube ads).

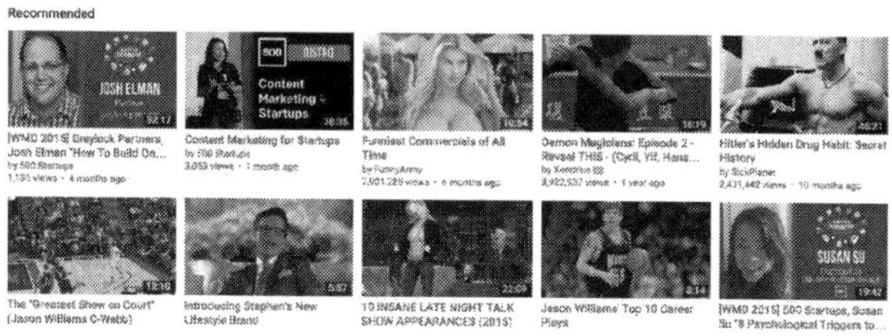

(*Note: I often get asked about the distinction between* viral media *and* open viral marketing. *There are a ton of similarities. However, one difference is that* ***viral media can also be created by the internal team,*** *while open viral marketing* always *involves user-generated assets and relies on the value of users self-promoting those assets.*)

Viral-Success Story: Udemy

Udemy is a much more niche example. This successful online course creator uses a similar open-viral-marketing strategy as Apple, in that course creators can create and sell courses on Udemy for a profit.

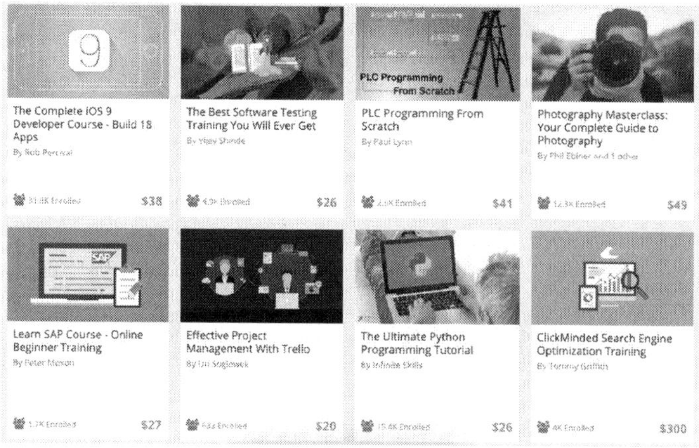

However, since the course-creation process is typically done start to finish by individuals rather than companies with staffs and marketing budgets, the user-driven viral loops are nowhere near as prolific.

To fuel its open-viral spread a bit more, Udemy recently began **giving up its commission** on user-generated sales. The goal is to increase user promotion. The hope is that new users who come to Udemy will be more likely to buy other courses or create courses themselves, thus spreading the platform's reach.

Viral-Success Story: Zapier

Zapier is a unique case of open viral marketing. Catering exclusively to B2B customers, Zapier provides software companies an easy engine for integrations. It's essentially become the "App Store" for service-to-service integrations.

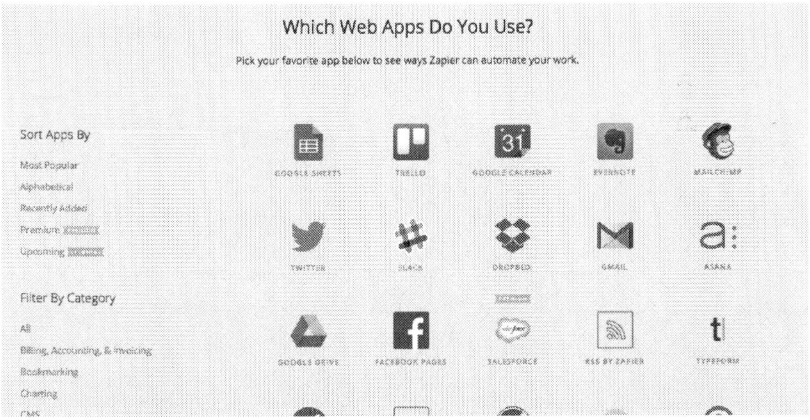

Companies typically become users on Zapier first, discovering new and powerful applications to help their businesses. They then often decide to open their own APIs to Zapier, allowing for integrations they can likewise promote to their own users on Zapier.

A company that uses Zapier adds value to its own users. It also becomes an asset creator for Zapier. Every user who then integrates that company's product will not only get a better experience but will be **exposed to Zapier's entire marketplace of integrations**. Users then find other sites to integrate with. Or better yet, they create integrations with their own platforms' APIs, if they have them.

In other words, open viral marketing is awesome.

To explore how the products you use—or even your company—can leverage these foundational viral engines, go through the various questions in the *Viral Hero* Workbook. Get your free copy at viralhero.com/workbook.

CHAPTER 3: VIRAL MARKETING ENGINES — SUPERCHARGERS

Viral Incentive Marketing—How Dropbox and PayPal Injected Steroids into Their Viral Marketing

The first four growth engines we covered are largely self-driving. Users invite others because it's obvious the value they get from a product is amplified by recruiting others, or they pay you to promote your product because it helps them advertise their own products. But what if the dynamics of your site don't include inherent viral marketing, viral communication marketing, viral collaboration marketing, or open viral marketing?

We've now arrived at one of the most powerful performance-enhancing drugs of viral marketing. Most products usually use only one of these first four forms of viral marketing; however, the next one *can* and *should* be utilized by pretty much every site or service trying to grow. It's called **viral incentive marketing.**

The Answer to "Why the Hell Should I?"

Let's assume you ask a user to invite others to your product. You have a solid product, and you ask them nicely in a ton of different places on your website to take action. You should be set, right?

Wrong.

You'll likely get a few shares from friends, family, and enthusiastic early adopters. However, for a significant percentage of your users (depending on how close you are to product-market fit), their knee-jerk reaction will almost always be something along the lines of the following:

- *Nope.*
- *This is annoying. I'm outta here.*
- *Why the hell should I?*

Not every user will feel like this, **but many of them will.** These are *exactly* the people we're targeting with **viral incentive marketing.**

The Six Categories of People

Remember the six "phases" of people from chapter 2? Your viral-incentive campaign should be the carrot you use to push acolytes to become advocates. The majority of your advocates will be acolytes first. If this is *not* the case, it means you have powerful incentives that compensate for a lack of product value. That's when you get people **gaming the system.**

Turn Acolytes into Advocates

Here are a few things to consider:

- **If acolytes aren't becoming advocates at all,** evaluate the value you're providing them. Do your research on what they want, what problems they're having, and what they truly find remarkable enough to talk about. Communicate with them as much as you can. Then make improvements accordingly.

- **If acolytes are leaving instead of becoming advocates,** you're likely being spammy or annoying. Your negative methods of acquiring shares or referrals are outweighing users' perceptions of the value you're providing. Go back to focusing on adding value, and *only* ask for shares or referrals when users feel good about their experience (typically when they first see the benefits you offer).

- **If acolytes are on the fence about becoming advocates,** you're likely offering solid value and not being overly invasive. However, you're just not quite where you need to be to push them over the edge.

Dealing with this last group is where incentivized viral marketing can shine. It can help convert those on-the-fence users from squeamish naysayers to loyal acolytes yelling your brand's name from the rooftops. However, the *degree* to which this happens will depend largely on the following:

- How **valuable** your product or service already is
- How **valuable** your additional incentives are
- How **relevant** your incentives are to the perceived **core value** and **viral value** of your product

(*Note: If you're starting to see the word* value *appear everywhere in this book, you're not crazy. Perceived value is an underlying foundation of viral marketing.*)

With and Without Viral Incentive Marketing

It's important to realize you're engaging in an implied conversation with users at all times. Depending on the scenario, the conversation can look quite different.

Scenario 1: You have *not* reached product-market fit.

YOU: *Do you like our product?*

USER: *No.*

YOU: *Well . . . shit.*

Work on creating more value until you reach product-market fit. (In other words, until users answer "hell, yes" to this question.)

Scenario 2: You *have* reached product-market fit.

YOU: *Do you like our product?*

USER: *Yes.*

YOU: *Will you invite others?*

USER: *Why the hell should I?*

YOU: *Because it's pretty and I'm nice to you.*

USER: *Umm . . .* [Awkwardly robot-walks out of the room.]

If you can't provide anything but a creepy and unsatisfactory answer to "why the hell should I?" you're failing.

Scenario 3: You've reached product-market fit, *and* you're using viral incentive marketing.

YOU: *Do you like our product?*

USER: *Yes.*

YOU: *Will you invite others?*

USER: *Why the hell should I?*

YOU: *If you do, you'll get *INCENTIVE.**

USER: *Seriously? Rock on! Okay, I definitely will.*

See the difference? This is a much more complete conversation that leaves both parties feeling satisfied.

Viral Incentive Marketing Done Right

The most effective viral incentives you can offer users are rewards that augment the core value that brought users to the product in the first place.

Think of any of the referral programs you've experienced. Many involve cash, which is typically why they fail, because this incentive doesn't blend with the product's core value and doesn't augment the experience you came for. Others provide an extrinsic benefit such as a discount, deal, or file download in exchange for inviting others to join a service or use a product. This works a bit better.

But the real veteran move is providing **a significant augmentation of your product's core value.**

Take **Dropbox** for example.

- Dropbox lets users store files and access them across all devices (this is Dropbox's core value).

- Users share the service because they want friends to easily have access to and be able to update those files.

- Dropbox then adds an **incentive**: for every person you invite who signs up, you get 500 MB of free space.

Get more space
You currently have 2.25 GB of Dropbox space.
Upgrade your account
Upgrade to Dropbox Pro to get the most space
50 GB
or more
Refer a friend to Dropbox
Spread the love to your friends, family, and coworkers
16 GB
500 MB per friend
Connect your Facebook account
Share folders with your friends and family in a snap
+ 125 MB
Connect your Twitter account
Invite your friends to Dropbox with a tweet
+ 125 MB

Dropbox's viral-incentive-marketing campaign rewards users with an augmentation of the reason why those users originally wanted Dropbox. The company expertly blends its core value with its viral value, and *that* is what makes the program so effective.

How effective? **Try over three hundred million users.**

When C4R Actually Works

A **Cash for Referrals** (C4R) program seems solid in theory. After all, you can pay people to do just about anything.

However, while you *might* get referrals, the actual **business value** (i.e., customer lifetime value) of the users you gain from C4R will most likely *not* be significant. While you may get new signups from a C4R system, you'll also get a lot of people gaming the system for a quick buck. As a result, your ROI will plummet.

But what if the transfer of money is the core value prop of your site?

Take **PayPal** for example. PayPal has actually seen success with a C4R viral-incentive-marketing campaign because the value it provides users is a means to transfer money to others.

By dropping twenty dollars into a user's account for inviting a friend to use its service, PayPal provides that user a risk-free method of trying out the service without depositing any funds. The value of money is something everyone knows, so this tactic massively increased PayPal's conversion rate of on-the-fence users to loyal repeat users.

Referral Bonus FAQ

What is PayPal referral bonus?
PayPal referral bonus is a bonus specifically set up for current users who successfully refer a friend to sign up with PayPal. Whenever such friend successfully signs up with PayPal through your referral link or PayPal logo and get verified, your PayPal account will be deposited with such referral bonus.

But that's not all.

Early on, PayPal used a "twenty dollars for you, twenty dollars for your friend" viral-incentive-marketing campaign to increase user-referral rates even further. Some users don't want to invite others if the reward is one-sided—**they feel guilty profiting from exploiting their friends.**

By providing an added incentive for the invitee as well, PayPal negated the guilt factor, which made it far more likely that referrals would occur.

(Note: PayPal did still see a tremendous number of "users" trying to game their C4R system. This ended up being the Russian Mob, and it came close to tanking their company early on.)

Using a Product Incentive / C4R Hybrid

DraftKings is a hybrid example of a company running a successful C4R viral-incentive-marketing campaign. Earning cash is part of their core value prop, but DraftKings (a fantasy-sports-contest provider) found a way to "monetarily" reward user invitations without the risk of bleeding the company dry.

Instead of adding free money to user accounts, DraftKings opted to use what they call "DK Dollars." They play the same as real money, but you have to use them on the site and can't withdraw them to your bank account.

Does DraftKings factor this into their cost of user acquisition? Of course. Those users can use DK Dollars to play in real games, and they (or their opponents) will win real money in return. However, the company knows these DK Dollars are spent giving new users value and that these users gain tangible value for inviting others.

Stay True to Your Core

Although C4R is attractive in theory, I stand by the assertion that the most cost-effective and powerful form of viral incentive marketing is a campaign that blends your site's core value prop with the value prop of your reward. If cash isn't part of your core value prop, **don't just settle for a lazy option** like C4R.

There's a better solution out there if you put a little brainpower into it.

Try incentives like additional access to your product, a discount, a free addition to an order, or a resource users couldn't otherwise get. If you have to **create a reward** specifically for your viral-incentive-marketing campaign, *do it*. It's absolutely worth it.

Remember also that viral incentive marketing is much more effective when the reward is two sided (i.e., a reward for the inviter *and* the invitee). This ensures inviters don't get negative feelings from taking advantage of friends. Instead, they feel as though they're adding real value to those who would truly be interested in the product or service.

How You Can (and Should) Benefit from Incentive Marketing

In summary, viral incentive marketing is the act of offering a specific incentive or reward for spreading the word about or inviting others to your site, app, or service. Ask the following questions to determine how to best put viral incentive marketing to work for you and inject a welcome dose of performance enhancement into your viral marketing:

- Why did users come to you in the first place?

- What problem are you solving for them?
- What's the core value for inviting others?
- Is there a way you can add even more value to your solution through a reward?

In my experience, viral incentive marketing is most underutilized in e-commerce, where *everyone* has a product to sell and *almost* everyone can offer a **discount code**. If you can, why wouldn't you?

Embeddable Viral Marketing—How YouTube Grew Faster than Any Company Ever

In this section, we're going to shift our focus to a type of viral marketing that's a bit different from viral incentive marketing, primarily because there's no tangible incentive encouraging users to share. It's called **embeddable viral marketing**.

Remember the six types of people we talked about in the last section? Here's how they fit into **the basic trajectory that every type of viral** marketing follows:

- A prospect is exposed to a product through an existing advocate within his or her network.
- The prospect is interested enough to request more info, becoming a lead.
- The lead is interested enough to begin using the product, becoming a user.
- The user, with an "Aha!" moment, realizes the core value of the product, becoming an acolyte.
- An acolyte reaches a second "Aha!" moment when he or she realizes the *viral* value of the product and sends one or more invites to his or her network, becoming an advocate.
- Rinse and repeat.

The mechanics of each type of viral marketing differ in where, why, when, to whom, and how advocates are exposed to the product. This is where embeddable viral marketing shines.

Why Do Most People Mistakenly Think That Videos Are What Goes Viral?

Let's get back to something I mentioned in the introduction of this book.

When people ask me what I do for a living, I typically say something about viral growth mechanics and growth engineering. Most people smile, nod, and ask the same question: *So when you say "viral" . . . you mean like a viral video?*

YouTube's imprint on society is ever apparent. Much like the common misconception that every type of facial tissue is a Kleenex, YouTube has created ubiquity with terms it's coined describing parts of its viral loop. Before YouTube, nobody would have associated the word *viral* with the term *viral video.*

I Say Viral, You Say Video

Before YouTube, people would probably have connected the phrase *viral growth engineer* to something more obvious. **Like . . . maybe . . . a virus.** But now, thanks to YouTube, no one associates what I do with transmitting infectious diseases. (Admittedly, this is a good thing.)

Don't get me wrong, I love that the term *viral* is now linked with *video* rather than with diseases. It allows me to do my job without my family constantly thinking I work for the CDC. However, it does breed a misconception that can hinder the effectiveness of a company's viral marketing, which I do not love.

Let's get one thing clear: when a video gets spread across the web, **the video is *not* what's going viral.**

So what is?

The Incredible Embeddable Product

Embedding describes taking a third-party product and plastering it right into your product as if it were a native part of your product's user experience. On the web, this usually involves the third-party product (such as a video player or an interactive tool) providing code that users can copy and paste onto their own websites. After a user does this, that third-party product lives on the user's website as a natural feature.

Utilizing embedding was a key reason YouTube blew up seemingly overnight. It allowed YouTube to spread virally early in its lifecycle. However, it didn't stop at just embedding. YouTube made **one key addition** that transformed plain old embedding into embedded viral marketing.

What YouTube Did

YouTube didn't start out as a video platform. Originally, it tried to be a dating service similar to Hot or Not, which had recently taken off as a massive viral sensation (more on this later). YouTube wanted in on some of that viral action, but rather than building its dating service around a photo platform, it decided to focus on videos. (Everyone knows it's easier to judge hotness when it's moving. That's just math.)

However, the founders quickly saw that most of YouTube's users were using the product primarily for one of its more innovative features—uploading and streaming videos—rather than as a dating site. They wisely made the decision to "listen" to this feedback and embrace the trend.

After that, YouTube went to work. Soon it came up with a platform that provided a quick, easy, and free way for you, the user, to upload your own videos onto the internet without having to host them yourself. Others could then watch the videos and share them via links to each video's hosted page on YouTube's website.

Alternatively, you could grab the **embed code and paste it onto your own website**.

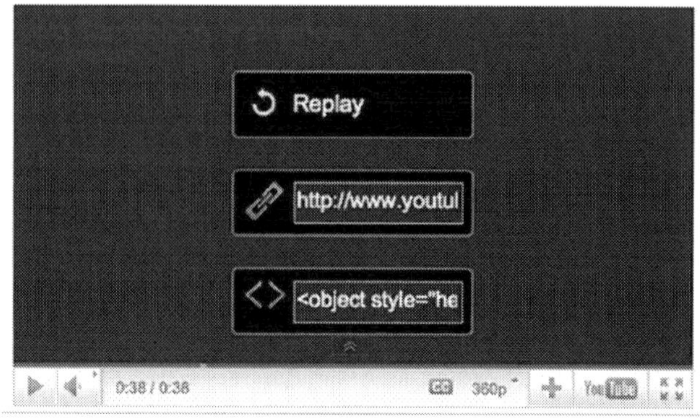

As you can see in the image above, with YouTube's new video player, three options appeared after a video was done playing:

- Play the video again
- Copy the video's link to send it to friends or to link text to it on a web page
- Copy the embed code to paste in so visitors could stream the video right on your web page

This simple offering was revolutionary. Not only could users benefit from a ready-made video player, but they didn't have to pay an arm and a leg to host large files on their sites.

Why Embedding Worked for YouTube

First and foremost, the entire platform offered substantial value to YouTube's market. Its product solved a real problem users were experiencing (i.e., it often took hours or days to download a video file and even longer to send one). And it solved this problem in a simple, low-friction way.

Sending links to hosted pages was a massive viral hit. However,

YouTube's true power was the embedding of the video player on a user's website. Suddenly, YouTube's player hijacked the audiences of every single website that decided it wanted to add a video, thereby exposing YouTube's product offering to millions upon millions of people practically overnight.

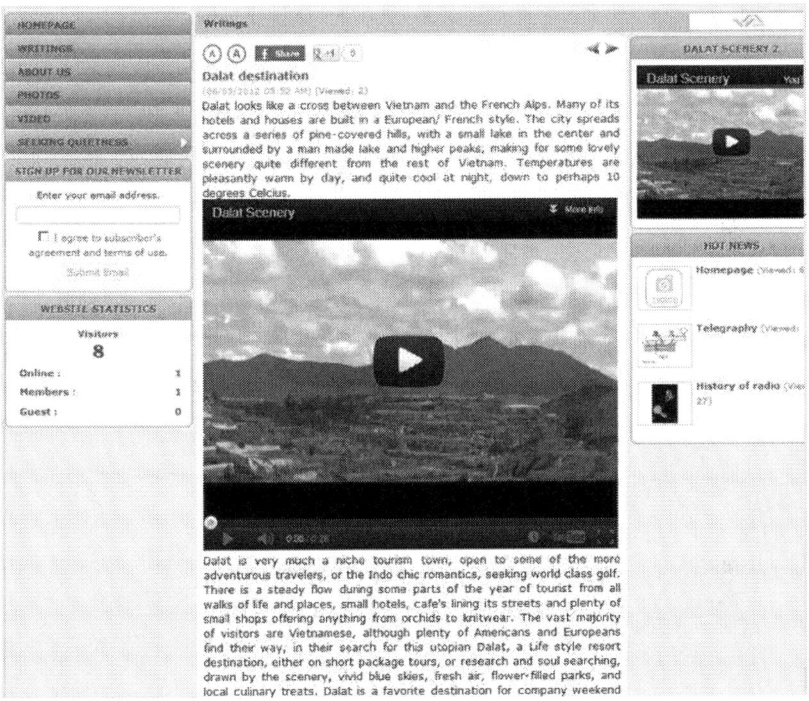

But **the embedding itself wasn't the secret sauce.** Remember when I mentioned that YouTube didn't stop at embedding? Nope—like a true viral superstar, YouTube took it to the next level:

- **YouTube's player showed its logo** on the bottom corner of every embedded video.

- **This logo linked back to the hosted version of the same video on YouTube's own site.** Neither the embedder nor the visitor minded because the link led to the same content anyway, and visitors were able to decide to seek more information *if* they chose (in other words, it wasn't forced down their throats).

- After every video (whether embedded or hosted), YouTube's player provided a **shareable link** and an **embed code.** The shareable link would *always* point to the hosted page rather than the page it was embedded on.

Most importantly, everything was done under the guise of users making conscious decisions. Nowhere in this experience were users shown anything they didn't want to see, and nowhere were they routed somewhere they didn't want to go.

A Voluntary Nudge in a Profitable Direction

The path a viewer takes while watching a YouTube video is always voluntary, but it *always* leads back to YouTube's website. Once there, visitors discover even more videos and learn how to upload their own.

In a nutshell, a video on YouTube functioned as what's called **viral media**. This is the content shared by a user to effectively demonstrate the value of the product. In YouTube's case, the viral media was essentially a way to demo the value and function of its video player to millions of people.

So I ask again, if the video is *not* what's going viral, what is?

It's YouTube. With every video that's uploaded and shared, YouTube is the one that leverages its own loyal users to expose its product to or infect new users (or reinfect dormant users).

Key Mechanics of Embeddable Viral Marketing

The short and sweet definition of embeddable viral marketing is embedding tools or content that adds value to users *while* serving as a demo of your product. **This includes generating a link** that allows additional users to add the tool or content to their own sites.

The content is typically the viral media, **not the product itself.** The viral media serves as a vessel through which to demo the product. This viral media (which we'll get into more later) can take a few different shapes.

- **It can be internal or curated,** such as the sharing tool from SumoMe.

- **It can be user generated in real time,** such as the conversation in a live-chat tool like Olark.

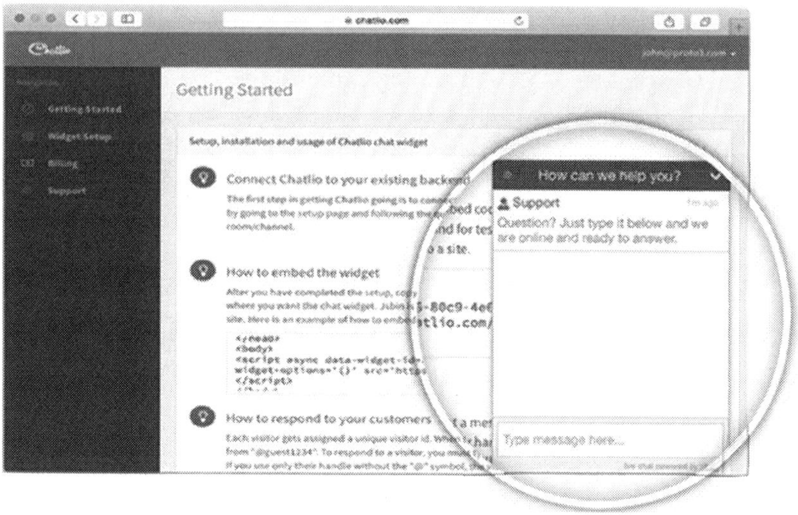

- **It can be user generated prior to being embedded,** such as a video from YouTube or a slide-based presentation from SlideShare.

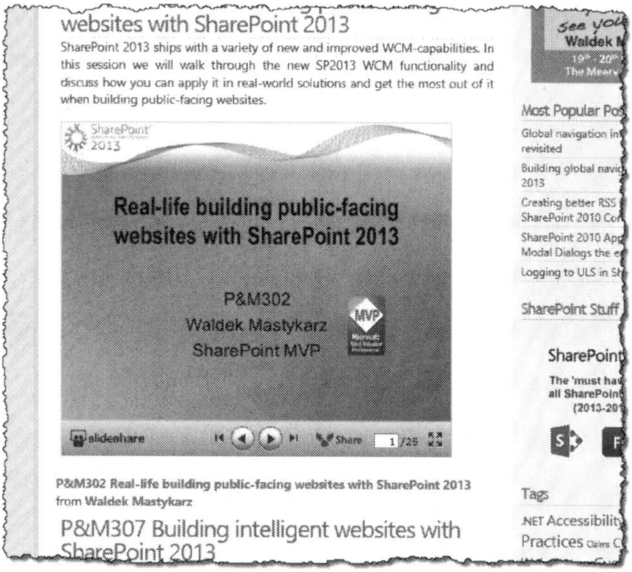

When new users see embedded viral media, the content (ideally) adds value to those users in various ways. This value is independent of the product. The product adds extra value by showcasing the media in a specific way, but the media itself can be a utility for entertainment, education, or anything in between. Ultimately, the way the viral media is consumed is always dictated by the product that transmits it.

Let Viral Media Show You the Way

Some users who see viral media instantly think of ways they could do something similar for their own purposes. This is where including the logo and link in an unobtrusive way becomes valuable. This subtle branding provides users a **quick and easy roadmap** to where they can learn more and potentially use the tool themselves.

With embeddable viral marketing, **the viral loop often looks something like this**:

1. You add viral media to a product you plan to embed (if applicable).
2. You embed the product within your own product.
3. Your users gain value from the embedded product through interacting with the media it contains.
4. Some of those users see the value of the product and want to use it as well.
5. Those users click the linked logo and proceed to the embedded product's site.
6. Those users embed the same tool on their sites with their own context-specific viral media.

7. Rinse and repeat.

Can you see how **powerful** something like this can become? If your product is valuable to users, if your linked path back to your site is unobtrusive, and if you listen to users and adapt to optimize this process, the sky's the limit.

Viral Signature Marketing—How WordPress, Typeform, and Zendesk Dominated Their Industries

You're likely starting to see some strong similarities between the various forms of viral marketing. Likewise, the next method we'll cover—**viral signature marketing**—works in a similar way to embeddable viral marketing.

With embeddable viral marketing, users experience a third-party product, notice how their own users can benefit from exposure to that product, and include it in their own product's user experience (e.g., embedding YouTube videos). This ultimately provides an on-ramp back to the third-party product's site (e.g., a link back to YouTube). As I said, viral signature marketing is similar to embeddable viral marketing, but it does possess a few key differences that influence **who** can implement it and **how** it can be enacted.

So what exactly are these differences?

Where the Third-Party Product Lives

The primary difference between embeddable viral marketing and viral signature marketing is not how the tool is used but where it lives. In other words, think about this question: Does your entire user experience live within your site, or do you bounce users out to a third-party location and then bring them back in?

If you've got a website and you're bolting on additions as if they're native experiences (like a video from YouTube), this is typically embeddable viral marketing. However, if you have a page on your website that's hosted elsewhere, *or* your entire website is built using a third-party tool, this is viral signature marketing.

But page location is not the only definer of viral signature marketing.

The Key Component of Viral Signature Marketing

An additional requirement of viral signature marketing is some sort of "signature"—for example, something like "Powered by PRODUCT NAME." This signature is then linked back to the third-party site. If this signature doesn't exist, it's not viral signature marketing. In fact, **it's not viral marketing at all** because users have no way of automatically passing it on to others.

For example, if you're using a website builder that you can completely white label so most visitors will never know what it's built on—this is *not* viral signature marketing. However, if the site you build using the tool includes a signature saying something like "Powered by WordPress" that's linked to a place where visitors can also use the service to build their own websites—that's viral signature marketing.

Viral Signature Marketing Done Right

Here are a few strong examples of viral signature marketing at work:

- Recurring billing platforms like **Chargify** and **Recurly** and affiliate marketing platforms like **ClickBank** use viral signature marketing via their hosted checkout screens. For example, users are exposed to the Chargify brand via "example.chargify.com" in the URL bar or a "Powered by Chargify" message at the bottom of the payment page. When users are done paying, they're dropped back onto the original site. (The first two also offer embeddable options. ClickBank is less subtle, and the entire checkout screen is very visibly branded as ClickBank.)

- **PayPal** uses viral signature marketing through its hosted payment forms. On a site's checkout screen, users click a button that says, "Pay with PayPal." They are then taken to a hosted checkout page on PayPal's website to pay for the goods. After paying, users are typically dropped back onto the original website. (This branded payment button is also a form of embeddable viral marketing.)

- **Typeform** and **SurveyMonkey** use viral signature marketing on their hosted surveys. (Both of these have embeddable options as well.)

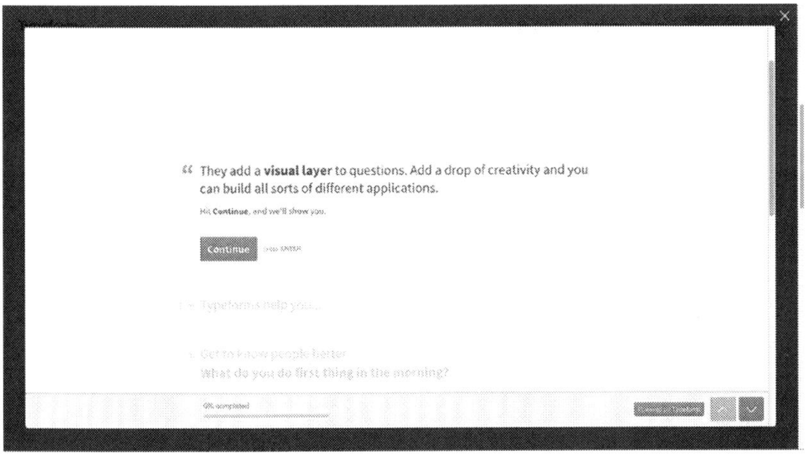

- **Zendesk** and **Groove** use viral signature marketing on their hosted customer-service tools (though again, both have embeddable options).

- **WordPress** and **Shopify** both have fully hosted website-builder options (and surprise, surprise—both also have options you can install and host yourself, which is a form of embeddable viral marketing).

Should I keep going?

Three Things to Remember

- Prospects **actively demo** all these products *while* getting value out of them through the use of another product—which is a strong conversion tactic. This allows prospects to visualize how they may be able to do the same thing for their own products.

- If prospects like what they've seen while demoing the product within another experience, this is another strong conversion tactic—especially if that experience is smooth and effective.

- Almost every example of viral signature marketing I've listed above **also has an embeddable option**. This is because not every user will want a hosted option, but the company behind the tool will want to keep leveraging viral marketing in some way. You'd be wise to do the same.

Some services allow users to "white label" their tools. This means you can actually remove their clickable branding element if you are willing to pay for the privilege. This is typically a desired feature if your linked branding element is an eyesore.

Alternatively, services like PayPal have created such incredible trust that site owners actually *want* to display their branding because it gives them a conversion lift on their checkout screen. Such a level of trust is something we all aspire to but only a handful ever succeed at.

Viral Transaction Marketing—How Spotify, MapMyRun, and Kickstarter Created Viral Powerhouses

Have you ever watched a video or been more willing to use a product because someone told you about it or you saw a bunch of other people watch or use it before you? Several forms of viral marketing heavily leverage this inherent tendency of human behavior, including the type we'll cover next.

Keep reading to tap into the power of social proof.

Endorsement through Achievement

When users take certain actions by using a product or service, those actions are often perceived as "achievements" to those around them. Our next type of viral marketing showcases these achievements publicly without overtly forcing them down anyone's throat. The result is a positive brand image and explosive growth.

Welcome to **viral transaction marketing**.

To understand the basic driving force behind viral transaction marketing, ask yourself these questions:

- How did you discover your favorite restaurants?
- How did you first hear about your favorite new band?
- What inspired you to travel to your most recent vacation destination?

Likely, you received some sort of a recommendation or review. Based on this, you probably gained enough confidence (or desire) to try that new thing yourself. These endorsements, whether from friends or online, are ways to "derisk" ourselves, because we trust the judgment of others. (Will trying the new sushi place around the corner be enjoyable or a huge disappointment? Yelp to the rescue!)

Most of us are followers in this way. Not because we can't make our own decisions but because we simply don't have the time or ability to make well-informed decisions about every product or experience out there.

These referrals and recommendations act as **filters**. The bad experiences are shared with us, and we avoid them like the plague. The good ones rise to the top, and we end up eating some delicious spicy tuna rolls.

Connect with Referrals

To a degree, all viral marketing stems from referrals. Viral transaction marketing, however, took things to a whole new level once social media came along.

Take music for example. Do you ever feel an odd sense of pride when you play a song you really love for a friend that they've never heard before? How do you feel when that friend absolutely loves it? Probably pretty good. After all, in that person's eyes, you've now become a **tastemaker**.

But what if that friend hates it? Do you find yourself trying to convince them they're wrong by playing other tracks by the same artist until they have no choice but to admit you're a musical wizard?

Most of us have felt this way at some point. It all stems from our desire to feel like a tastemaker or trendsetter.

Thanks to social media, we can now amaze many more than one friend with our impressive tastes. This is exactly what the digital music service Spotify took advantage of in its journey to becoming a viral powerhouse.

How Spotify Turned Users into Tastemakers

In the early days of Spotify, users logged in to the service with Facebook. As they listened to new music, they could **broadcast** on their Facebook newsfeeds what they were listening to on Spotify. Facebook users could then check out what their friends were listening to and **get on Spotify to hear it themselves**.

With a single click from its users, Spotify got their permission to share *what* they were doing *as* they were doing it with their Facebook friends. The users were fine with this because they loved being considered music aficionados. The more friends who "liked" what they were listening to, the more they felt they were in-the-know tastemakers. And since this broadcast was a wall post, the branching factor—or individual invites sent per invite session—was *huge*. (We'll talk more about branching factor later.)

To ensure all this worked well, Spotify was wisely transparent about what it was doing. In the past, certain black-hat sites and apps found ways to auto-post for users or auto-invite users' friends without being forthcoming or honest about it. While you as a company might get some **short-term benefits** by being shady like this, the bad perception you generate about your brand is hardly ever worth it. So it's better to follow Spotify's lead.

How Spotify Became the Pied Piper of Viral

You know the Pied Piper—that guy who induced others to follow him by enticingly playing his musical pipe? Spotify works kind of like that, only on a much more engaging scale. And those being drawn in by the music (Spotify's, not the Pied Piper's) also end up sharing their own music choices as well, creating a massive network of people simultaneously following and leading one another via some sweet beats.

Discovering new music you love is a unique and satisfying feeling. Especially when you do so on the recommendation of a trusted friend. As a result, Spotify broadcasts received an absurdly high viral conversion rate. Users trusted that the social broadcasts were authentic, and they didn't feel manipulated or pressured to engage. Especially since there was no push to try Spotify—they could just listen to music they loved.

Through Spotify, friends were merely sharing music they enjoyed in a way that sparked curiosity and a click through. Spotify didn't make it about itself; it was just the vessel for adding value to the user.

And that's where **a new viral loop began**.

Spotify's viral loop blends very well with its retention loop and revenue model:

- A user visits Spotify to see what music his or her friends are listening to.

- Since those friends likely have similar tastes, the user listens to those same songs.

- The user then sticks around for more songs by the same artist. Then different artists. Then different playlists, and so on.

- Soon a whole new world of musical entertainment opens up right there on the user's screen.

- The new user is now a tastemaker, and the process repeats as that new user's *friends* now visit Spotify to see what music he or she is listening to.

So what did Spotify do here?

It effectively leveraged viral transaction marketing by playing one heck of a captivating pipe.

Good Feelings Act as Fuel

When is **the perfect time to present an opportunity** for a user to enter your viral transaction loop? Right when they acquire a positive feeling of accomplishment or achievement from your product. You're not asking users to share because using your product is so important but because they achieve something of note through using your product, such as finding a great new song.

Your loop's call to action should never be spammy or forcibly induced. Instead, you're giving users a quick and easy opportunity to show off an accomplishment or experience they're proud of. They should *want* to take this action because you're making it about them, not about you. **They did *not* start using your product to become your sales rep.** They signed up to gain value, and you're providing them an opportunity to share that value.

Most often (and easily), this is executed amid networks on social media, but it **can be done offline as well.**

As an example, consider Tough Mudder, the endurance event series in which participants attempt obstacle courses that test their mental and physical strength. Upon successfully completing a course, each participant receives an orange headband. This is an excellent example of offline viral transaction marketing. The headbands can't be bought and are instead **earned** by those who complete the obstacle races hosted by the company.

Others then consider the headbands achievements, or badges of honor. Those who wear them are riding high on their accomplishment of something awesome. This in turn fuels others to want to do the same (i.e., participate in future Tough Mudder events).

New users are always more inclined to join or sign up because of the value they see one of their peers gain through an action. But it's the result, not the action itself, that is the key here. Your product, service, and brightly colored headbands simply fuel the opportunity to **achieve through action**.

More Examples of Viral Transaction Marketing Done Right

MapMyRun is another great example of an opportunity to showcase achievement through action. When users complete runs, MapMyRun does not ask users to share MapMyRun. It provides them with a voluntary way to share their achievements, which in this case is the run they just completed.

Ollie O'Brien
19 April via MapMyRun
13.1 km Run / Jog with MapMyRun
http://www.mapmyrun.com/workout/262088526
Distance: 13.1 km
Duration: 1:01:17
Pace: 4:40
Like · Comment · Share

This method also helps create **user-generated benefit-driven sales copy**, which can help your company get the maximum benefit from this type of viral marketing. Users sharing their achievements motivates others to use the tool to achieve similar feats.

Yet another good example is **Kickstarter**.

People love a good underdog story. Many of those people also feel intrinsically satisfied by being the benefactor in those stories. When a user decides to financially back a new founder, Kickstarter prompts the user to share the project with his or her own social network while still riding the high of having backed the campaign. Not only does this promote the user's accomplishment, but it posits the user as an in-the-know trendsetter. This broadcast then acts as **a form of social proof**: *Wow, Melinda backed this campaign? It must be awesome—I'll check it out.*

Because Melinda's friends dig her taste in clothing or know she's always on the cutting edge of new technology or art, they'll take a look. Then Kickstarter's viral loop kicks in, and many of these people back the project as well.

If you want to dig deeper into how you can use these viral superchargers to skyrocket your company's growth, start by filling out your copy of the *Viral Hero* Workbook. Get yours now for free at viralhero.com/workbook.

Chapter 4: Viral Marketing Engines — Psychological Engines

Viral Credibility Marketing—How Rolls Royce, Gibson, and RED Use It to Do Their Branding for Them

You may have noticed that the last two types of viral marketing—viral signature marketing and viral transaction marketing—involve establishing a reputation as a trusted recognizable brand. In this chapter, we're going to explore a few more types of viral marketing that depend on this same concept—a brand or product's positive reputation and user endorsement.

While most of the twelve types of viral marketing are almost exclusively focused on product development and growth engineering, one could argue our next type, **viral credibility marketing**, is a hybrid of viral growth engineering and branding.

In reality, viral credibility marketing is more product focused than all the rest. This leads to a higher-quality product that generates a high-quality perception and creates a high-end brand. In other words, this high-end perception is what *defines* the branding of the product.

But we're getting ahead of ourselves.

Viral Credibility: The Intersection of Growth Engineering and Branding

In any industry, there's often one brand that stands out above the rest. It's usually a more expensive luxury brand catering to a more serious or wealthy market. By aligning itself with wealthy individuals and celebrities (or whoever tops the hierarchy in that industry), the brand creates a sense of credibility that passes to the person using it.

This creates a **"chicken or egg" scenario**.

- Person X is more credible because he or she uses Brand Y.
- Brand Y is more credible because it's used by Person X.

Which of these statements is true? Both, eventually, but to seed this never-ending loop, you'll have to convince the first few high-end users pretty heavily.

Who Needs All the Extras?

Top-of-the-line brands aren't appropriate for users who are beginners or bargain hunters because these market segments don't need all the bells and whistles typically included in high-end brands. They need the basics. Anything more will hinder their experience. However, more serious aficionados often want these extra features. So that's exactly who these top brands cater to.

A great example of viral credibility marketing utilized by a higher-end market is RED, the top-of-the-line DSLR camera manufacturer.

RED is an incredibly expensive DSLR camera that, if used correctly, will shoot cinema-quality footage without endless rolls of old-school film. Top-quality DSLR cameras like RED are part of the reason the cost of making movies has been cut in half over the past decade.

Serious cinematographers know that the footage they shoot essentially becomes their business card, so they invest in a RED camera in order to stand out from the crowd.

This investment sets them apart from cinematographers who shoot lower-quality footage. Because REDs make this footage look better, cinematographers using REDs often get jobs simply because **they've got a RED** available to them to shoot with.

Think about these questions:

- Are serious cinematographers more credible because they shoot footage with a RED?
- Or is RED more credible because serious cinematographers shoot footage with it?

It doesn't matter. What matters is the product's quality and output are great, and cinematographers using it get higher-profile gigs as a result. In response, other cinematographers then want to up their quality and get higher-profile gigs as well, so more REDs get sold.

Value is provided, the word spreads, and the loop continues.

"What Do You Do, and How Do You Do It?"

There's a scene in the movie *The Pursuit of Happiness* where Will Smith sees another guy drive up in a fancy sports car. He looks at the car longingly before saying, "Wow . . . what do you do, and how do you do it?"

The answer didn't really matter. The car said it all. It instantly passed on credibility, and Will Smith's character found something to aspire to.

This **"status symbol" perception** is the foundation of viral credibility marketing.

- With a brand like RED, that status is "serious cinematographer."
- With a brand like Rolls Royce, that status is "seriously rich."
- With a brand like Gibson, that status is "serious musician."

The credibility of the brand responsible for creating a top-notch product rubs off on the person who's using it. Others view the person using it as a "power user" getting serious value. They then aspire to obtaining that same value.

While not every user may have the same talent as that "power user" (e.g., the ability to rock out like Jimmy Page or capture a scene like Steven Soderbergh), they can still up their game and enhance their own experience by upgrading their product choices.

The problem with viral credibility marketing is that it's often not something a startup can create from day one. The level of quality needed to successfully achieve this method takes time and money, something not many startups have. Not to mention, as the whole "launch early and imperfectly" mantra indicates, startups often need to move fast and break things. That said, those who have the luxury of ignoring this rule and shooting for the moon with a viable viral-credibility-marketing strategy can often activate the potential this viral engine has to offer.

Online Viral Word-of-Mouth Marketing—How BuzzFeed Joined the Media Elite

The majority of viral marketing techniques involve viral structure and viral value. We've seen this over and over as we've moved through the first of the twelve different types of viral marketing. The funny thing is, when most people think of the term *viral marketing*, these are not the techniques that come to mind. Instead most think of one thing in particular: **online viral word of mouth.**

Online Viral Word of Mouth: The Most Common of Confusions

The best viral marketing shouldn't seem like viral marketing at all. That's how you know it works. It should seem like **a core-value**

add-on of the product. Otherwise, we'd see it as an ad, which many of us resent.

The confusion typically stems from the association most people make between a social media share and "going viral." In other words, many people think something like clicking "Share on Facebook" is all it takes. They then think of a site like BuzzFeed as the vessel through which virality occurs.

Viral-Success Story: BuzzFeed

Unlike sites like Dropbox and Skype that rely mostly on user interaction within their products to drive virality, BuzzFeed relies heavily on viral media to drive online viral word-of-mouth marketing.

In a nutshell, this is the "do something really cool, funny, terrifying, awe-inspiring, infuriating, or controversial so people tell their friends about it" approach. It's what BuzzFeed and sites like it rely on to grow—especially when combined with a strategically designed interface to leverage sharing via social media.

How well this type of viral marketing works depends on the **quality, controversy, or value** of your online content. If it evokes a high-arousal emotion in the user (e.g., nostalgia or laughing so hard milk shoots out your nose) so that the content practically *requires* the user to talk about it with somebody, then your content has succeeded. The million-dollar tasks then become **finding core interests** and **testing content** until you learn which are positioned to spread the fastest.

The Science of Hijacking Users

Many well-marketed blogs or websites leveraging online viral word-of-mouth marketing will carve a deep niche. This makes it easy for them to successfully optimize their entire experience for one specific subset of users who, by and large, respond to similar things.

However, BuzzFeed is a more general online publication. Its core focus is gaining readers and delighting them to the point of sharing content, and instead of concentrating on a single content topic, it throws a wider topical net. That said, most of these topics are strategically crafted to elicit one of the following responses:

- Anger
- Humor
- Fear
- Controversy
- Fascination

This may sound easy, **but it's not**. In fact, it's quite the opposite and often requires far more research and resources than most bloggers have access to.

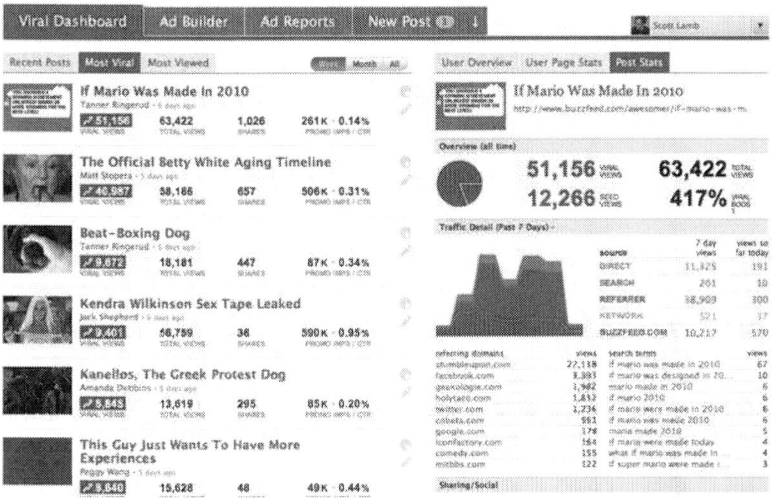

In addition to a top-tier writing staff schooled in strategically crafting content with the goal of spreading it virally, BuzzFeed invests heavily in behavioral user data. Its content creators endlessly tinker with content, page elements, headlines, and recommended content (among other elements) to maximize four key things:

- Shares
- Number of articles read
- Time on the site
- Repeat visits

The goal of online viral word-of-mouth marketing is to **hijack the user's attention span** and implant a certain topic, idea, or product in place of what was there before it. This hijacking is typically temporary, but the goal of a site like BuzzFeed is to **prolong the length of this hijacking as long as possible.** The more engaging its content, the more it has control, and the more likely you are to take actions like sharing, viewing another article, sharing *that* article, and so on—all of which builds more ad revenue for BuzzFeed.

Your Source for All Things Funny and Interesting

So what provides a site like BuzzFeed with the most control over your mind? As I mentioned above, BuzzFeed's strength lies in its ability to strategically create **high-arousal emotions**. From there, it simply needs to relay a message you believe is "remarkable" (i.e., worthy of remark), especially one that your network might find interesting.

Consider these examples:

- BuzzFeed creates an article with hilarious headlines that instantly reminds you of your friend's cat. Obviously, that friend needs to know about it.

- BuzzFeed compiles the latest memes about *Game of Thrones* and adds some great descriptive text. You can't help but chuckle reading them, especially that one about your favorite character's head getting chopped off. Think you'll share that with people you talk about the show with? Highly likely.

BuzzFeed rounds out its viral one-two punch by perfectly blending its viral loop with user retention.

- Users visit BuzzFeed because they want to see funny, fascinating, or timely content.
- Users want to share that content with friends to amaze and entertain them, which in the users' minds ups their social status.

Most of us have an unconscious desire to be the friend that is "in the know." We want to make our friends laugh or break the news about an important topic. We want to be known as the first person to know things because **it gives us a feeling of importance**. This is the core value of passing things on through word of mouth.

In this way, BuzzFeed is simply the vessel. It puts us in the driver's seat to start conversations within our networks, and BuzzFeed does its best to motivate this action through design and content testing.

However, at the end of the day, it all comes down to our own emotional reactions to what we see.

Offline Viral Word-of-Mouth Marketing—How Apple, theCHIVE, and Cards Against Humanity Crush It

The *most common* form of viral marketing is . . . (drumroll, please) . . . people talking to each other.

Sorry to be anticlimactic, but **offline viral word-of-mouth marketing** is far and above the most prevalent form of viral marketing. Think about it: online viral word-of-mouth marketing may be a viable strategy, but 90 percent of actual word-of-mouth communication happens *offline*.

You may not realize it, but nearly every product uses offline viral word-of-mouth marketing. Companies that use it purposefully and strategically are the ones that end up household names. This has been true throughout history, and it will continue to be true until the robot aliens take over and we're all assimilated.

But *why*? Why is this true when brands like Skype and YouTube and Dropbox have become viral hits using more product-focused forms of viral marketing?

Offline Viral Word of Mouth: The Common Denominator

The answer is simple: offline word of mouth happens for every single site, even if you don't know it.

- When Apple includes free stickers with every product, many people stick them on their notebooks and laptop cases, **just because they're there**.

- When a friend invites you to play Cards Against Humanity and you end up laughing your faces off, **you'll want to buy a set yourself**.

- If somebody sees you wearing a T-shirt from theCHIVE

with Bill Murray's face on it, **that person will ask you where you got it.**

To sum up, offline viral word-of-mouth marketing is deeply rooted in the core value of the product. If you spend time and energy trying hard to satisfy your customers, they are going to talk about your product with others. Which is why this marketing strategy is incredibly common.

How Do You Get People Talking?

Getting people talking about a product is so rarely done well because **most companies don't *purposefully* create offline viral word-of-mouth marketing.** If word of mouth about a specific item occurs, it usually happens as a byproduct of that item's amazing usefulness for solving a problem. The company likely didn't begin the product-development process with the intention of subliminally encouraging users to talk about the product.

However, the businesses that purposefully do so often win big.

Viral-Success Story: Sincerely Truman

About a year ago, I was living in a tech incubator house in Venice Beach. It was a fascinating experience. I was exposed to so many ways of doing business and building companies that I hadn't experienced before.

These guys weren't cheap, but they were incredibly good at what they did. However, before signing on with Sincerely Truman, my friends' company did its research and had conversations with a few other firms to test the waters.

Then one day, **three packages showed up on our doorstep**. Each was addressed to one of the cofounders of the company. Inside was a wooden crate that contained a large bottle of microbrewed beer called Seasoned Traveler—a brand that none of us had ever heard of. But the packaging was impressive, as was all the cool stuff that came with it.

Next to the bottle and all the fun extra swag was a full brand-identity package, **all designed and created by Sincerely Truman**. There were handwritten notes to each of the founders thanking them for their consideration and offering this free gift as a sign of their appreciation. There were no obligations or expectations. Just a warm thank-you and some beer.

Here's the interesting thing: these bottles of beer were so well crafted and cool looking that nobody wanted to actually drink them. They instead sat on display in the house.

We had people in and out all the time and hosted some larger events like concerts every few weeks. Like clockwork, **people would ask about the really cool bottles of beer on display**. The founders would then tell them about Sincerely Truman, the pleasant surprise of receiving the package in the mail, and the whole story about their experience.

That's what we in the viral marketing biz call a *win*.

This entire experience was deliberately built to showcase Sincerely Truman's creative chops and get people talking. I don't know how much business they, as a high-dollar creative firm, got from this sort of offline word of mouth, but I know they got more than enough to offset the cost of creating the package. Overall, this is the perfect example of **offline viral word-of-mouth marketing done well and on purpose.**

Online versus Offline Word of Mouth

Many people think the word *viral* is interchangeable with "word of mouth" (a belief that's ironically driven by word of mouth). At this point in your journey with *Viral Hero*, you should already know there's much more to it than that.

While, yes, word of mouth is a type of viral marketing, it is by no means the *only* type (or the most effective). That said, both offline and online viral word-of-mouth marketing can be incredibly effective if done well and to scale.

But which **type of viral word-of-mouth marketing** should you focus on? Don't be tempted to take a shortcut and focus on both offline and online equally. Select the one most appropriate for your company, and go all-in on executing it incredibly well.

How to Decide Which Word-of-Mouth Strategy Is Best for You

Need a little help deciding whether to go with offline or online viral word-of-mouth marketing? Consider these questions:

- Do you have a high-dollar agency like Sincerely Truman? Or a remarkable product like the Soma water pitcher that people will ask about every time they see it? **Go with offline.** People can see it and touch it and tell their friends about it—especially if you provide some fuel for the fire (such as two free gift coupons for 20 percent off a Soma product for a friend).

- Do you have a publication like BuzzFeed or a platform showcasing the latest and greatest startups like Product Hunt? **Go with online.** Your customers make a few clicks, and you'll see higher viral branching through social media. You'll also likely be catering to an audience that's already active on many social networks and online communities, which makes this strategy even more effective.

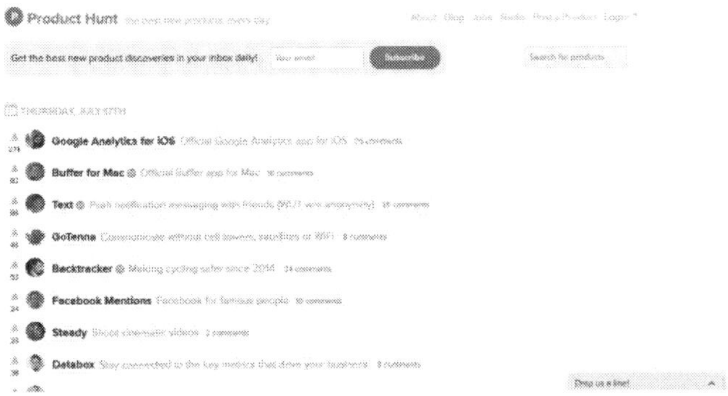

Any type of word of mouth, whether it's offline or online, always speaks to the quality, controversy, and value of your product as it relates to the interests of your users' networks. The more you connect with your niche and **speak directly to them**, the more word of mouth you'll spark.

Viral Satisfaction Marketing—How Zappos and Basecamp Grew into Juggernauts

Congrats! You've reached the last section of our chapters covering the twelve different types of viral marketing. (Viral Panda and his sidekick Red are very impressed.) In a few moments, you'll be one giant leap closer to building scalable, sustainable growth for your product.

As you've probably already figured out, there are many ways you can make your product more viral. However, the next strategy is one of my favorites. But before I dive into it, I want to first stress something very important—something that I've said before and will say over and over again. No matter which type of viral marketing you choose for your product, **the foundation of all viral marketing is value**. Not value for *you*, mind you—I'm talking about value for your *users*.

Value Stems from Your Product . . . Right?

The perceived value of your product is one of the most important items you must address to achieve success.

For viral marketing to work in any capacity, you must provide an elevated value to users that drives them toward inviting others to also become users. This value is important because it creates a feeling of

satisfaction for the user. In today's wide sea of low-quality products, a truly satisfying experience is well worth telling others about.

However, satisfaction **does *not* have to come from a product** to still be worth talking about.

Sure, it must come from somewhere. And that somewhere needs to be an absolutely incredible touch point with your brand (i.e., the point of contact between a buyer and a seller). In other words, you need to provide the user an experience so uniquely great compared to what everyone else is doing that it becomes the remarkable "purple cow" that dot-com-business-exec-turned-author Seth Godin so often refers to.

So, let's think for a moment. Where could such a key touch point exist?

Customer Service and Virality

Viral satisfaction marketing is a form of viral marketing that occurs when a user has had such a great experience with your team that he or she tells others about it. Through this interaction, **you've given that user value** with an altogether different experience than the user typically receives from other brands in every industry.

Viral satisfaction marketing may not seem like a form of viral marketing. If you're understanding viral marketing through a structural lens (think inherent viral marketing or viral collaboration marketing), you may have a point.

However, **Zappos would argue otherwise**.

Viral-Success Story: Zappos

Originally the Amazon of online shoe sales, Zappos became famous for its unrivaled customer support. There was no script. No automated robots. No outsourced call center in India. Just real people whose primary goal was to **absolutely delight customers**. So much so, it began airing commercials showing off *real* customer-service calls.

Tony Hsieh, CEO of Zappos, knew that these customer touch points were traditionally a source of **friction and frustration** for customers. Most companies would do just enough to ensure customers didn't hate them and not much else.

At the time, most companies deemed personalized customer service too expensive or not "innovative" enough to be worth the effort or had some other equally wrong and stupid opinion.

For Hsieh, however, it was a no-brainer. He created a culture within Zappos of genuinely happy employees who were interested in and passionate about helping customers solve their problems. Their job wasn't just about assisting customers. It was about brightening each customer's day and ensuring they all felt like they mattered.

And guess what? Once customers got off calls with Zappos support, they *raved* about how incredibly well they'd been treated, rhapsodizing about how Zappos's agents went above and beyond to help them.

Do you think these ringing endorsements helped Zappos acquire new customers? (Here's a hint: if you said, "Not likely," go sit in the corner.)

Satisfaction Virality versus Word of Mouth

If you tried to argue that viral satisfaction marketing is simply a form of viral word-of-mouth marketing, you'd be (mostly) correct.

"Word of mouth" is so broad and vague that cramming every subset into one crowded chapter **wouldn't be useful or practical.** It's implemented in different ways by different companies. My goal is to give you an actionable view of each viral engine and the intricacies that must be considered in each case.

The mechanics of creating viral word-of-mouth marketing in the ways we've previously discussed deal mostly with the product, not with **support interactions**. That's the key difference here. It's important to separate these two because only *some* companies can leverage viral word-of-mouth marketing, but *every* company can leverage viral satisfaction marketing. You can even leverage it from day one, well before you have a product. In other words, before your product can speak for itself, **you must speak for it**.

Give People Something to Be Happy About

Basecamp founder Jason Fried has publicly boasted that his company's customer-support response times are often within one minute. Not surprisingly, Basecamp has proudly showcased this spotless support record on its website.

Think this is by accident? It's not. It's a form of viral marketing. Because good customer service is such a rare experience, users talk to others about it immediately. It gives them a sense of confidence that if anything goes wrong, help is just a minute away.

The Right Time to Ask

Not all support interactions need to be organic. In fact, with the right tools, the right automation, and the right planning, you can create other support interactions to keep your viral satisfaction marketing engine chugging.

For example, many apps (including Circa News) use this simple flow to ask for either a rating from satisfied customers or feedback from an unsatisfied customer:

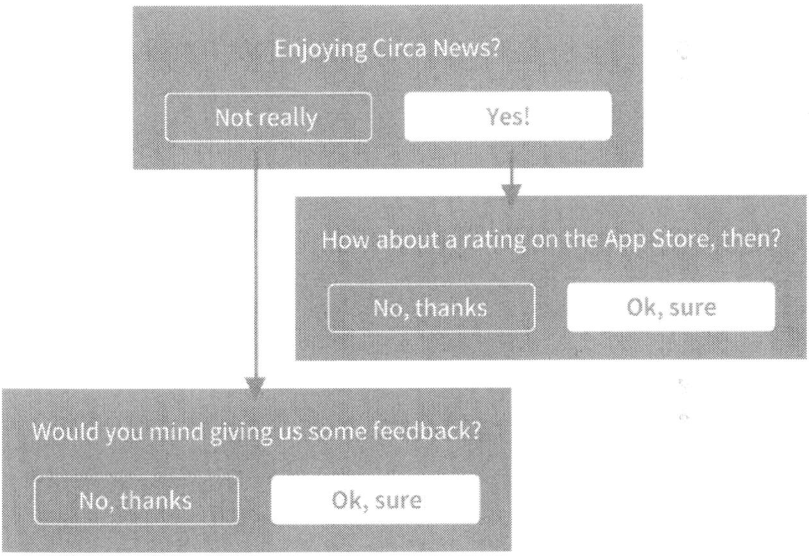
Enjoying Circa News?
Not really
Yes!
How about a rating on the App Store, then?
No, thanks
Ok, sure
Would you mind giving us some feedback?
No, thanks
Ok, sure

This feedback not only helps Circa improve but is also an opportunity to provide support to a user who may be at risk of churning otherwise. (We'll discuss churning in a bit.)

Turning an unhappy user into a delighted user is often the mark of a successful viral satisfaction engine. Why? Because the shift is **so rare that it's worthy of conversation.**

I'd suggest including a steady balance of the following in this interaction flow:

- **Ratings**—social proof is a powerful conversion tool.
- **Invite CTAs**—happy customers will be your most viral customers, so it's sensible to ask users to take actions here.

Be Remarkable All Around

Just as you want your product or service to be remarkable, you also want your customer support to stand out, and each additional touch point you have with customers can help boost virality. This could be a postcard in the mail or helping a frustrated customer at two in the morning while their toddler is screaming in the background. You're not there to judge, just help.

In other words, don't measure the amount of time it takes to resolve each problem a user has. Resolutions can be quick, but **delighting the customer** requires added effort. So offer stress-free support. Have fast response times. Create a remarkable, conversation-worthy experience. Work hard to help customers as much as possible in order to stand out from the competition and leave the customers satisfied—even if it means singing "Rock-a-bye Baby" to help put their toddler to sleep.

Succeed, and I guarantee they'll be coming back for more—and bringing their friends with them.

Learning from Measles

Let's shift gears back to virology for a moment and look at a disease we've all heard of: the measles.

Simple diseases like the measles allow new epidemiologists to use simple models to study them (we'll go through a specific model they use, SIR, a bit later). Projecting and tracking the spread of measles is a bit easier than doing so for other viruses for these reasons: there's a single strain of the measles virus, everybody who catches it shows symptoms, and once you recover from it, you can't get it again.

What's more, once a large-enough group of people get vaccinated, they experience a phenomenon called *herd immunity*. This is what happens when a disease has too few opportunities to spread, so it effectively dies out.

Herd immunity is what organizations like the CDC are hoping for. It's also what we—the entrepreneurs and growth engineers working to spread our products virally—desperately want to avoid.

So what can we learn from measles?

1. First, we want our "virus" to be as effective as possible, so we need to utilize several types of viral marketing (i.e., multiple strains instead of a single strain).

2. Next, we not only want to present the benefits of our product to target prospects, but we also want to inexpensively promote our product to groups that interact with them often—even if they aren't as likely to become users themselves (i.e., nonsymptomatic carriers).

3. Then, we want to ensure we have reactivation campaigns (effectively specialized messaging campaigns dedicated to resurrecting dormant users who haven't been active recently) in place. We'll talk more about reactivation later.

4. Lastly, we want to keep a close eye on the number of people we expose our marketing materials to, compared to the estimated size of a niche market, and diversify our targeting or radically change our marketing messages before we approach saturation (i.e., herd immunity). We'll discuss market saturation later as well.

What's Next?

You didn't think we were going to stop here, did you?

You may know all twelve forms of viral marketing, but knowledge without action is worthless. You can read these lessons all day long, but without *implementing* them, you'll never get anywhere. Now you need to **create your viral engine**—which is precisely what we will be diving into next.

Get your party pants on!

Psychological viral engines aren't appropriate for every company, but they could be for yours. To find out more, answer the corresponding questions in the free *Viral Hero* Workbook. Where can you get it? You guessed it - viralhero.com/workbook.

Part 2: Building a Viral Business

Chapter 5: Initial Viral Architecture

Step 1: Viral Marketing Structure—Six Magical Questions to Transform Your Site and Grow Virally

In the next few chapters, we'll walk through fifteen steps for building your own viral engine for your product or service. If you follow these steps, you'll have the tools you need to build your product into a viral superstar.

But before we begin discussing your viral marketing structure and the fifteen steps, it's worth reiterating something I've already said several times. **The foundation of *all* viral marketing is value**—namely, the value you provide to your users for inviting others to your product. As we move forward, it's important to always keep that in mind.

Viral Marketing Structure: Creating Valuable Touch Points

Asking nicely is for amateurs.

No matter how nicely you ask people to do something, they won't do it unless they expect to gain value from it (or you threaten them with a really big stick). Your mom may get value from making you happy after you ask for something nicely, but random strangers on the internet won't be so kind.

To truly make your site viral, you have to **create new value**—value that your users can unlock by inviting others. However, simply *offering* that value is only one piece of the bigger viral puzzle.

Start with Your Viral Loop

To effectively build your viral loop, you must **consider the following four things**:

- The value for inviting or sharing must be **easy to see**.
- How the invite or share occurs must be **obvious**.
- The action to invite or share must be **quick**.
- Most importantly, the user must **actually want** to invite others.

To make this chapter even more helpful for you, I'll provide a simple example of a viral loop I personally built as the head of growth for a brand called Lottery.com.

Lottery.com's Viral Structure: Answering Easy and Important Questions

There are six "magical" questions that can help transform your site and successfully map your viral loop. I've listed them below and included how we answered each at Lottery.com.

Some of these are going to seem like obvious day-one-level questions that any Joe Schmoe could answer. **That's exactly why they're tricky.** If you don't ask or answer these questions in the proper context, they won't serve the right purpose for you.

Most of the time, founders and growth engineers view these questions through the lens of product development or ideation, not through the lens of viral marketing and mapping viral loops. But trust me—we'll get to your million-dollar revelation quicker than you think.

Okay, let's dive in.

1. **Why Does a User Come to Your Product?**

    Lottery.com's main business is a mobile app that allows users in select states to play the lottery on their phones from start to finish (i.e., from getting their tickets to cashing out winnings into their bank accounts). Users typically begin using the Lottery.com app because they've found it through organic search, have been exposed to it via an ad, or have been invited by another user.

    Often, users are not proactively searching for a new, more frictionless way of playing the lottery. They've been conditioned to think the game is only played using paper tickets they get at local convenience or grocery stores. They've often also seen fake products on the internet promising similar value but not delivering. For this reason, **brand awareness and trust** were our most important commodities.

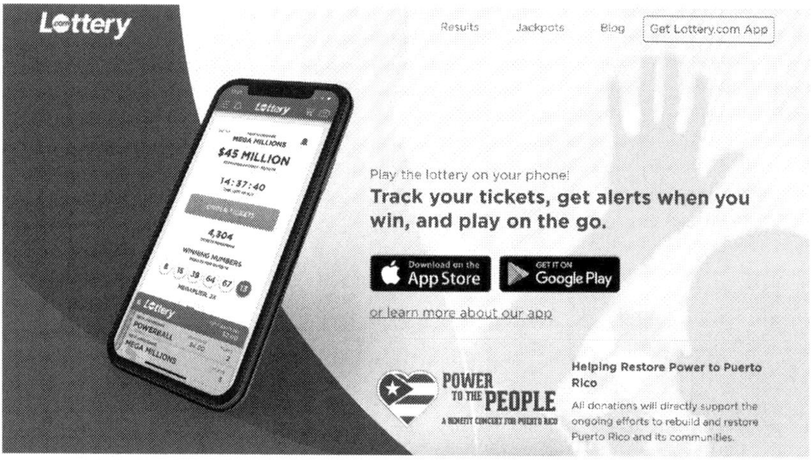

Sub-Questions:

- Based on how users are exposed to your product, are they adequately introduced to who you are and what you do?
- How can you more effectively smooth their transition from prospect to lead by creating one cohesive storyline with zero interruptions or confusion?

2. **What *Core Value* Do You Pass On to Users?**

Lottery.com gives users a way to skip the simple yet annoying process of physically going to the store to purchase paper lottery tickets, checking their numbers, and cashing in their winning tickets.

In short, **Lottery.com acts as a concierge service for users**, doing all the manual work for them. It allows users to sit back, relax, and enjoy the fun of playing the lottery (e.g., imagining all the crazy, lavish things they'd do with the jackpot if they became the next lucky winner).

Sub-Questions:

Are you sure that users can instantly see the core value you provide them? What evidence are you using to justify your claim?

Do you have to convince users that they need your product? How could you simplify your product, your language, and your marketing to make them instantly see the value you provide?

3. **What Have Users' Experiences Been to Date?**

Lottery players are used to **the annoying, antiquated process** of going to the store, buying paper tickets, manually checking their tickets, manually calculating how much they've won, and then remembering to go to the store to cash in their winnings. If they've won over a certain amount, they actually have to go to the lottery commission in their state to cash in their prize, fill out tax forms, and go through the whole ordeal of claiming their funds.

While this seems like a small price to pay for a nice chunk of change, most players would disagree. In fact, over $2 billion in winnings go unclaimed every single year in the United States.

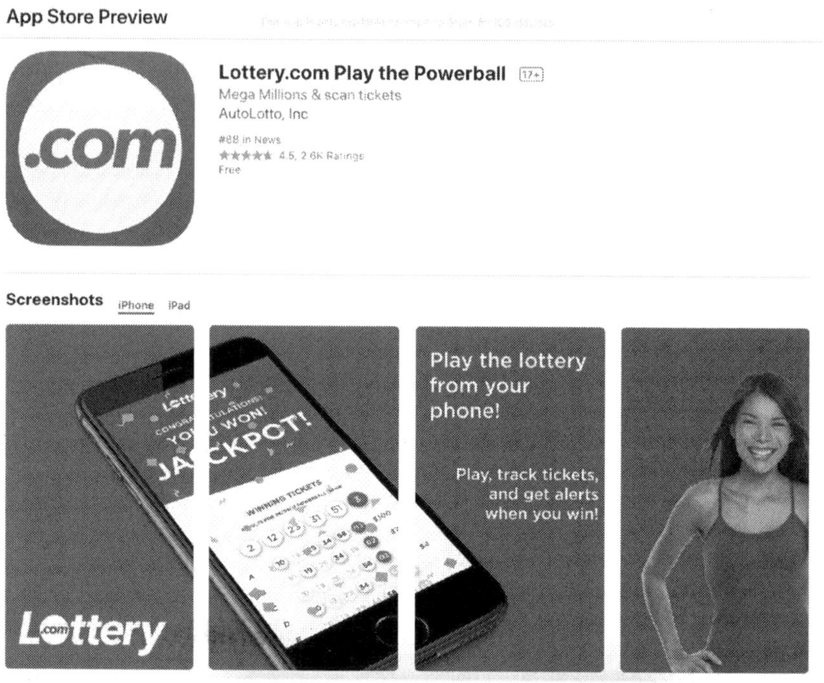

Sub-Questions:

- What was life like for users before your product?
- What is life like for users after your product?

4. **How Is Your Product Different?**

Lottery.com gives users a well-designed, smooth lottery experience on their mobile devices. In about sixty seconds, they can actually use the free ticket incentive we've added to their account that they unlock by completing the new-user activation funnel. This allows them to demo the product and see the value it provides without any financial commitment or perceived risk.

Once they've tried the app for free, they can continue to play every week by linking a credit card, debit card, or bank account. In fact, they don't even have to manually play every week; with the AutoPlay function, Lottery.com gets users their tickets automatically every week and notifies them when they win. If they don't want to play every draw, users can set their preferences so that the app will only activate AutoPlay when the jackpot is above a certain threshold.

When they win, the cash-out process is even easier. Users just link up their bank accounts in the app and receive their winnings instantly. If they prefer to let it ride and use their winnings for more tickets (as most winning tickets are in the four- to ten-dollar range), we provide that option as well.

Lastly, users never have to worry about losing, damaging, or forgetting to check their tickets. Lottery.com takes care of this entire process for them. Tickets are insured, and winning notifications and cash-outs happen automatically.

In short, Lottery.com provides users with **the quickest, easiest, safest, and securest way** to play the lottery everyone already knows and loves.

Sub-Questions:

- Have you done a thorough sweep of the competitive landscape lately? If no one else is doing what you do, why do you think that is?

- Is your product actually different, or are you just trying to convince yourself it is?

5. **How Do You Know the Value You *Think* You're Providing Is Actually Valuable?**

   This one's easy. Here's the answer: **retention rates are stellar.**

   At Lottery.com, of users who proceed through the on-boarding flow and redeem their free tickets, more than 75 percent stick around for more than thirty days. Compare that to most mobile apps that boast "good" thirty-day retention rates anywhere from 10–20 percent, depending on the industry, and you've got a solid foundation upon which you can build scalable growth engines of any kind—including viral ones.

   Sub-Questions:

- Does your product provide what you *yourself* consider value, or have you done qualitative research on the aggregate?

- Why aren't more competitors trying to provide this value currently? What happens when they do?

6. **How Does a User Share Your Product?**

   To work well, the viral loop within Lottery.com had to be as simple as the product itself. And that's exactly how we built it. For every friend you invite to join Lottery.com, both you and that friend get a free Powerball ticket.

What's more, there's no limit to the number of friends you can invite.

Right now, the viral carrier is SMS, but the goal is to experiment with other methods.

Sub-Questions:

- Do you have to extensively explain to users how your viral loop works, or is it instantly obvious and intuitive? How can you make it even more simple or easy to understand?

- Based on users' experiences with your product to date, what would be the most obvious method of sending invites if it were to happen organically (i.e., outside of your viral loop)? Is this how you've designed your viral carrier?

Turn Your Answers into Action

Now that you have the core questions to ask yourself and you've seen some real-world answers from a product I've personally helped build, it's time to turn these seemingly menial answers into **things you can actually use to improve your viral engine**.

Here's a short list of expansion questions to help move you forward (we won't get too deep into these here because we'll explore them further in later chapters):

- Is there a way you can make the benefits of sharing your site more **obvious**?

- Is there a way you can augment this value to make the decision **easier**?

- How **intuitive** is it for users to see when and how this value transfer happens?

- Do the requirements needed to invite users make the path to value **shorter**?

- Have you added your metrics to each step in your loop to **make bottlenecks reveal themselves**?

- Could you combine or remove any steps in your viral loop to make it **faster**?

If you don't have answers to the questions above, or if the answers you've come up with aren't the answers you want, it's time to make some changes.

Step 2: Viral Marketing Optimization—Five Simple Steps to Go from Hundreds of Users to Millions of Acolytes

Viral success will never happen overnight. In the first iteration of any product, funnel, or process, meticulous optimization is what leads to the overwhelming success we all want.

Two Magical Steps to a Successful Company

There are **two initial steps** to building a successful business:

1. **Get people in the door** (acquisition).

2. Once they're in the door, **get them to repeatedly buy more** (optimization).

Okay, you're right. This may be an overly simplified view. But both are critical steps—and both can be accomplished through **viral marketing optimization.** Many newbie founders or marketers assume the first is the most important (or sometimes even the *only*) step to success. These founders believe if they can just get people in the door, those people will come to their senses and realize that they need to buy the company's products.

After all, your product is the most amazing product to have ever been created in the history of humanity, right? **Wrong.**

Optimize Conversions the Right Way

Conversion rate optimization (CRO) is the process of increasing the likelihood that the people who walk through your door will take a conversion action (such as buying what you're selling).

When done right, the optimization process is **a continuous (and lucrative) cycle**:

- Build
- Measure
- Learn

This is identical to the process taught by Eric Ries in *The Lean Startup*. It may seem basic, but this iteration loop is the bedrock of optimization.

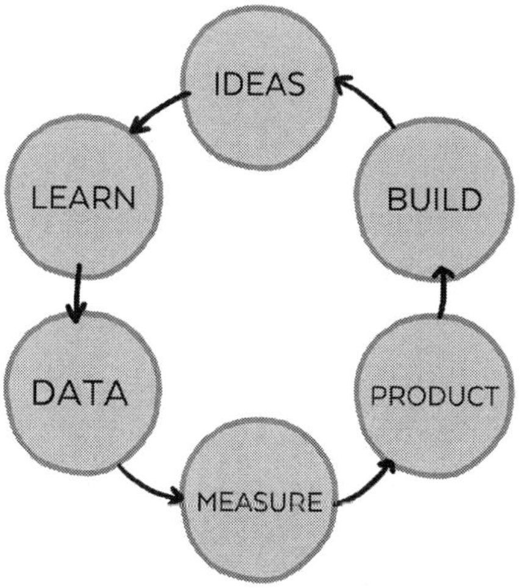

You've likely seen all this before, but I wanted to go over the foundations of optimization first before I show you some things you likely haven't seen anywhere else.

CRO and Viral Marketing Optimization

We've established that viral marketing can be powerful if used correctly. But how powerful can it be?

Let's say you have a product with the potential to be **very viral on a per-user basis**. As such, it has a viral coefficient (or K factor) of **2.0**. (This is obscenely high, but let's just use it as an example for now.) I'll explain exactly how to calculate viral coefficient in a later section, but in a nutshell, a K factor of 2.0 means every user who comes to your site will recruit two more users for you.

Scenario 1: Five-Day Cycle Time

Let's say it takes a user five days to recruit those two users for you. Let's also assume that you've recruited ten of your friends to be your first ten users. After ten days, you'll have a little more than **three hundred** users. I know what you're thinking: *Wow, that's awesome! And I didn't even have to pay anything—where do I sign up?*

But wait—there's more.

Scenario 2: Two-Day Cycle Time

Let's say you do a little **viral marketing optimization** and you employ the same tactics you'd use to optimize a sales funnel—only this time, you use them to optimize your viral loop (i.e., the actions users need to take to complete the invite process).

You make some solid improvements to speed and efficiency of the invite process, and by doing so you shave down the cycle time of your viral loop. Everything else remains the same, but it now takes a user only two days to recruit those same two users.

This means that after the same twenty-day period, you'll end up with **over twenty thousand users**. Pretty wild, isn't it?

The point here is that because your viral factor is so high, you can expect **exponential growth**. You have now allowed for more viral loops to happen because there's more time for more waves of invites to be sent out by more people during that same twenty-day period. That's a whole lot of "more."

And that's why viral marketing is so powerful.

But we're not done yet.

Scenario 3: Twenty-Four-Hour Cycle Time
Let's say you manage to optimize that process yet again.

By adding a few extra improvements, such as making it easier to invite more people at once or showing users the value in inviting others sooner, you shave your cycle time down to just one single day. Run the same twenty-day scenario over again, and you end up with over **twenty million users**. *What?* Yep.

But let's not congratulate ourselves for being so hypothetically awesome quite yet. Is this a feasible example that anyone can use to build a billion-dollar company? **Unfortunately, it's not quite that simple.**

The example above describes an inherently viral product with a viral factor considerably higher than 1.0, which isn't possible for 99.9 percent of products out there. Even in the fringe cases where it is, this number can't be sustained for very long. These scenarios also assume you're solving a real problem, offering real value, and working with a few really smart people who can map your viral loop in detail to improve it bit by bit.

That said, the example above *should* be dramatic enough to get my point across: **viral marketing optimization is the most important and impactful form of optimization you can use to improve your**

product's growth. Even if you're able to increase your viral factor from 0.2 to 0.25 or shave a few hours off your cycle time, the difference over the course of a month or a year can be the most significant improvement you make all year long.

How to Get Started with Viral Marketing Optimization

It's much easier than you might think to get started with viral optimization. All you need is a good behavioral-analytics tool (e.g., Google Analytics or Mixpanel) and a tool to create a diagram. For diagramming, I like services such as Lucidchart, but hell, a good old-fashioned piece of paper and a pen will work just fine.

Step 1: Map your viral loop.

- Create a visualization of every single step users *need* to take from the time they're first exposed to your product to the point they expose somebody else to it.
- Create a second visualization of every step users *currently* take to do the same thing.

Step 2: Find your Value Hook Point (VHP).

- Mark where the two visualizations you created in step 1 don't match up.
- You'll see exactly where and when users acquire enough value from your product to trust it, realize the value in sharing your product, and actually take action to share it.
- This is your **Viral Hook Point.**

Step 3: Add conversion metrics for each step.

- Using your analytics tools, add metrics to each step in your current viral loop. These can include click-through rates, average time on page, bounce rates, etc.

- If you can, segment some of this data to show how different subsets of users behave differently.

- Try to hypothesize why that's the case. This will help you pinpoint bottlenecks.

Step 4: Run simulations, and prioritize your focus.

- Based on the visualization you've now created, create a simple spreadsheet with a field showing traffic into the entry point of your loop. That's phase one of your viral loop.

- Create subset fields for each subsequent phase of your viral loop. Structure their formulas to apply the conversion rate from that phase to the traffic flowing to it from the one before it.

- Go through each phase, and list the potential improvements you could make as well as a conservative estimate of how much these improvements might enhance the data for that phase.

- Run the simulation you created on the spreadsheet, making a note of the overall impact that each proposed improvement would have on the final numbers **individually**.

- Rank your task list, prioritizing the estimated highest-impact changes you've identified.

Test, Test, and Test Some More

Early on, many of your tests will yield big improvements because there's so much low-hanging fruit. However, once you've spent a fair chunk of time on optimization, it's likely that most of your tests will fail. But when you reach the point that you're relatively well optimized with your current architecture, some of your tests *will* continually succeed and in big ways—especially if you have smart, capable people interpreting your data and forming hypotheses.

It's important to note that **speed matters here**. The quicker you iterate on versions of each page, the quicker you'll learn why your users behave the way they do—and the quicker you'll achieve success in growing more virally.

- **High-Tempo Testing**—Release an iteration every two days, and you might see success in two weeks.

- **"Just often enough to say we do it"**—Release an iteration every three to four weeks, and it might take half a year to nail your model.

Use A/B testing and optimization techniques on all the steps of your viral loop as much as possible. Pay close attention to metrics like these:

- Sources of traffic

- Landing page views

- Percent of users that register
- Percent of users that send invites
- Number of invites sent per user on average
- Number of invites sent per invite session
- Percent of invites delivered successfully
- Percent of invites viewed by users
- Number of virally added users per user on average

Optimizing these metrics individually will help make users feel that sharing your product is efficient, valuable, and even necessary.

Optimize What You Know

To be clear, **you do not need hundreds of viral features to succeed.** You only need a select few, as long as these features create value in an intuitive way.

Even huge sites like LinkedIn that have thousands of product features only have a few significant viral loops. The takeaway is to avoid spreading yourself too thin and concentrate on the features that will have the highest impact. (Wondering what those features might be? Go back and review our list of the twelve types of viral marketing for some ideas.) Then you can optimize those for maximum performance.

If you're already schooled in CRO, you have a huge head start here, as there are a *ton* of resources out there on conversion optimization. In fact, only a few CRO-savvy folks manage to unlock new traffic sources **that their competitors can't** because of how optimized their sites are for conversions. This allows them to **pay more** for acquiring visitors because those visitors will turn into customers far more often.

So do yourself a favor, and learn about testing and optimization theory and tools first. Only *then* should you start with viral marketing optimization. The impact can (potentially) mean the difference between startup life and death.

Step 3: Viral Value—How User Guilt Can Destroy Your Viral Campaign, and What to Do about It

As we saw in the last section, an optimized viral loop is critical, but it relies heavily on one core thing: value.

Value is the be-all-and-end-all foundation on which your entire viral campaign will hinge. You're probably not surprised that viral marketing relies on value, but you're also likely not utilizing it to the level that you will after reading this section.

Few products are capable of using viral growth exclusively as their primary growth engine. But it's not their creators' fault. Most marketers, heads of growth, and founders have not been educated in viral growth mechanics. And even if they have, rarely do they give it much thought until after they've finished development—which is a mistake.

Before you can create a product that can grow, you need one thing: **value**.

Viral Value: A Requirement for Viral Marketing Success

I'm not talking about value to *you*. I'm talking about value to *your customers*. They are your *real* boss. You cannot succeed in the long run without first satisfying them. So to generate large amounts of revenue, you must consistently and repeatedly deliver value to your customers.

You must offer so much value that your customers are willing to trade you something valuable (e.g., money) for the product or service you're offering. In simplistic terms, you're bartering. You're creating value, and you're getting value in return. This might sound like Business 101, and that's because it is. But many businesses forget this because it's all too easy to fall into the trap of looking at things through our own perspectives more than through the eyes of our customers.

You don't have to do something crazy or tabloid worthy to become remarkable or valuable in the eyes of your users. Value can be created simply by solving a common problem well. When you add remarkability to that value by delivering it in a way that inspires customers to tell others about it, well then, my friend, **you've stumbled upon viral value**.

Why Customers Buy, and Why Customers Talk

Consider this pattern of perception:

1. People visit your site because they think you may have **value they want**.

2. People buy from you because you've convinced them that you have enough **new** value (your product) to part with the **existing** value they have (money).

3. People share or invite others because you've convinced them that you can offer **additional** value (e.g., elevated social standing, incentives, etc.) in exchange for **the risk of parting with the existing value** they have (their current social standing in the eyes of their network).

Perceived value is the foundation you need for users to complete your sales funnel. It's also the foundation you need for users to complete your viral loop.

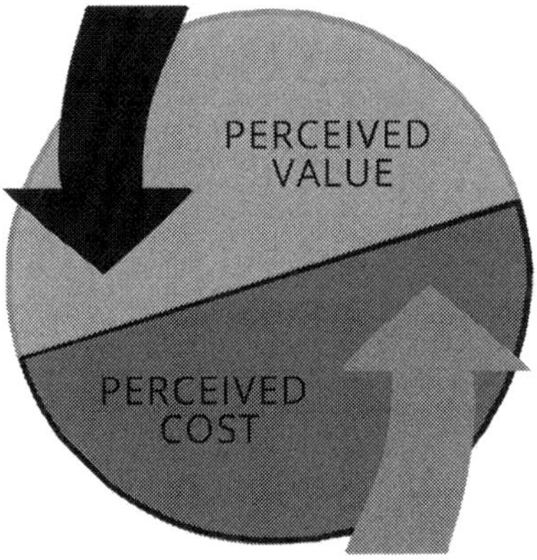

However, there's **one key difference** between completing your sales funnel and completing your viral loop. If users buy your product and it ends up being a mistake, nobody else has to know. They can choose to publicly complain (e.g., leave bad reviews), but this is a voluntary and relatively rare action. However, if users *share* your product and it ends up being a mistake, **that mistake is public.** They put their own credibility on the line to promote you, and as it's often more difficult to build and maintain social credibility than it is to make a few bucks, losing it can be more detrimental.

This public mistake is the **perceived cost**, and it's what you must ensure your perceived value outweighs in order to get (and keep) your viral marketing machine humming like a champ.

You win when you can successfully create enough perceived value in the minds of your users to outweigh or erase the perceived cost. In this case, you replace the fear of losing social credibility with a feeling of being "in the know." This then plants the idea in the minds of your users that sharing or inviting others will actually *increase* their social credibility.

You Can't Buy Viral Value

A common mistake is to think a viral incentive is the only form of viral value you need to offer.

Sure, supplying extrinsic rewards and incentives can **augment** the rate and frequency at which users send invites. But unless your incentives are ridiculously outlandish (which slashes profitability), it won't convince users to do something they don't see any value in otherwise.

Take PayPal for example.

Viral Value Success Story: PayPal

When PayPal first appeared on the scene, users received twenty dollars for every friend they referred to the service, who in turn also got twenty dollars for joining. A pretty nice incentive. Who doesn't love free money?

However, the real key to PayPal's viral marketing success was that this **incentive was not its core value**.

PayPal's core value was the ability to send and receive money. The cash bonus simply **pushed on-the-fence users over the edge**, inspiring them to take more immediate and profound action.

If PayPal hadn't offered this viral core value, it wouldn't have acquired **active, high-quality customers**. Sure, it still would have seen invites sent out from people trying to game the referral program and make a quick twenty, but PayPal wouldn't have experienced substantial and profound viral growth **in a cost-effective way**.

Overcoming "Inviter's Guilt"

A common phenomenon in any viral marketing program is what I call **inviter's guilt**. This is when users see the value *they* get from inviting others, but the guilt they feel about exploiting their friends to acquire that value prevents them from taking action.

Thankfully, this is easily overcome. You simply need to inject **double-sided value** into your viral value proposition and augment it with double-sided viral incentive marketing.

In the PayPal example above, as a member, *you* got viral value from using the service and being able to send and receive money online. As a sweet bonus, you also got twenty dollars for every additional member you referred.

But if that's as far as things went, inviter's guilt would have inhibited PayPal's viral growth. So PayPal added a double-sided viral value prop and a double-sided incentive. Not only did users see the value their friends would get from joining PayPal (i.e., the friends could also use a quick and secure way to send money), but **their friends also received twenty dollars for signing up**.

Get the picture?

Viral Value Success Story: Dropbox

PayPal's legendary referral program inspired another titan of viral we've discussed: Dropbox.

The online file-hosting service similarly used viral value wisely as the foundation of its viral marketing strategy. Only instead of waving around money to kickstart growth, it offered something just as—if not more—valuable.

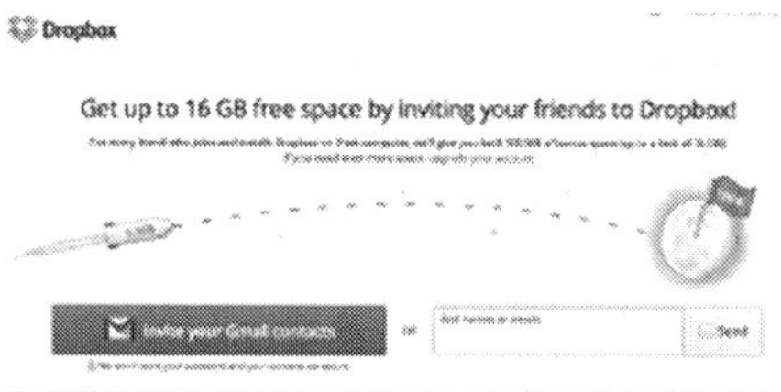

Here's a simple breakdown of the viral value Dropbox provided:

- **Users sign up for Dropbox** because they want space to store their files.

- They get *more* **value** when they share access to those files with others.

- They get ***even more*** **value** by inviting new users.

Just like PayPal, Dropbox offered both a double-sided viral value prop and a double-sided incentive. When a user invited a friend who successfully signed up, both received 500 MB of free space, and they both could benefit from Dropbox's file-storing and file-sharing services. It was **a win-win-win** for all parties involved.

Starting to make sense?

Measuring Viral Value

Viral value is not a soft-skill metric. It has very little to do with branding and a lot more to do with how quickly, easily, and cost effectively you **solve your users' core problems**. Branding is a fun thing to show your mom, but if the changes you make to your branding don't drive key metrics in a significant way, it's just more wasted time and resources.

So keep in mind the following when evaluating the true impact of your product's viral value:

- Focus more on specific metrics than on branding. (This will provide a quantitative, data-backed view of the value you're *actually* adding.)

- Take steps to **increase your viral value in comparison to the user's perceived cost**.

- Mitigate perceived cost by adding elements like **social proof** (such as tweets from influencers).

- Make sure any share or invite CTAs within your viral loop **lead with the benefits** users get from completing the action.

Your users **hate being "sold"** but they **love getting value**. Ensure they see the viral value *first* before they learn what they need to do in order to unlock it.

The Million-Dollar Questions

Want to achieve financial success and blow up all over the interwebs? Ask yourself these two questions:

- Are your users *currently* sending out a ton of shares and invites?
- If not, is the viral value prop you have *really* compelling enough to get customers to share?

Determine the answers to these questions, and you'll have a good idea where you need to start in achieving viral success. If you're having trouble finding the way, go back to the drawing board, and figure out how to add either more *actual* value or, at the very least, more *perceived* value to your viral CTAs.

Every great building starts with a great architect. The same is true for a great viral loop. To start architecting yours, make sure you fill out the corresponding sections of your *Viral Hero* Workbook - available for free at viralhero.com/workbook.

Chapter 6: Viral Loop Basics

Step 4: Your Viral Loop—How It Can Make You Absurdly Rich but May Also Make You Its Bitch

I've been talking a lot about your "viral loop" but haven't given much of a robust definition or visualization of what this is yet. That's what we'll cover next.

Your viral loop is the meanest, most generous, most incredible, most viciously humbling thing you will ever work with as a growth scientist. Not having one that works at all is a strong indicator that your product or service totally sucks. Having one that's absurdly effective can be just as catastrophic, as it may require you to scale well before you have the capital or manpower to do so.

But what the hell is it?

Your Viral Loop: Many Sides to the Same Coin

Simply put, your **viral loop** is all the steps a user goes through from becoming aware of a product to inviting the next set of new users to it.

Most business owners don't map out their viral loop. Instead, they think something along the lines of the following: *I'm going to create a product and add in these cool sharing buttons. If people like the site, they'll share it and tell their friends. Because . . . I've got these cool sharing buttons.* After that, business owners never give their viral loop a second thought. They then go back to working on their products and listing all the things they'll buy when they strike it rich.

Shortly thereafter, they fail.

However, some business owners put time, effort, and focus into mapping their viral loops with the most intricate detail possible. They then begin the process of systematically improving each step in their loops one by one. In no time at all, they find themselves on stage at some massive event talking about how they **acquired millions** of users by creating a product people love. Though if that's all they're telling people, they're leaving out an important step—namely, that they acquired millions of users by creating a product that people love *and* **share with others**.

To explore this idea, let's revisit the concepts of epidemiology, how actual viruses spread, and how they help us understand viral marketing.

One basic model epidemiologists use to project the spread of disease is called the SIR model, which was first conceptualized back in 1927.

This model states that there are three "buckets" that people fall into: susceptible, infectious, and recovered (which, oddly enough, is the category that dead people fall into as well, as they can no longer spread the disease).

- S (susceptible)
- I (infectious)
- R (recovered, or deceased)

While more complex viruses render a model like SIR obsolete, it works well for viruses like the flu, the measles, and others for which the progression through the model is pretty much linear. Based on what we talked about earlier (i.e., not needing our models to be 100 percent accurate in order to make sound decisions), it should work for us as well.

That said, know in advance that projecting virality, in our case, is going to be a bit paradoxical. While it helps epidemiologists and organizations like the CDC deal with a virus that behaves in a simple, predictable way, the viruses that spread the most effectively are the ones that break the projection models.

- They're the ones that can reinfect recovered individuals (or, in our case, reactivate former users or prospects who we previously deemed "dead").
- They're the ones that may spread through people who don't show symptoms at all (or, in our case, "believers" who are exposed to our product, don't have a use case for themselves at the moment, but still promote it to others).

- They're the ones that spread without a super-high-touch interaction, or are "airborne" (or, in our case, they use more than one viral marketing channel).

In other words, for tracking and projection purposes, we'd rather have simple, linear viral growth—but to maximize growth, we'd rather our viral growth be a bit more . . . complex.

It's important to know that epidemiologists use models like SIR specifically to project—and *prevent*—the spread of disease. In our case, we want to project and *promote* the viral growth of our product. Given this, we'll use a model that's more specialized for building viral products and acquiring users—viral loop.

To illustrate things a bit better, how about an example?

A Common Example of a Viral Loop Structure

Viral loops come in all shapes and sizes. Without knowing what you do or how you do it, it's impossible for me to map your unique viral loop.

That said, here's a walkthrough of a common viral loop structure to keep in mind while you're developing your own viral loop:

Step 1: Awareness—a Prospect Hears about Your Product

This awareness can come from an external "viral feeding" traffic source like a paid ad or organic search result in a search engine. It can also come via a viral invite from another existing user.

Once prospective users, or prospects, are exposed to your product, the next step begins.

Step 2: Interest—a Prospect Has a First Experience with Your Product

Somehow you've snagged enough of a person's interest to convince him or her to experience your product (e.g., come to your website, walk through your door for the first time, etc.). The person is now a "visitor" wanting to learn more about what you do and the value you offer.

You typically only have a brief amount of time (a few seconds, in fact) to make an impact and instill enough trust and confidence that the prospect moves forward in your viral loop. Let's assume the next action a prospect takes is to sign up for your product.

Step 3: Decision—a Visitor Signs Up as a User

You may have several steps in your user-signup funnel, and that's okay. Your signup funnel should itself be an optimized process—however, it's often at least partially contained within your viral loop, and step 3 assumes that this process has been a success.

You've shown enough perceived value to convince a user to sign up. Now you can demonstrate *actual* value by delivering on the promises you made to the user before he or she made this commitment (hopefully even *outdelivering* to really "wow" your users).

Step 4: Action—a Visitor Understands and Wants Your Viral Value

The new user has started receiving your product's core value. Here's where you reveal that the new user can get even *more* of that *same type* of value by taking a certain action to help spread your product to others.

This is your **viral value**.

Step 5: Recommendation—a User Shares or Sends Out Invites

To unlock your viral value, the user must invite others.

Invites could be anything, such as email referrals, Facebook shares, invites to collaborate, embedded tools, physically taking friends by the hand and leading them through your door—whatever option works best for your product.

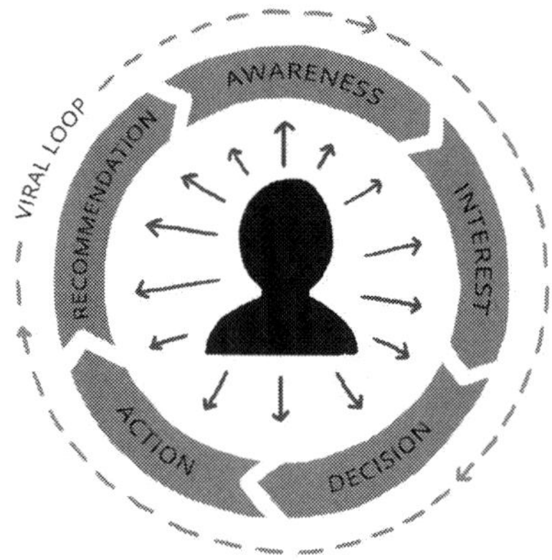

This invite then exposes your site or service to a new prospect (creating new awareness), **which closes one loop**

and starts a new one.

Let's take another glance at the epidemiology world.

Learning from Vaccination Behavior

Remember when we talked about epidemiologists using the SIR model to create projections to limit the spread of viruses? Well, in our case, we actually *want* our virus to spread, so we won't be trying to learn from epidemiologists here.

We'll be looking at the behavior of the viruses themselves.

First and foremost, it's important to note that the simple projection models (such as SIR) used in epidemiology assume that everybody in a population thinks and behaves in the same way. But the reality is that, as much as we may not want to admit it, different groups of people (i.e., different age groups, races, genders, religions, etc.) don't always think or behave in the same way.

These different groups of people are often more likely to consume different forms of media or be influenced by different brands, celebrities, or causes. Most importantly, they're much more likely to hang around with other people who think and behave like they do.

In epidemiology, this would make certain groups of people more susceptible to certain diseases—and more likely to be vaccinated for those diseases—than other groups, based on whom they intermingle with most frequently.

Here's an example: Let's say good ol' Bill is susceptible to a virus. If he thinks he's more likely than not to become exposed to the virus, he'll be more likely to get vaccinated. For example, if his neighbor

Lucy gets sick, or Lucy's daughter Jane catches the virus, Bill will take the risk of contracting the virus more seriously, and the probability that he'll get vaccinated will increase. If he sees a report about the virus on a news outlet he follows, he'll take things even *more* seriously. But if he doesn't encounter either of these situations, it's a lot less likely he'll take action, as the threat of catching the virus doesn't really hit home.

What can we learn from viruses and vaccination behavior that we can use to spread our product?

1. First, we need to comb through our data to assess who our most and least viral users are. What do the top 10 percent most viral users have in common with each other? What about the top 10 percent least viral users?

2. Once we've grouped these users, we should objectively assess how we can acquire more of the most viral ones and avoid paying much to acquire the least viral ones (unless, of course, they're valuable in some other way).

3. One of the most helpful things we can do is reach out to and have conversations with as many of our most and least viral users as possible.

4. We should then create psychographic personas for each category and figure out how each group found us, the value they get from our products, whom they hang around with socially, whom they interact with professionally, where they spend most of their time online, what apps they use most often, and so forth.

5. As often as possible, we must show prospective users which of their friends, colleagues, or coworkers are using or are "fans" of our product. We want the spread of our product to hit home with prospects, making it far more likely they'll take action.

In Summary

To understand your viral loop, you must create a detailed, metrics-backed map of all the steps that must occur for a user to successfully do the following:

- Have a first experience with your product
- Understand your product and the value you offer
- Make the decision to share or send an invite

Diagram this viral loop as a cyclical process that you can visualize, discuss, and brainstorm around. **Make sure to include your data at each step so you can see where your bottlenecks are** (we'll talk more about bottlenecks in a bit).

Also, try to include the segmentation factors that describe your most likely converters through your viral loop. Try to figure out why those users behave the way they do, and assess how to either attract more of those users or make other users behave in a similar way.

At the end of the day, successfully improving each step in your viral loop involves **increasing the perceived viral value** for users who send invites or referrals and adding an additional, often time-sensitive reward (e.g., viral incentive marketing). Of course, the overall goal is to incite more immediate and profound action that can be repeated.

Step 5: Your Viral Carrier, and the Two KPIs That Can Make or Break Any Viral Marketing Campaign

Now that you're in the loop (see what I did there?), let's kick this viral game up a notch.

Getting users to send their first invites is the first step toward viral success. If that's all they do, you're winning big. But what if you can get each of them to send another? And another? Then three? or five? or twenty?

That, my friends, is what we'll dive into next.

As you build and examine your viral loop, you'll soon find that you're leaking users in various ways. This can happen for any number of reasons, such as the following:

- High bounce rates on specific parts of the experience
- Broken features that make users think ill of you
- A plethora of little hiccups within your user journey

Finding these leaks and putting **corks** in them will make things incrementally better every day.

Your Viral Carrier Starts with the "Cork"

If your analytics tools are reporting data correctly, they'll reveal exactly where the corks in your funnel should go, whether that means fixing a bug or addressing a bounce-rate issue. Then you can effectively eliminate these leaks and get users flowing through your funnel like they should.

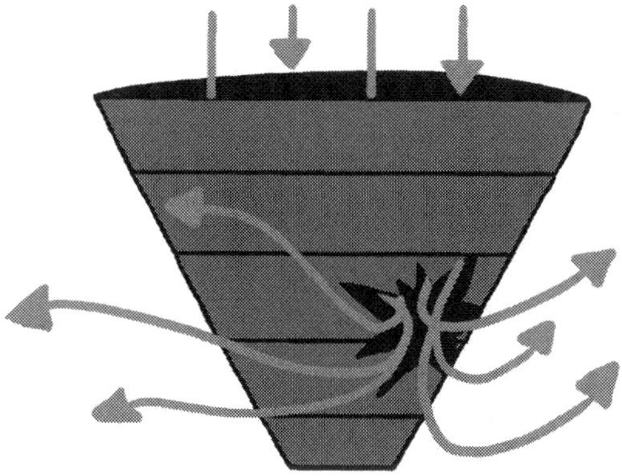

This process will occur often within your traditional sales funnel. That's just the nature of optimization. Which is why the same process should take place with viral optimization. And it all begins with your **viral carrier**.

The Bottom of the Viral Funnel

A **viral carrier** is the method through which invites are sent to potential users by existing users. In other words, it's *how* people share your product with or invite others.

Most sites don't think twice about this. They assume sharing is a spur-of-the-moment thing and hope and pray for a miracle. Usually one never happens. Why?

Because good viral marketing is engineered. It happens on purpose, and it's carefully thought out, planned, and optimized by analyzing live interactions with users, visitors, and customers—all of which results in informed decision making.

So, based on what you know about your users, how does your typical user send invites? Is it via email? social media? snail mail? text? paper airplane? tying it to the ankle of a pigeon? **Do you even *know*?**

Regardless of what your answer is, ask yourself this even better question: *Based on my service, what is the most **relevant and logical method** for sending invites?* If it's a social service, sending invites through social media makes the most sense—so social media is your best potential viral carrier.

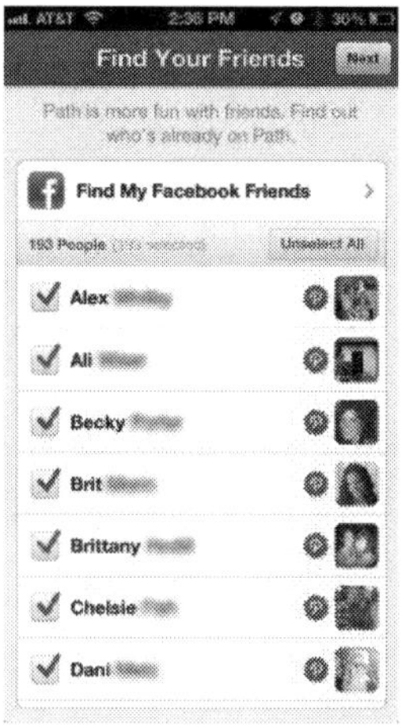

If it's a team collaboration tool used to manage employees or co-workers, email is far more logical—so email is your best potential viral carrier.

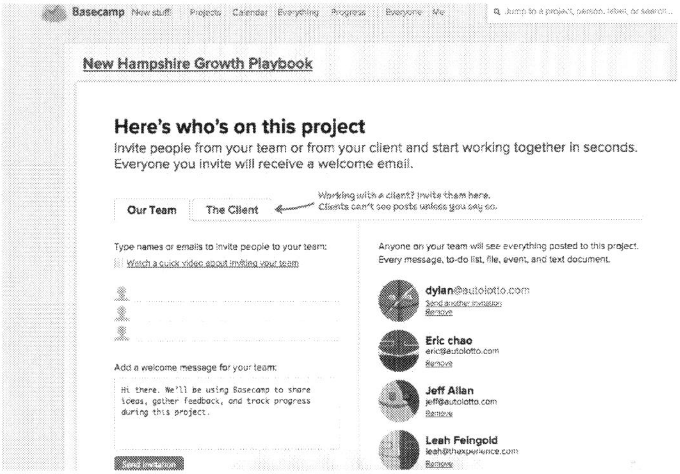

Get the picture?

Great. Now, let's look at . . .

A Few Relevant Viral Metrics

Before we talk about your specific viral carrier, let's talk a bit about viral growth metrics and the two KPIs that can make or break any viral marketing campaign. To help, we'll be joined by our good friend Math.

The first metric we'll explore is the following:

- The number of invites sent per user on average. Let's call this *i*.

Let's say **User A** has sent out **two** invites to other users in the past month, and **User B** has sent out **four** invites in that same time period. We need to find the **average** of these two numbers during this time, which is represented by the following equation:

i = (total number of invites sent) / total number of users

In this case, this is what our equation looks like:

i = (2 invites from User A + 4 invites from User B) / 2 total users = 3

So during this time period, *i* = 3. Not bad, right?

But wait, the math doesn't end there!

The variable *i* only refers to the number of invites *sent* per user on average, not the number of new users you get in return. You don't care about *i* by itself; you care about *growth*! To find out how many users you get from these invites, you need to factor in the **average conversion rate** on invites sent out by your users. We'll call this *conv%*.

Let's assume you have that same *i* value of three invites sent out per user on average. Let's then assume that, out of those three invites, **one of those people** who received an invite **becomes a user**. Here's this equation:

conv% = total number of new users / i

Plugging in the numbers, here's what we get:

conv% = 1 new users / 3 invites sent = ***33.3%***

So 33.3 percent of all invites convert into new users. *Math strikes again!*

How to Boost Your Viral Carrier like a Boss

Both *i* and *conv%* are incredibly important viral metrics to consider when performing viral optimization. **And both are heavily dependent on the viral carrier.**

Here are a few questions you need to ask yourself (and test ruthlessly) to ensure you can boost these two metrics as much as possible:

- Is there a different type of viral carrier that increases *i* more?
- Which viral carrier are you using that yields the highest *conv%*?
- Is it necessary to activate users (e.g., sign them up) before they invite others, or is your *i* value independent of user activation?
- Do you have a way of measuring any of this?
- Are there certain segments of users in which *i* or *conv%* is higher? lower?
- Why do you think this might be happening?
- Is it time to get rid of those messenger pigeons?

Work through these questions, and your viral carrier will turn into one of your most powerful growth assets.

Step 6: Your Viral Branching Factor, and How It Can Help Grow Your User Base like a Weed

Your *i* value (number of invites sent) will heavily depend on two things: how quickly and noticeably your invites are delivered through your viral carriers, and the **saturation level** of your viral carriers—meaning, how many competitors or other services are using these carriers or have used them in the past.

However, before we dig into the finer nuances of all that, there is something that will affect your *i* value even more: your **branching factor**. And that's exactly what we'll discuss next.

Now that we've covered your viral carrier, it makes sense that the next step is to make that carrier more effective. So that's exactly what we're about to do with a viral branching tune-up.

One Critical Micro-KPI of Viral Growth

One of the key performance indicators, or KPIs, that can help you amplify your viral growth in a big bad way is **the number of invites sent out per user on average**, which we went over in the last chapter and lovingly refer to as *i*.

As we discussed, you can estimate your viral growth over time by combining this metric with two other key players:

- **The conversion rate on those invites** (a.k.a. *conv%*)

- The "**cycle time**," or amount of time it takes for each viral loop to happen (a.k.a. *ct*)

Each of these KPIs has smaller micro-KPIs involved in calculating them. Your *i* value—the number of invites sent per user on average—largely depends on the average number of invites the average user sends **each time that user sends any invites at all**. (Try saying that ten times fast.) This is called your **branching factor**, and improving this is one of the quickest ways to increase *i*.

Before we dig too deeply into branching, let's take a look at another virus, shall we?

Learning from MRSA

MRSA is a tricky virus to model, so there's a lot we can learn from it. It's an antibiotic-resistant staph infection that can cause normal cuts and scrapes to become potentially life-threatening infections.

MRSA can spread through contact such as hugging or kissing, through transmission of bodily fluids from open wounds, or through other contact. However, it can also live on surfaces like countertops, tile floors, and even towels. The multiple transmission paths make settings like locker rooms ideal locations for the virus to spread, as it can lead to a higher branching factor (e.g., one person infects a tile floor in a locker room, and multiple people step on the infected area).

What's more, some people who carry the MRSA bacteria don't show any symptoms, making it even more difficult to model or track; thus, groups of people like sports teams are more likely to experience rapid group infections.

Epidemiologists look at a disease like MRSA and ask themselves questions like these:

- Which groups of people are more likely to hug, and which are more likely to keep their distance?

- What types of individuals cover their open wounds with bandages, and which are less likely to?

- How many people in a neighborhood are regular gym goers or regularly visit other environments where the spread of staph infections is more common?

- Which environments are most conducive to a high branching factor, therefore making it extra important to clean and disinfect them regularly?

So what can we learn from MRSA?

1. First off, we want to deeply investigate how our most viral prospects interact with each other, and we should attempt to make our viral message mirror that type of interaction, if possible.

2. Next, we should interview our most viral prospects to assess which products they strongly dislike and what their pet peeves are regarding how companies communicate with them. This will help us determine what forms of marketing or messaging will be most or least effective, and we can try to validate those answers with real behavioral data.

3. After that, we should determine where we find large clusters of our most viral prospects. Where do they congregate in the highest density? What places do they frequent most often in their daily lives? We can try to expose and reexpose prospects to our product there.

4. Lastly, we should explore the best way to encourage branching in a high-density area. More specifically, we should ask ourselves these questions: Which carrier feels

most "natural" for multiple rapid invites? And how can we craft a process to make branching more likely?

Types of Viral Branching

Your users have a short attention span. **The more work you require them to do to complete a task, the fewer will complete it.** It's not that your product necessarily sucks or that your reward incentives are too low—it's that you're battling against the rest of your users' lives. Your users are busy people. They have other things they need to do that require their time and attention. Like binge watching Netflix, or trying to figure out what they should binge watch on Netflix next. Therefore, if your invite process is too time consuming or labor intensive, your branching factor (and your *i* value) will be minimal.

So what can you do?

Selection Branching

Say you've analyzed the data and observed that a good percentage of users will invite one friend. That's a fine place to start. Knowing that at least some of your users are willing to invite at least one friend tells you that your process isn't too time consuming or intense.

But why stop there? Why not try employing a different invite flow that requires the same amount of time or work from users but allows them to invite multiple friends in one shot?

This is called **selection branching**.

Here's an example: replacing a good old-fashioned email-invite flow (where users manually enter friends' emails into a field) with a bulk-invite opt

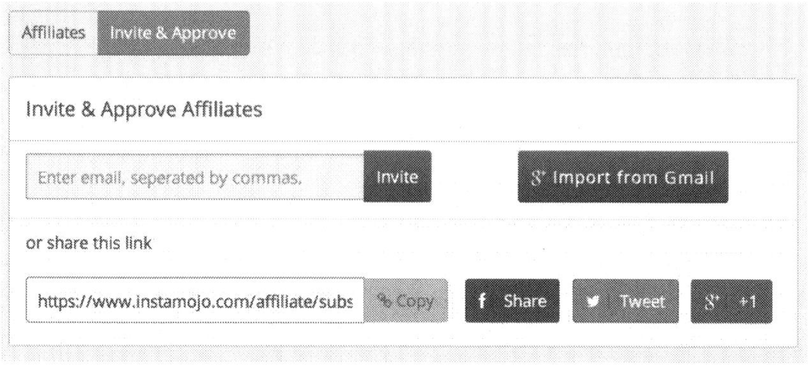

You don't need to completely replace the single-entry email field—some users might still prefer it. But having the option of selecting from an address book or Gmail contacts list makes inviting fifty friends as easy as inviting one.

The great thing about this is that not every user needs to invite multiple people for your *i* value to increase significantly. In fact, if just a small portion of users use your bulk tool, you'll see an increase.

Selection Branching in Action (a.k.a. Math!)

Let's say you have ten users who each invite one friend. This means that, through those ten users, ten invites have been sent out.

$$i = 10 / 10 = 1.0$$

After you add your bulk-invite tool, nine of those ten users still each invite one friend, but the final user invites six friends. You now have the same ten users, but fifteen invites have now been sent out.

$$i = 15 / 10 = 1.5$$

Pretty sweet, right? Each time one user invites more than one friend in the same action, your branching factor increases along with your *i* value—and your viral awesomeness.

High fives!

But wait—we're not done. There's something else we can do to increase branching even more.

Prediction Branching

Every product is unique. Given the differences of your product, who your users are, and how your users prefer to use your product, there's going to be an ideal method for sending invites that's best for your product.

If you can use your data to **predict** (or at least retroactively analyze and locate) what this method is, not only will your *i* value increase but your *conv%* too. (*Note: Be sure to test for this last part. In rare cases, you'll see* i *increase but* conv% *decrease to the point where the math doesn't work in your favor.*)

For example, if you are a B2B SaaS tool, your users will probably be much more likely to invite friends via email. However, if you are a mobile game app, you may see considerably more success with bulk Facebook-friend invites.

What's more, if you've done any work in CRO, you know that the farther users have to scroll down a page, the more likely it is they'll drop off. So ideally, you'll want to get creative by displaying the friends your users are most likely to invite **right at the top of their invite lists**.

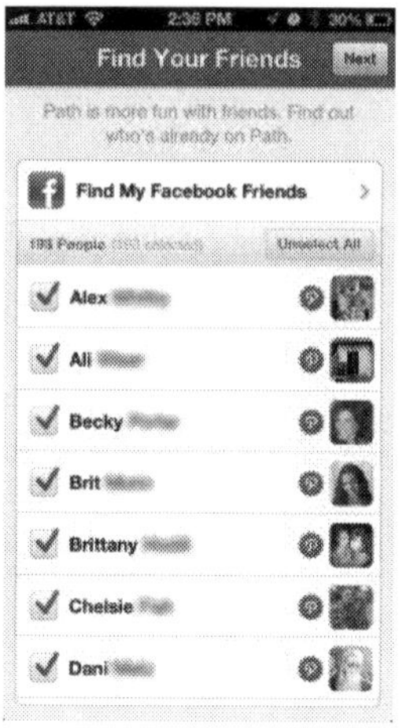

Here's an example of how to do this: say you have an SaaS tool that uses viral collaboration marketing. You could try building a custom function showing users their Gmail contacts **with the same email suffix** (e.g., @yourawesomecompany.com). If they're within the same organization, it's more likely they'll want to collaborate on projects.

Showing your users' most relevant friends at the top of their invite lists will not only increase their likelihood of inviting these friends but may even remind them of people they should invite but otherwise would have forgotten about.

This is viral branching at its best. You want to predict *how* your users will want to send invites to the friends they're *most likely* to send invites to.

Boom! Boom! *Pow!*

Step 7: Your Viral Marketing Hook, and Getting Users to Take the Bait by Making the Bait Awesome

Creating a well-built viral product is the bee's knees in a big way, *but* architecture is only one piece of the puzzle. To fill in some of the missing pieces, we're going to dive back into one of the foundations of viral marketing. You guessed it: fishing.

I'm going to start this discussion with a little anecdote. It may seem pointless at first, but stick with me.

A few months back, I tried fly fishing for the first time. I was on a remote mountain in Utah, and the weather was beautiful. I was with a group of friends, and we had an instructor who had been fly fishing for fifteen years.

As a former athlete, I'm obsessed with mastering the mechanics of an activity. I firmly believe that with sound fundamentals, even mediocre athletes can compete at the highest levels. So after about an hour of practicing the mechanics with the instructor, I was ready to catch every fish in the world. The instructor helped me prep my rod for the first cast, and I caught a fish within the first three minutes.

Clearly I'm the best fly fisherman here. Come at me, fish.

What Fly Fishing Taught Me about Viral Marketing

Feeling brassy as all hell, I made a bet with a friend that I could catch more fish than he could in two hours. Filled to the brim with my newfound confidence and perfectly executed mechanics, I promptly began casting the crap out of those waters.

An hour later, **I hadn't caught a thing.**

Something was wrong. Was it my mechanics? I rewalked through every step and asked the instructor to show me a few more times. Everyone around me was catching fish and having a grand ol' fishy time, but I wasn't making any progress. And I had a bet to win!

Sensing my growing frustration, the instructor came over, took one look at what I was doing, and chuckled to himself.

"Did you rebait your hook after your last catch?"

. . . *Shit.*

Once we put a fat night crawler on my hook, guess what happened only a few minutes later?

The moral of the story: The fish didn't care about my mechanics. Or how awesome I was. They just wanted the worm I was throwing in the water. The mechanics helped once I had a worm on the hook, but without the worm, the mechanics were meaningless.

Viral Marketing Hook: Using the Best-Possible Bait

The core reason a person shares your product with others is called your **viral marketing hook**. (*Note: This should not be confused with your viral hook point, which is the moment at which users actually* become aware *of the value sharing your product provides.*)

> The viral marketing hook is determined by a few key things:

- The **dynamics** of your product
- The **core value** your product provides
- Which of the **twelve types of viral marketing** you're using
- What **additional value** users unlock when they share your product

While a poor product can adversely affect your user experience and viral loop (with poor content, a poor slideshow, a poor widget, etc.), most people place the blame on the viral marketing hook by default. What they *don't* consider (but should) are the other influential factors that have an impact on the user decision-making process.

B = M + A + T

The **Fogg Behavioral Model** (shown above) tells us that behavior, or **B**, comes from three things:

- **Motivation (M)**: Why should people take an action? Why should they do it *now*? Is this obvious at a glance? The higher the motivation, the more likely your users are to take action (which in this case is sharing or sending invites).

- **Ability (A)**: Does anything prevent users from taking action? Is your interface even semi confusing? Is it too much work to act? Too expensive? Is the process intimidating, or is it *super* quick and easy?

- **Trigger (T)**: What tells the user that it's now time to take action? For example, the ringing of a phone tells us there's somebody calling and we need to answer the phone. What's the "ringing phone" of your viral loop?

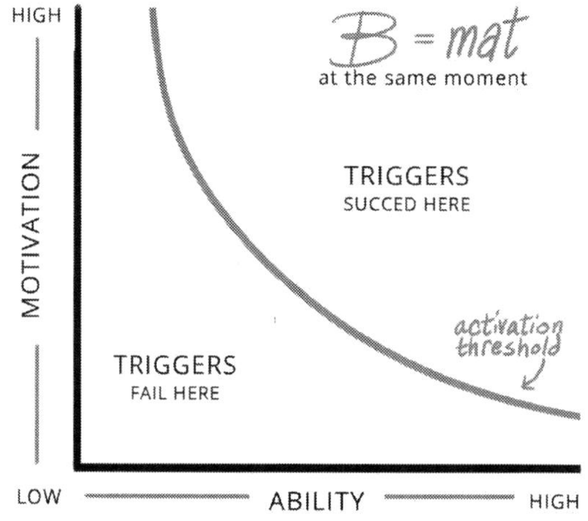

Your viral hook is a **combination of the M and the T** in the Fogg Behavioral Model above.

When you identify when you can most clearly communicate that it's the right time for users to share and that their experience will be enhanced when they do so, you've identified your **viral hook point**.

To help yourself find this hook point, look at your application, and ask this question: *Within which of my features* ***does it actually make sense to*** *encourage a user to reach out and connect with a nonuser?*

And without further ado, how about another virus?

Learning from Rabies

Rabies is a relatively well-known virus spread through the saliva of infected animals. We've had vaccines for rabies since the twenties, but the virus still causes problems in places like India and Africa. With all the vaccines and treatments available, an infected person who gets treatment promptly can be easily cured—but if this person does not seek treatment, he or she is 100 percent going to die. This is an incredibly high-stakes situation that drives successful vaccination behavior in most parts of the world.

The unique aspect of rabies, obviously, is that it's spread through animal bites. It's not airborne, but human beings are so drawn to cute, furry creatures—even wild ones—they'll often voluntarily put themselves in harm's way for the "hook" of getting to feel soft fur and being looked at lovingly by a cuddly, cute creature. (Kind of ridiculous, but it's part of our nature as human beings.)

Also, approaching a wild or stray animal can activate the nucleus accumbens in our brains, which stimulates the brain's addiction center with the anticipation of a variable reward. *Will the animal like me, shy away, or attack?* (More on this later.)

So what can we learn from rabies?

1. First, we must communicate the stakes of the situation. Why would users care about what we're trying to get them to do? What would reality look like if they did *not* take action?

2. Then, we must examine the role human nature plays during times of high-arousal emotion, specifically as it relates to our hook. Can we tie our hook to feelings of compassion? awe? rage? amusement?

3. Finally, we should determine whether we can activate the nucleus accumbens by communicating the variable nature of what might happen next after a successful invite action.

A Butterfly Halfway across the World Can Create a Typhoon . . . or Something

You know that old saying (hopefully better than I do) that basically means it takes just a small action to create a huge impact.

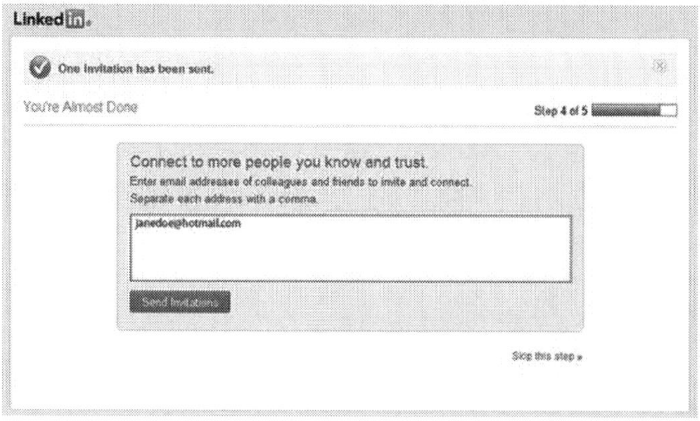

According to LinkedIn cofounder Reid Hoffman, in the early days of LinkedIn, only a half dozen out of thousands of features actually encouraged this sort of viral impact. And of those, **only two** made any real difference. **These two would be considered hooks.**

The important thing to understand is that LinkedIn integrated these features from the start and was able to test which of them best meshed with its core value. Those special few created a butterfly effect.

When to Bait Your Viral Hook

Viral marketing mechanics can't be easily grafted into a service when there's no real value to be gained from them. The creators of the best viral products build their viral loops *before* building their core products, ensuring they can engineer and optimize both the loops and the hooks before embarking on the epic, arduous journey of starting a new company.

This doesn't mean you can't build a viral marketing engine after you've built your product. You'll just need to accept that it might be a long, hard road full of serious changes and potentially even major pivots. After all, to get what you've never gotten, you must be willing to do what you've never done . . . or something.

Hey, give me a break here. I'm a growth engineer, not a motivational speaker.

(Oh, and in case you were wondering, I did *not* win the bet I told you about at the beginning of this section. But I did get a great anecdote, so I'll count that as a moral victory.)

To begin planning your own viral loops, check out the corresponding sections of the *Viral Hero* Workbook. Get your free copy at viralhero.com/workbook.

Chapter 7: Key Pieces of Virality

Step 8: Your Viral Invite—Level One in the Game of Viral Growth

If you've reached this point, congrats! You've built your viral engine.

We started by answering six magical questions to build your viral marketing structure. We then took the five simple steps of optimizing it, formed your viral loop, and expanded your user base with viral branching. At the end of the last chapter, we discussed how to bait those users with the perfect viral hook.

But where's the growth?

Just because your users are *sending* invites doesn't mean the people *receiving* them are actually doing anything.

Let's change that, shall we?

The Intersection of Internet Marketing and Virality

Ever hear of "the big orange button"? If not, you've got some homework to do. (It's a pretty famous concept in conversion rate optimization.)

The big orange button essentially refers to a low-tech, high-impact color change of your call-to-action button—making it stand out in contrast to other page elements—that will increase your conversion rates.

Whether you believe it or not, this is a cornerstone concept of conversion optimization.

Zero times out of ten does the process of improving your conversion rate involve slogging through a swamp of math and tech wizardry. You just need to **educate yourself** enough to know how to make some simple yet beneficial changes, in the right order and at the right time—sometimes it's as easy as changing the color of a button on your webpage.

Thankfully, if you've educated yourself on the subject of viral marketing (which you're currently doing if you're reading this. *Huzzah!*), you'll know that one of the more important yet wildly underappreciated aspects of any viral loop is also one of the easiest aspects to improve: the **viral invite process**.

Viral Invite: Growth Made Easy

A **viral invite** is the act of a user sending out an invite from your site or application or sharing a link to it with the goal of recruiting others—in other words, it's users physically carrying out the action you want them to take that directly contributes to your viral growth.

Everyone's familiar with the concept of invitations. (Unless you have no friends—in which case, consider this your formal invitation to be my and Viral Panda's friend. Welcome.)

Take everything you know about invitations, and combine it with what you've learned about sound viral marketing strategy. The result is nothing short of awesome, so long as you put in the work.

Without a doubt, all the viral factors we've discussed so far are critical. You cannot achieve viral growth effectively without those factors. But once you've created your viral value, added your incentive, identified your hook, and optimized your mechanics, you must spend considerable time and effort making it as **quick, easy, and intuitive as possible** for users to invite many others in one shot.

How are you going to do this? This is where conversion rate optimization comes in.

Optimizing for Viral Invites

The first thing to keep in mind is that conversion rate optimization is not specific to sales.

A conversion action is whatever **you want your users to do**. Conversion rate optimization (CRO) is improving the rate at which users take that action.

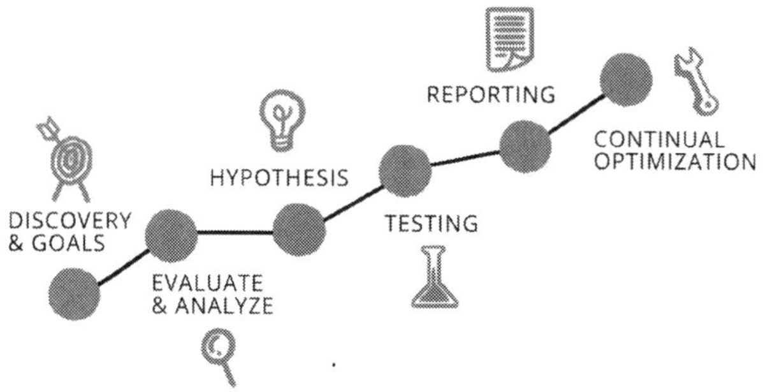

When you improve your sales funnel's ease of use, decrease the number of steps it requires, and reduce possible friction points, your sales will inevitably increase. The same holds true in your viral loop.

The first step is asking a few key questions:

- What is the process of sending an invite like? Map it out using a tool like Lucidchart.
- How can you make the above process quicker and more efficient? Think from both a design and a technology perspective. Use resources like ConversionXL, the Unbounce blog, and the Conversion Rate Experts blog to find all the conversion factors that can help.
- Is every step absolutely critical for users to take *right now* to

reach the end goal? Can any of it be done later, or dropped completely? Use common sense and logic for this.

- What viral value does a user gain by sending an invite? Try to quantify this, make it more obvious, and increase it.

- How can you augment that value even more with viral incentive marketing? Get users who are on the fence about acting off that fence and on your side of it.

I could continue to bloviate about how important CRO is, but I'll save you some time and instead encourage you to check out the resources I've listed above. You can use these to supplement what you'll find here, and in no time, you'll have everything you need to create an optimized viral invite process that delivers the goods.

Step 9: Your Viral Marketing Message—Five Steps to Doubling Viral Growth

You're officially past the halfway point in our discussion about creating your viral marketing engine. Everything you've done so far has been critical to your success. And let's say that looking at your analytics, you see you've got great data. Pat yourself on the back!

Have a drink (or some bamboo if you're a panda), and take pride in how far you've come.

But wait—do you feel that? Something just . . . ugh. **Something just isn't right.**

That viral machine isn't humming along like it should, and your growth curve isn't sharpening like you (and potentially your investors) want it to.

What's going on?

When an Old Loop Ends, a New Loop Begins

Just because your users are inviting others doesn't mean those invitees are opening the invites. And if they *are* opening the invites, they might not be taking any action once they do. As a business, you could get users to send a million bazillion invites or share a billion gazillion things across every major social network, but by themselves, those actions will be totally meaningless. The invites and shares won't get you more new users or more sales. Heck, they won't even buy you a cup of coffee at Starbucks.

The real value comes from what happens next—specifically, new prospects being exposed to your product or your message **and then actually taking the action you want them to take.**

This, my friend, leads us to your **viral marketing message**—the beginning of any new viral loop.

The majority of your prospective users will become aware of your site or app through an invite from a friend or colleague. For a percentage of them, that's as far as they'll go. However, **if you do your job**

correctly, most of those prospects will come see what all their friends and colleagues are fussing about, which gives you a great chance to convert them into a user.

The End (and the Beginning) of Your Viral Loop

While the middle of your viral loop will usually be unique to your site or app and will depend on the experience within your product and the types of viral marketing you've activated, the beginning and the end of all viral loops are the same:

- **The end** is when a user you've recruited to your site experiences enough value to send an invite to a friend or colleague.
- **The beginning** is when a person the previous user invited receives the invite.

Every viral loop starts and ends with one person. As soon as the first person transfers the required action to another person, the first person's loop is over, and the new person's loop begins.

We talked about the end of your viral loop in the last section, but we haven't spent much time on the beginning of your viral loop. That's what we'll discuss next.

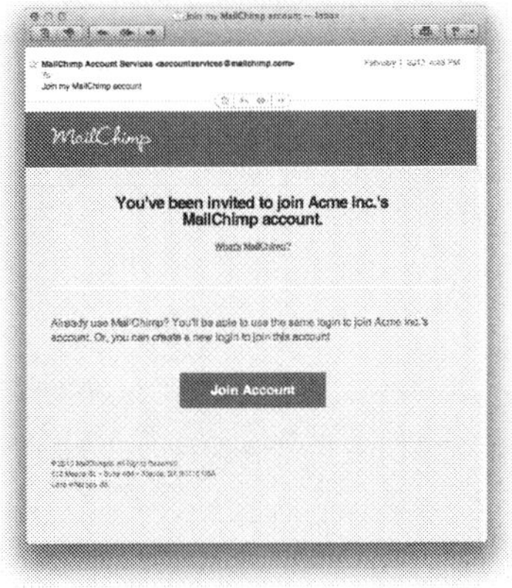

The Composition of a Great Viral Message

A great viral marketing message has **five distinct components:**

- **The Attention Grabber:** This is how your viral message steals receivers' attention away from the rest of the noise in their lives. For email invites, this is the subject line and sender name standing out from the rest of the garbage in receivers' inboxes. For social broadcasts, it's the imagery and the headline.

- **The Referrer's Name:** Referrals tend to have a far higher conversion rate than ads or cold outreach. That's because the invitations come from known and trusted sources (i.e., friends or coworkers). But to feel this trust, receivers must *know* whom the referral came from as quickly as possible. For example, the referrer's name must be in the headline of the invite email. Otherwise, the receiver won't see it unless he or she opens the email, which few people will do if they think it's spam.

- **Short yet Compelling Message Content:** A great viral message must account for receivers' short attention spans while simultaneously doing its job. So get right to the point. In one or (at most) two sentences, tell receivers what they're being referred to and why. This looks something like this: "John Doe is inviting you to join him on Dropbox—the easiest way to store and share files." Curate this text as much as possible to maximize click-through rates.

- **Proper Context:** Receivers need to know not only what they're being referred to but also why they'll love it and why they need it *now*. In certain cases, you'll be the best person to curate this message, as in the previous step. In others, the referrer may be the best person to customize this message with his or her own content. It depends on who your users are and how many use cases you have. This looks something like this: "John Doe just shared a folder named World Domination Plans with you on Dropbox—the easiest way to store and share files." See the difference? Use your best judgment here, and test, test, test.

- **A Clear Call to Action**: Once users know who referred them, what they're being referred to, and why they need it, your final task is to give them a clear and intuitive next step. Ideally, your call to action should tell users exactly where they'll land after they click. This means following the example statement above with "Click Here to Join This Folder" or something of that nature.

The **click-through rate (CTR)** from your viral marketing message will depend entirely on how well you execute the above five items. You may only have a few short moments to convince invited users to both pay attention and make the decision you want them to.

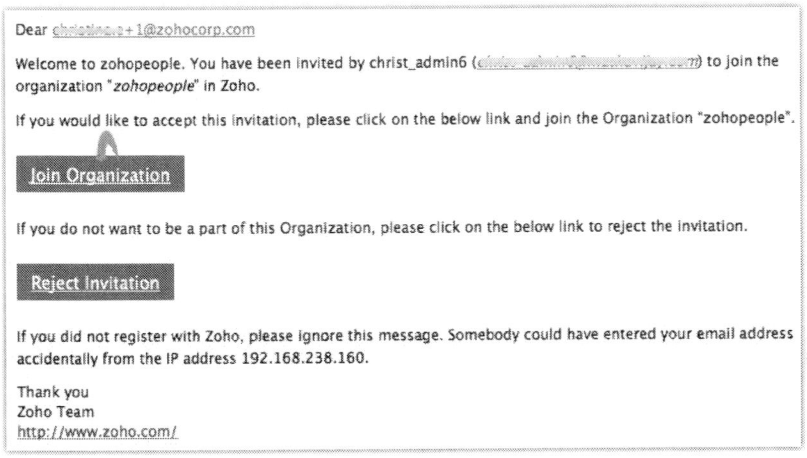
Dear [illegible]+1@zohocorp.com

Welcome to zohopeople. You have been invited by christ_admin6 ([illegible]) to join the organization "*zohopeople*" in Zoho.

If you would like to accept this invitation, please click on the below link and join the Organization "zohopeople".

Join Organization

If you do not want to be a part of this Organization, please click on the below link to reject the invitation.

Reject Invitation

If you did not register with Zoho, please ignore this message. Somebody could have entered your email address accidentally from the IP address 192.168.238.160.

Thank you
Zoho Team
http://www.zoho.com/

Conversion rate optimization techniques lead to huge virality wins if you apply them to your viral marketing message. I strongly encourage you check out other resources like ConversionXL and the Unbounce blog to help educate you further in this area.

Step 10: What Your Viral Media and "Love at First Sight" Have in Common

So you've enticed your users into sending out invites. In turn, their friends are taking the bait of your well-crafted message hook, line, and sinker. You've won this battle, **but the war is far from over**.

The logical next step is to strategically create the place those newly invited visitors will end up after accepting the invite. After all, everything you've done so far is meaningless if you haven't optimized that "unboxing."

You get one chance to make a good first impression. So the first-ever experience these visitors have better *wow* them into taking further action.

This is the big money moment. Don't screw it up.

Life after the Click

Once people click on an invite or something that's been shared with them, what do they see? What's their experience after that first click?

This is where your **viral media** takes over.

Your viral media is what the invite or shared content looks like or says. To give you a better idea of what this entails, below are a few examples of viral media that several companies with prolific viral-success stories use to impress—and later convert—their prospects.

- For YouTube, it's the **content of shared videos**. The primary goal is to get prospects to watch more videos, be exposed to more ads, and potentially make and upload videos of their own to share with others.

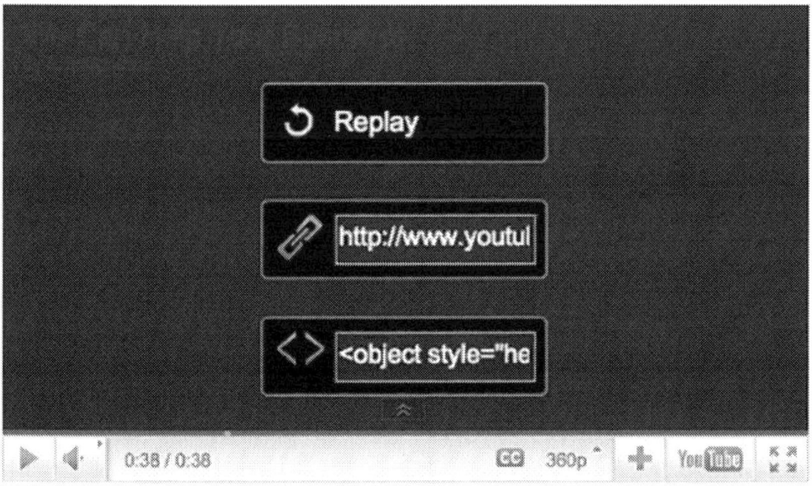

- For SlideShare, it's the **content of shared presentations**. The primary goal is to get prospects to consume more presentations, sign up for accounts, and potentially make and upload presentations of their own to share with others.

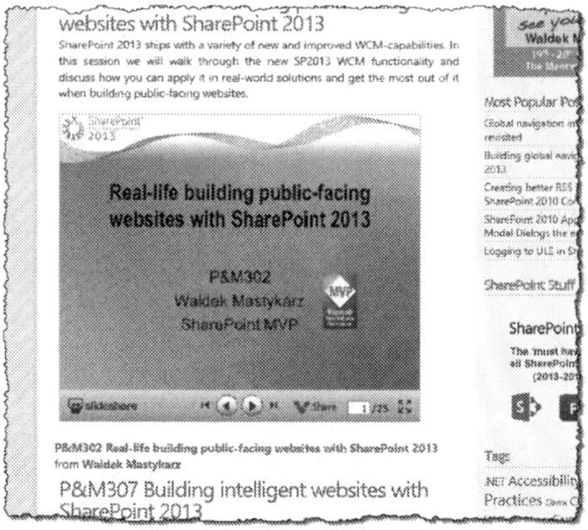
websites with SharePoint 2013
SharePoint 2013 ships with a variety of new and improved WCM-capabilities. In this session we will walk through the new SP2013 WCM functionality and discuss how you can apply it in real-world solutions and get the most out of it when building public-facing websites.
Real-life building public-facing websites with SharePoint 2013
P&M302
Waldek Mastykarz
SharePoint MVP
P&M302 Real-life building public-facing websites with SharePoint 2013 from Waldek Mastykarz
P&M307 Building intelligent websites with SharePoint 2013

- For BuzzFeed, it's the **content of shared articles**. The primary goal is to get prospects to click on and consume more articles, be exposed to more ads, and potentially find content they want to share with others.

BuzzFeed
LOL
win
omg
cute
fail
wtf
News
Buzz
Life
Entertainment
Quizzes
Videos
More
TOP POST
2,001,682 VIEWS
33 Startling Photos Of Porn Stars With And Without Their Makeup On
BuzzFeed NEWS

- For DropBox, it's the **content of folders or files shared by inviting users**. The primary goal is to get prospects to sign up for accounts themselves, upload some of their own files, and potentially invite others to gain access to those files.

Get extra space free!
Complete these simple tasks and instantly boost your Dropbox space!
Like Dropbox? Tell your friends on Facebook
128MB
Tell your friends on Facebook why they would like Dropbox and get some extra free space!
I love Dropbox because it's so easy to use, and I never have to carry my flashdrive around.
Post on Facebook
Tweet about Dropbox for more free space!
128MB
Tell your friends on Twitter why you love Dropbox and get some more free space!
I love Dropbox because it's so easy to use, and I never have to carry my flashdrive around.
Post on Twitter

- For Basecamp, it's the **content of the projects prospects are invited to view or collaborate on**. The primary goal is to get prospects to interact and collaborate on that first project, create accounts and projects of their own, and potentially invite others to collaborate on future projects.

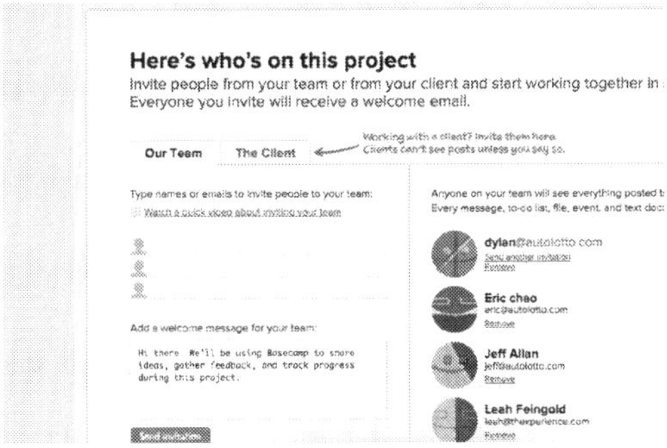

- For TED, it's the **content of shared videos**. The primary goal is to get prospects to watch more videos, find videos they find fascinating, and share those with others.

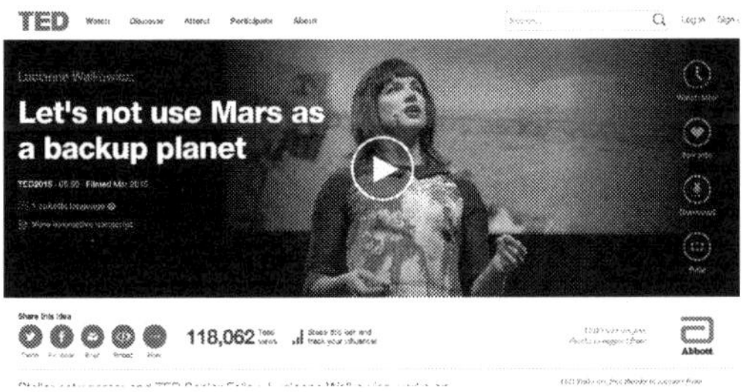

Viral media can be user generated, such as with YouTube or SlideShare. It can also be generated in-house, such as with BuzzFeed or TED.

Either way, the viral media is new prospects' very first exposure to the value a product offers. Sometimes it's through an embedded video on someone's blog; other times it's through a link to collaborate on a project. The quicker this value is recognized by prospects, the more often they will become users, and the more likely they are to complete viral loops of their own.

Creating Viral Media That Converts

The conversion rate (*conv%*) on your invites depends largely on your viral media. This is because, as I've said before, the foundation of a good viral marketing campaign is value, and your viral media provides the first glimpse of that value.

In a way, it's kind of like love at first sight (assuming that you're a viral Casanova; if you're not, it's more like repulsion at first sight, which is far less cool).

Those same conversion rates also **depend on the relevancy of your viral media** to your viral message. Did you know that a paid ad with a matching landing page converts better than one whose landing page looks completely different from the ad? Similarly, your viral media and viral message need to sync up.

This relevancy is vital because you're beginning a narrative. By clicking on your message and granting you a small amount of their time, prospects indicate that they've started to buy in to that narrative. So it wouldn't make sense to completely derail that narrative in favor of something more canned or mass marketed.

Instead, **continue that narrative with the viral media.** Provide prospects the experience they expected to have when they clicked on the invite. You only have a few moments to convince prospects to stay, so this experience must be carefully crafted and well thought out.

In other words, blow their freakin' socks off.

Step 11: Viral Marketing Conversion—Why Your Entire Viral Marketing Campaign Is Wasted without It

What do we do now that we've exposed prospects to some kickass media showcasing all the wonderful value your product has to offer?

It's time to convert those prospects into users.

It should be self-evident that your viral loop is intended to help you grow. However, "growth" can mean different things to different people. Depending on your specific business and goals, you may be trying to grow in users, revenue, or some other KPI.

So, in that regard, everyone's viral loop is unique. But there's still a general outline that all follow.

The Basic Composition of Every Viral Loop

As we've been discussing, a sound viral loop is comprised of a few distinct steps:

1. Make a prospect aware of your product through a viral invite.

2. Communicate initial core value to the prospect through your viral message.

3. Demo your product's full core value to the prospect through your viral media.

4. **Convert the prospect into a user (this is *viral marketing conversion*).**

5. Communicate your viral value to that user at the viral hook moment.

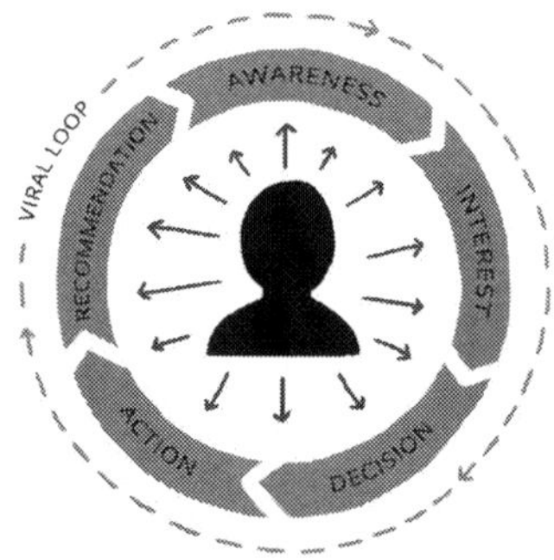

Most products can leverage some big wins to make things work even better within your viral loop, such as branching or viral incentive marketing. But with or without these, for nearly every product, the viral loop starts over again when new prospects receive invites once the five steps above have been completed.

Notice how I bolded number four—viral marketing conversion? That's because without users converting, your viral campaign (and business) might as well be dead in the water.

This topic just screams, "Teach me how a virus can help me grow my product," right?

Okay, maybe not—but I'm going to do it anyway, so buckle up.

Learning from Influenza

You probably can't even count how many times people have told you about their experiences with the flu. Because it's so common, it might not seem like such a big deal, right? Wrong. It's a very big deal. So big, in fact, that every year, about half a million people die from one of many strains of influenza, or "the flu" for short.

The most dramatic flu was in 1918, when the Spanish flu infected upward of 40 percent of the worldwide population, killing nearly fifty million people. The fact that influenza is so incredibly common and still actively spreads every single year like clockwork makes it one of the most effective viruses to study for our purposes.

First and foremost, it morphs and adapts into different strains, making it resistant to herd immunity as well as many vaccinations. It's also airborne and can spread to a new host up to six feet away from an infected person through tiny droplets of water produced when that person coughs, sneezes, or even speaks. These droplets get inhaled by others, and *boom*—infected.

So what can we learn from influenza?

1. First, we must continually alter the messaging and media used during both our marketing and viral campaigns (i.e., different "strains"). If we've had a specific ad running in a market for several weeks, it's likely in danger of saturation (or herd immunity). We should refresh this collateral to resonate with folks on whom the old messages didn't work. The same rule goes for existing users on whom our previous viral hooks didn't work.

2. Next, we should ensure our primary marketing message, or our tagline, can be easily connected in conversation to solving a problem prospects may be having. Sounding cool or impressive isn't a tagline's purpose; it should ensure that even a one-line mention of the product during the right conversation takes hold in the hearts and minds of prospects.

3. Finally, we should attempt to increase our "conversion radius" by examining just how "close" an existing user has to be to a prospect to invite that person to our product in a way that genuinely adds value to their interaction. Would it make sense to users to speak about our product even to somebody they barely know? Or do they feel like it's only safe and sensible to mention it to folks they work or interact closely with?

Switching Funnel Goals

When you acquire a new prospect or lead through viral means, your first and foremost goal is to convert that prospect or lead into a user. While you may get a little bit of virality from users who like your product without using it, **you'll get ten times the virality** from those same people if they become users themselves.

But, Travis, why does this happen?

I'm glad you asked.

An endorsement from a friend is great. But an endorsement from that same friend combined with **anecdotes of his or her own personal experiences** and the ability to **answer basic questions** on various use cases is as big a viral win as you can get. With this, *conv%* goes through the roof.

To get you closer to the pantheons of viral glory, below is a short list of things you can do today to convert more prospects.

- **Shorten and simplify the conversion process.** If you reduce the friction, effort, and information required to act (e.g., sign up, download, make a purchase, etc.), you'll start seeing a big jump in conversions.

- **Minimize or eliminate distractions.** Any graphics, colors, or elements within your prospect-to-user conversion funnel that don't directly support a conversion action in your viral loop are distractions and should be removed. So put away all those bells and whistles unless they're helping the cause. Boring pages often convert better than ultraartistic, flashy designs. Remember, you're growing a *business*, not making an art project.

- **Do your homework.** Check out some of the more specialized conversion-rate-optimization educational resources like ConversionXL or the Unbounce blog. Use what I'm presenting as a starting point, and from here, research deeper into conversion tactics. After all, this is a book about viral marketing, not CRO.

Remember, your most glowing endorsements (and thereby the most virality) will come from satisfied customers for whom you've worked your ass off to provide value.

As the saying goes, a happy customer is a viral customer. (That's how the saying goes, right?)

You're probably starting to formulate some ideas on how to make what you're building more viral - but the key pieces we just touched on can trip you up if you don't give them the necessary attention. Follow the steps in the *Viral Hero* Workbook to make sure this doesn't happen to you. If you haven't yet, head over to viralhero.com/workbook to get your free copy.

Chapter 8: Measuring Viral Success

Step 12: Your Viral Marketing Funnel, and How a Basic Visualization Can Help You "See the Matrix" like Neo

In the last three chapters, we covered pretty much all the key steps of any viral loop and explored some effective augmentations. Now, let's take a step back and look at some practical visualizations we can actually use on a day-to-day basis to increase virality.

Remember the end of the movie *The Matrix*, when Neo finally embraces his true gift and can see the world around him as binary code rather than as people and things? You're not there yet. But after this chapter, you'll be a whole lot closer to Keanu Reeves–esque levels of "*Whoa.*"

(*Note: If you don't have a clue what I'm talking about or you're not a fan of the first movie in the Matrix series, we can't be friends. Also, you probably won't get some of my jokes in this section. But trust me—these jokes are hilarious.*)

Seeing the Viral Matrix

As part of our process of creating your viral engine in fifteen steps, we've dissected the basic structure and critical points of standard viral loops.

That said, knowing what those steps are can only get you so far. Or as Morpheus would say: "There's a difference between knowing the path and walking the path." Theory is great, but putting theory into practice involves creating a practical method for implementation that can be sustained over time. To do this, you'll likely have to create a visualization of your viral loop complete with data and context.

> **Here's how I'd recommend doing this** (other than by swallowing a red pill):

- Use a tool like Lucidchart to diagram each step of *your* viral loop using boxes.

- If you've already got metrics from your site, drop them in next to each corresponding box. Include things like the time it takes to get to each step, the conversion rate on that step, and even a small screenshot of that step.

- On an accompanying spreadsheet, **run a few scenarios**. Choose one or two steps in your loop, and increase them marginally. Notice how your overall virality increases.

- Carefully examine your loop as it stands, and try to diagnose the bottlenecks and the weakest steps. Where can your biggest improvements happen, and how much improvement can you realistically expect?

- Document everything, but make it short and digestible. Each page is a barrier you're asking users to jump over. These metrics should show *only* how much of a barrier each step is so you can know what to focus on improving. Any more and it's overkill.

Drawing the Line in the Sand

You obviously want to make each metric in your viral loop as awesome as possible. But how awesome is "awesome enough"?

This is never an easy question to answer. After all, if you're just getting your data for the first time, you likely have nothing to compare it to. **So do your research.** (In other words, don't think you are—know you are.)

For example, let's say your viral carrier is SMS (meaning users send out invites via text). You might not be familiar with the average open rate of an SMS text message, but after doing a little research, you'll find that this number is around 36 percent. Is this specific to your app or your industry? No. But it will give you some sort of a benchmark with which to set more accurate expectations.

You can do research like this for each step in your funnel. You should be able to find general benchmarks of what you can expect. If your metrics on any step are severely undershooting these benchmarks, you'll likely be able to diagnose that step as a **bottleneck**. You can then place more focus on lifting those metrics rather than others that are closer to the benchmark average.

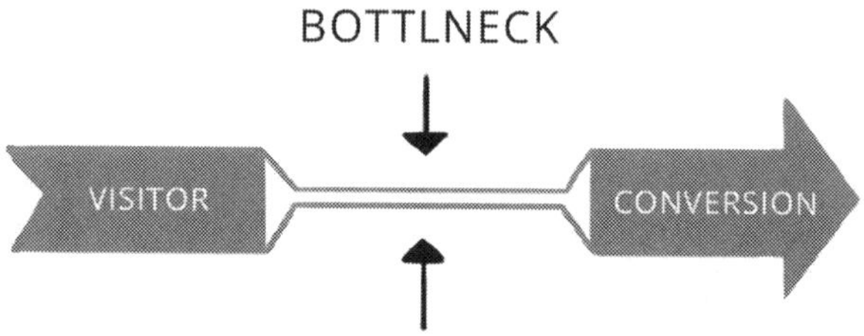

In general, if you make each step in the process incredibly short and clear with slightly progressive commitments of information, you'll win. Optimize this viral funnel as if it were a landing page or sales funnel, and test for drop off at each step.

Step 13: How to Calculate Your Viral Factor, and What It Means for Your Growth

The difference between optimizing a landing page and optimizing a viral loop is that a landing page is a static metric. Throw people in the top, and customers come out the bottom—plain and simple.

However, **viral growth is a compounding process**—so optimization can be a *lot* bigger deal if done correctly.

Let's dive into some basic viral math so you can see exactly what I mean.

If you're as big a fan of the latest and greatest tech talks as I am, or you do any combination of reading books and blogs, attending growth and marketing conferences, talking to other founders and growth engineers, and hanging out with anthropomorphic panda bears who occasionally wear capes, you've probably heard the buzzword *viral coefficient.*

> However, most people who throw this term around never bother explaining the following:

- What is a viral coefficient?
- How do you calculate a viral coefficient?
- What kind of an impact can a viral coefficient have?

Lucky for you, these big "secrets" are about to be revealed.

Granted, no one in the history of words has ever enjoyed hearing the word *coefficient.* In fact, its mere utterance is usually enough to send people running or into a deep sleep—which is probably why *viral coefficient* is just as commonly referred to as *the viral factor.*

You have to admit that sounds way cooler and could easily be the name of a popular TV game show hosted by Wayne Brady: *Do you have . . . the VIRAL FACTOR? Let's play to find out!*

Basic Viral Marketing Math

Your **viral factor** tells you to what degree your users will power your growth by inviting others to try your product.

While it would be a bit more intuitive to name this variable *V* (which I almost did, as you can see in our jazzy little panda art above), since most existing resources call this variable *K*, let's adopt *K* as our variable here so other past or future resources make sense to you.

Your viral factor = *K*

(See? I told you this would be basic math.)

To elaborate more, you need *K* to calculate the average number of new prospective users each existing user will successfully bring back to your site or app and into your viral loop. In other words, ***K* is a measure of the magnitude of virality your site or app possesses on a per-user basis.**

Not quite getting it yet? Hang in there.

No Sharks Here

Let's say *K* = 0.5.

This means for every user you recruit via nonviral means, that user will bring 0.5 prospective users into your viral loop for you. (We'll talk extensively about nonviral marketing later; for now, all you need to know is that it's methods of spreading your product that don't involve users sharing it themselves.)

Wait . . . a half a user? I still don't get it. That makes no sense. Did the other half get eaten by a shark or something?

Nope—no sharks here.

Let's think of this a different way. When $K = 0.5$, this means for every *two* users you recruit via nonviral means, they'll collectively bring *one* prospective user into your viral loop for you.

How to Calculate Your Viral Factor (a.k.a. K)
K is made up of **two smaller KPIs:**

- The total number of invites sent out per user on average during one cycle of a viral loop (which we've previously labeled *i*).

$$\{ K = i \times conv\% \}$$

K = for each user you have how many new ones they create.

i = number of invitations each user sends out in one cycle of the loop.

conv% = rate at which invitations convert into new users.

- The conversion rate on those invites (or the percentage of those sent invites that result in new prospective users coming to your site and starting new viral loops—we've previously labeled this *conv%*).

As you start to think about this, you'll inevitably want to factor in time. So it's worth noting that *K* is typically calculated over a fixed time period, such as one month. Don't use an average *i* value from the last ninety days with an average *conv%* of the last two weeks. That's just silly.

As you optimize, *conv%* should eventually become relatively stable (unless you experience heavy seasonality). This will be great for the projections we'll begin doing shortly. However, *i* will vary significantly over the life of each user, so measuring for month one is a good starting point.

(*Note: If your loop has been rocking and rolling for a while and you've got enough data to measure* K *over the life of a user, we'll use a different variable, which we'll call* K'*—but more on that later.*)

Pretty exciting stuff so far, right? *Yay, Math!*

Here's a Viral Use Case

Let's assume you're building a live-chat tool, such as Olark or Intercom. The goal is to help brands engage prospective and existing customers in a more efficient way.

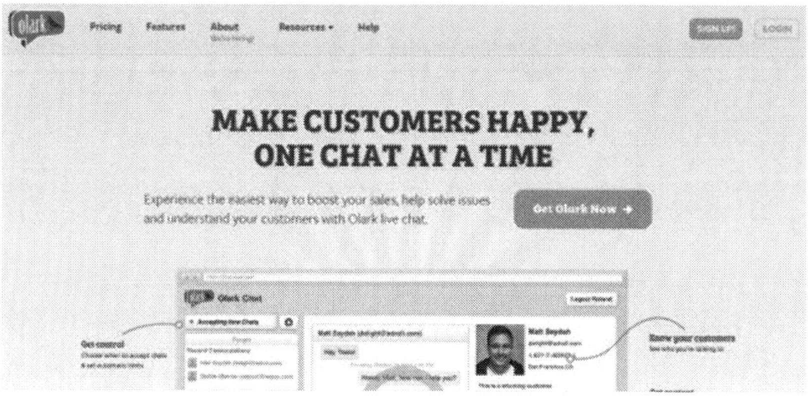

So how could this tool be viral?

- It could use **viral collaboration marketing** by adding a feature that lets users incorporate their team members in providing customer service through the tool.

- It could use **viral communication marketing** by adding a feature that lets users email a transcript of a conversation to friends or coworkers after it's over.

- It almost certainly *will* use **embeddable viral marketing,** as companies will typically embed a tool like this within their own website or app, exposing it to that site's visitors.

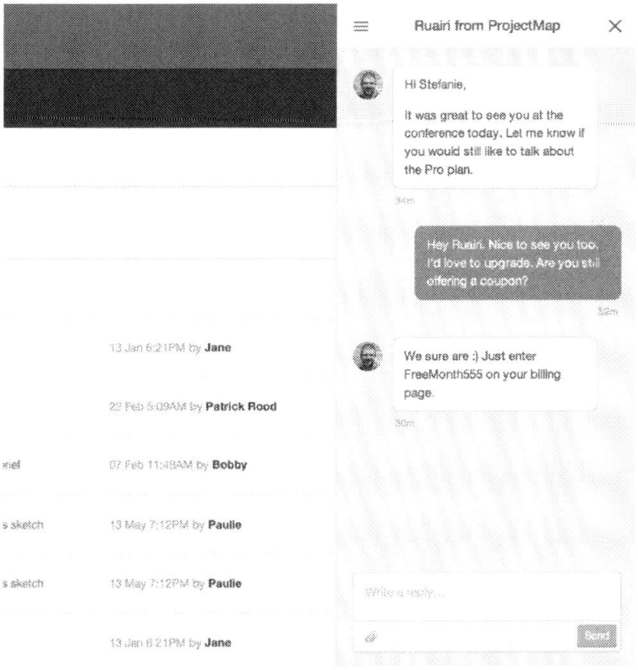

You could also use other types of viral marketing engines beyond these examples with a tool like this. For this reason, *and* because you've spent ample time developing the product and making it legitimately valuable compared to other solutions available at the moment, let's assume you've built what you believe is a strong viral loop.

And now you need to quantify its growth.

The First Bit of Viral Math

As we said, you've worked hard on your product and your viral loop, and you've finally decided that it's time to expose your amazing product to the world. You start by inviting ten of your closest friends. Since they know and love you, they all sign up as your first ten users. (It pays to have friends—am I right?)

This kicks off our math with a base number of **ten users**, or $u(0) = 10$.

That wasn't so hard, was it? See, math can be easy *and* fun.

Your initial **ten users** seem to totally get the product. They all love the experience, and you've made the additional value they receive for inviting others both obvious and compelling. As a result, they each send out an average of **ten invitations** to *their* friends, generating **one hundred invites total.**

Now, remember that our variable i is **the total number of invites sent out per user on average** during a selected period of time. So for this example, $i = 10$.

Still with me?

For every batch of ten invitations that get sent out, say **two** of the people who received those invites respond favorably and sign up to use your product.

Let's add in our other variable, *conv%* (the conversion rate on invites).

$$conv\% = 2 \text{ new users} / 10 \text{ invites sent} = .2\ (\text{or } 20\%)$$

Mow we're really moving!

Summing It All Up

So we started with a base number of **ten users (*u(0)* = 10)** who ended up sending **ten invites each (*i* = 10).** Those invites had a **20 percent average conversion rate (*conv%* = .2).**

Using these numbers, we'll now calculate your viral factor, or *K*—remember that we find *K* using the following formula:

$$K = i * conv\%$$

Plugging in our numbers, here's what we get:

$$K = 10 * .2 = 2.0$$

This leaves us with a ***K* of 2.0.**

This tells you that on average, for each user you acquire through nonviral means, that user will bring you two additional users via your viral loop. In other words, *K* quantifies the level at which these users will "infect" others around them. (*Note: A* K *factor of 2.0 is absolutely incredible and also very rare.*)

Since we initially seeded our viral engine with ten nonviral users (a.k.a. your awesome friends), applying this *K* to them gives us twenty *more* users by the end of the first full "cycle" (or the amount of time it takes for all this to take place), for a total of **thirty users.**

Piece of cake so far, yeah?

Those new twenty customers will likely send out a similar number of invitations themselves, beginning brand-new viral loops. The users they recruit will then similarly recruit new users from their own viral loops, and so on and so on.

Now, it's important to understand that even if you achieve an extremely high viral factor, like in our example, your user growth *will* slow down over time. The original ten users with which you seeded your viral engine may continue to sporadically send invites. However, the invites they send will drastically drop off as they both max out their perceived viral value and run out of other people they want to invite. This is called **viral decay**, and it's something we'll go into later in a lot more detail.

Likewise, it's highly unlikely (scratch that—impossible) that your entire population of users will continue to send out invites during every cycle. Expect to see a quick user-growth spike when users initially see viral value and then a dramatic drop to a slow trickle after that.

Finding the Holy Grail of Viral Marketing

If you reach anything near a ***K* of 2.0**, you'll see true viral growth.

But this is a compounding, exponential process that's as rare and difficult to achieve as it is lucrative and powerful. Call it the Holy Grail of Viral Marketing. It may be incredibly hard to obtain, but it's not impossible. With a substantial viral education (like the one you're currently receiving), you can gain a massive edge in the probability of reaching it.

That might sound intimidating (and a little messy), but don't worry—it's actually very straightforward. Once you get the hang of applying these equations to your marketing campaigns, the impact they'll have will blow your mind.

Step 14: Viral Amplification Factor—the Key Ingredient in Most Growth Recipes

Let me guess: you just ran to a calculator or a spreadsheet to see what sort of an impact a $K > 1.0$ would have on your product, and you're currently flipping out.

If that's you, **take a deep breath**.

I hate to be the bearer of bad news, but as I mentioned at the end of the last section, even if you hit $K > 1.0$ (the holy grail of *K*s), this can't last for long. As you'll soon see as we move forward, if it *did* last for long, you'd end up with more users than currently inhabit the entire planet. While that might sound awesome to your bottom line, unfortunately it's impossible (unless your product goes viral on Mars too).

Fear not—you can still harness the incredibly profound power of *K*. But believe it or not, *K* is *not* the most powerful viral KPI we have. **Amplification factor** is even more powerful.

The Recipe for Scalable Viral Growth

As you may remember from one of our early chapters, most products will never "go viral"—meaning, their *K* will never even get close to 1.0.

Does this mean all is lost? Is your viral marketing campaign doomed to fail? Is your company destined for the wall of shame and all its employees sentenced to having tomatoes thrown at their faces?

Certainly not. Viral marketing can still be one of the most effective things you utilize for growth, even with a $K < 1.0$. In fact, if you have a $K < 1.0$, you're in the same boat as 99.9 percent of startups. With this in mind, we need to use a new KPI as **a more practical measure of virality.**

Transitioning from *K to A*

Again, most sites, no matter how hard they try, will never achieve true viral growth (meaning, a $K > 1.0$). For those who do, it won't last long. So the primary metric for us moving forward will *not* be our viral factor. It will be our amplification factor.

An **amplification factor** is a simple multiplier that indicates how many total users you can expect to acquire for every user you gain through nonviral means **after viral marketing does its job.**

For example, if your amplification factor is 1.3, this means for every 1 user you acquire via nonviral means, you can expect 1.3 users total after viral marketing is all said and done.

Here's how to **calculate your amplification factor:**

Viral factor = *K*

Amplification factor = *A*

$$A = 1/(1 - K)$$

If you're having trouble wrapping your head around the equation above, take a deep breath. I promise not to throw too much math at you, and when I do, I'll explain it in so much detail, you'll think you're the second coming of Einstein.

Moving on.

Let's say *K* = **0.2**. We can then calculate *A* in the following way:

$$A = 1/(1-0.2) = 1/(0.8) = 1.25$$

You've now found that **your amplification factor is 1.25**. Great work!

Let's Try a Use Case

Ready to observe this equation in action? Let's see what we can do to adjust our *A* value.

In the last section, we looked at a hypothetical, incredibly viral SaaS application and how the basic viral formula may work in a vacuum. Let's now talk about a model that can be a *lot* more hit or miss—an online media outlet.

Since this model is drastically different, the goal is no longer to create application-specific viral value for users to directly invite others, as it was in the last example. Instead, the media-outlet model usually means that viral invites come via online viral word-of-mouth marketing, most often a share on social media.

Some of the world's top viral media properties like BuzzFeed and Dose *crush* this method, but most small teams don't execute it nearly as well.

Let's say that we've got a relatively popular blog that caters to an active market. For now, we'll assume that you're the typical new blog, and instead of a *conv%* of 20 percent (as we had in our previous example), let's decrease ***conv%* to 5 percent**. Also, we'll say our *i* value remains the same as it was in the last example—each user you recruit exposes **ten new people** to your product. This means that for every ten people who see an invite that has been sent (e.g., every ten people who see a post that's shared in their feeds), 0.5 of those people come to the site and become readers.

Wait, how can we recruit 0.5 readers? Do we need to saw them in half?

(*IMPORTANT: Please do not attempt to saw anybody in half, and if you do, please find a better tux than this guy.*)

No—remember? No sharks eat anyone, and you don't cut anyone in half.

What having 0.5 readers means is you'll need two users executing your full viral loop and exposing your product to ten new people each (for a grand total of twenty) in order to recruit **one single new user through viral means.**

In short, if our *i* value stays the same (*i* = **10**), this one simple change of decreasing our ***conv%*** from 20 percent to 5 percent will alone reduce ***K*** **to 0.05.**

How to Calculate Amplification Factor

Remember how you calculate your viral amplification?

$$A = 1/(1 - K)$$

By inserting our values from the use case above, here's what we get:

$$A = 1/(1 - .05) = 1/.95 = 1.05$$

Basically, what this says is that for every one hundred users you drive to your site, they will collectively recruit an additional five users for you.

This isn't great a number for *A*, but it's often typical for sites of this type that have given zero attention to improving their viral metrics. An amplification factor this low would likely only be a needle mover for sites spending a ton of money to acquire users through nonviral means.

But hey, it's better than nothing.

Turn That Viral Dial Up

Let's now assume you and your team conduct some research into online viral word-of-mouth marketing. You realize that while you're evoking at least *some* **high-arousal emotions** (which you know because your *i* is fairly average), there's still room for improvement.

Fortunately, you can often increase your content's shareability by improving its headlines and imagery. This will better catch people's attention by igniting curiosity, controversy, or awe (or any other high-arousal emotion), thereby increasing your *conv%* on those shares.

Ever hear the term *clickbait*? This is exactly what media outlets use to increase their viral numbers.

TRENDING IN THE WORLD
This Roller Coaster Doesn't Have Flips, Turns, Or Speed But Is The Most Terrifying Of All
If you're scared of heights just click the back arrow now.
Read more >

The image above shows how Chicago-based online-media juggernaut Dose uses clickbait on its homepage with a catchy headline that's almost impossible not to click.

So you've gone ahead and made some awesome improvements to your blog by harnessing the power of clickbait. As a result, you've successfully **driven your *conv%* up to 40 percent**—meaning, people who see something of yours that's been shared in their feeds have a **40 percent chance of doing the following:**

1. Clicking

2. Coming to your site

3. Becoming readers

With that boost, here's what our equation becomes:

$$A = 1/(1 - .4) = 1/.6 = 1.667$$

That's a little better. An amplification factor like this means for every one hundred users you pay to acquire, they bring back **sixty-seven new users**.

Although this isn't the sort of wild, self-driving, exponential growth we all dream of, an *A* value of 1.667 is a *huge* needle-mover metric for even a brand-new bootstrapped startup. If this is your company, you can likely afford to profitably dump more cash into nonviral acquisition channels and unlock additional channels that were previously not cost effective.

Getting the Most Out of Your A
So what do you do with *A* once you have it?

To get to the bottom of this, let's introduce a new variable, ***nU***. This stands for ***nonviral users*** and is the total number of users you acquire in one day through nonviral channels.

We'll use *nU* to find ***tU***, or the ***total number of users*** you acquire in one day overall from *both* viral and nonviral channels. We calculate *tU* by multiplying our *nU* by *A* (the amplification factor).

$$tU = nU * A$$

For simplicity's sake, let's say we acquired exactly one thousand users today from something like an AdWords campaign. As this is the only nonviral campaign we have running, we don't have any other sources of traffic (very unlikely, but we're just trying to make the math easy here). **This means *nU* = 1,000.**

As those one thousand nonviral users make their way through their viral loops, they begin inviting friends. But how many total users (*tU*) can we expect after that loop does its thing? This is where *A* comes in. For this example, let's use the *A* value from our first example in this section: *A* = 1.25.

$$tU = 1{,}000 * 1.25 = 1{,}250$$

Fantastic! But wait—what does this mean for our business?

The Business Value of *A*

If you're like most companies and have a *K* < 1.0, you'll need to continuously acquire traffic through nonviral means to allow your viral loop to continually do its thing.

That said, with a strong *A* factor, you'll have a huge advantage compared to your competitors with unoptimized viral loops because you'll now have a significant discount on your ad spend.

Here's how this works.

Let's assume our data from our last example is still true: our ***K* = 0.2**, our ***A* = 1.25**, our ***nU* = 1,000**, and our ***tU* = 1,250**.

Now, let's factor in our **advertising costs** with a new variable: ***cN***. This refers to our *cost per acquisition of a new user through nonviral means*. As you probably guessed, we'll also add in ***tN***, which gives us our *total cost per acquisition of all users on average* (after factoring in virality).

For simplicity's sake, let's assume ***cN* = $1.00.**

By multiplying our nonviral costs per acquisition (*cN*) by our total new users acquired (*nU*), we'll get our total advertising costs (*aC*) for this specific nonviral campaign to date.

$$aC = cN*nU = \$1.00 * \$1,000 = \$1,000$$

This tells us that we've spent $1,000 to seed our viral loop with 1,000 nonviral users.

But wait—we don't have 1,000 users anymore! Our viral loop has now done its job. Our users have invited friends, and we now have 1,250 users. Let's then assume our viral value and viral incentive per user don't cost us anything extra, which means we've still spent the same $1,000.

This is our equation now:

$$tN = Total\ costs\ /\ tU$$

When we plug in the numbers, here's what we get:

$$\mathbf{tN = \$1,000\ /\ 1250 = \$0.80}$$

In other words, **you've decreased your total costs per acquisition from $1.00 to $0.80**. If you're doing the math—and I know you are, New Einstein—that's a 20 percent discount in your per-user ad spend!

High five!

This may not seem super incredible with regards to this example, as that 20 percent discount only yields twenty measly cents, but when you're spending *millions* of dollars a month on advertising, **this can help you**

- achieve a profitable ROI from a channel and use it cost effectively;
- avoid spending an extra $1 million on ads you could have spent on five new high-level hires;
- pump an extra $1 million back into advertising and seed 20 percent more users into your viral loop;
- dominate a market rather than getting buried by a competitor; and
- not get a tomato thrown in your face.

. . . and it's all thanks to *A*.

Step 15: Viral Cycle Time—a Bird's-Eye View of the King of All Viral KPIs

We've made it! This is the last step in our process of **creating your viral marketing engine**. Well done. *Clap*, *clap*, *clap*, and all that jazz. Do you feel different? You should. You're practically a viral superhero (almost).

By now, you've gotten to know your viral factor (*K*) and how good a friend it can be to your growth (and your valuation). You've also learned how your amplification factor (*A*) is an even more practical measure when you calculate day-to-day growth.

But remember when I mentioned earlier in this chapter that *K* is *not* the most powerful viral KPI you'd be learning about? Well, it actually isn't *A* either. Ready to learn the KPI that will have the most profound impact on your viral growth—and what you can do to make it the best friend you've ever had?

Let's get this party started.

Completing K to Reveal Virality

K is a key measure of the magnitude of your virality (also known as the overall growth potential your viral engine has *if* time were not a factor). However, by itself, *K* will not predict your actual viral growth over time.

Why? Because it's an incomplete equation. For example, if you asked, "If I get ten new users today, how many new users will they bring back to me total?" you might have a shot at a ballpark figure using *K* and *A*. However, if you asked, "If I get ten new users today, how much will my total user count grow over the next twenty days?" you would have no way of answering—yet.

This question can't be answered with just *K* because *K* doesn't factor in time. To get projections like this, you need to complete the picture by factoring in two new KPIs:

- Viral cycle time (*ct*)

- Time (t)

Good Growth Takes Time to Prepare

Viral cycle time (ct) is the amount of time it takes for a user to become aware of your product and go through all the steps required to reach the point at which they invite a friend or colleague to it.

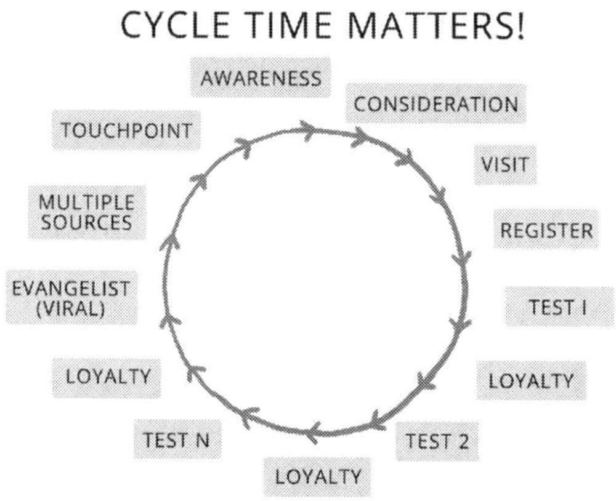

Most ct equations you'll be working with will measure in days. But for practicality reasons, we'll convert things into minutes or weeks when necessary so they're easier to understand in future chapters.

For example, say you have a ***ct* < 1 day**. For our equations to work out, this must be a decimal-based fraction (1.0) to make sure many of our higher-level equations (which we'll cover shortly) work as planned.

This means that a ***ct* of 1 day = 1.0**, while a ***ct* of 12 hours = 0.5**, and so on.

Got it? Good.

But hold on a second—what makes viral cycle time so important anyway?

To explain how powerful viral cycle time can be, we must look no further than everyone's favorite furry forest creature.

Why Do Rabbits Have So Many Babies?

Have you ever had friends pop out multiple children in quick succession and thought to yourself, "Wow, you guys are like rabbits!"? I think you might know where I'm going with this.

Allow me to elaborate.

Understanding the Finer Nuances of Rabbit Sex

(Disclaimer: I am not a rabbit-mating expert. That would be weird. So I borrowed all my example numbers from a paper published by the University of Miami's biology department.)

Let's start with a few assumptions to make our math easier:

- A single female rabbit has an average litter size of **six** babies.
- **Half** of new baby rabbits are female, so **three** new females are produced in each litter.

- We're only discussing reproductive **capacity**. As such, we will not factor in *churn* (i.e., baby rabbits dying for ungodly reasons) or *carrying capacity* (i.e. , baby rabbits dying for ungodly reasons) or carrying capacity (i.e. environmental limitations). We'll cover these two terms later.

For context, while human mothers have a nine-month gestation period before birthing one (or very occasionally a few) offspring, rabbits have a **one-month gestation period** and typically produce a half dozen offspring at a time. *Wowzers!* This speeds things up a bit.

What's more, human females must be a certain age before their bodies actually allow for reproduction. (I believe it's something like fourteen or fifteen, but don't quote me on that. I'm a growth engineer, not a doctor.) Female rabbits, on the other hand, can begin reproducing at **six months old**. *Double wowzers!*

If that's not crazy enough, a female rabbit is biologically capable of getting pregnant again within *minutes* of giving birth. So a female can literally have a new litter every month if she's around a totally horny male rabbit (which we'll assume, for our purposes, she is).

So if our first female rabbit begins reproducing when she's of age and reproduces as frequently as her body is able (*and* if all the female babies behave in the same way), I ask you, **how many actively reproducing female rabbits would we have at the end of each year**?

- Year one: 37 rabbits

- Year two: 1,369 rabbits

- Year three: 50,653 rabbits

- Year four: 1,872,792 rabbits
- Year five: 69,293,304 rabbits
- Year six: 2,563,852,248 rabbits
- Year seven: 94,862,569,180 rabbits

You probably assumed it would be quite a few. But you probably didn't realize that after seven years you'd have almost **ninety-five billion rabbits.** ***And that's only the females!*** If you add all the males to that count, we'd have **184,597,433,860** total rabbits in seven years. *MIND BLOWN.* That's very impressive and, if you're a rabbit, probably reason to celebrate.

What Rabbit Reproduction and Viral Marketing Have in Common

Two questions remain:

1. **How is this even possible?**

   Well, first off, since rabbits have so many natural predators, their reproductive rate (and more specifically, their reproductive *cycle time*) is their main defense mechanism as a species. However, while it's mathematically possible, **nature wouldn't allow** rabbit numbers to get this high. Predators would eat a ton of them, food would be too scarce, Elmer Fudd would undoubtedly blow a few away, or any number of other factors would "thin the herd" to prevent such rapid population growth. We only went through this to show a real-world example of how the math of viral cycle time works. (And to talk about rabbit sex.)

2. **Why should I care?**

   Other than to prepare you for the very real possibility of rabbits taking over the world, the point of this whole conversation is to demonstrate how something so dramatically explosive can happen (in terms of growth)—and to set the stage for how it relates to your virality. The thing to keep in mind is that rabbit population growth is so insane not because of the size of their litters—six is a lot from a human perspective but pretty average in the animal kingdom—but because of their extremely fast cycle time.

Getting Back to Business

Many engineers, marketers, and founders with a bit of viral knowledge choose to focus on optimizing their viral factor (*K*) to max out invites per user (i.e., trying to get each rabbit to have eight babies instead of six). However, reducing viral cycle time (i.e., reducing a rabbit's gestation period from thirty days to twenty days) is *much* more impactful.

To better understand this, let's look at a basic equation:

$$x^y$$

(*If you've never seen the ^ symbol before, it denotes exponentiation. So another way to state this equation is* x ***to the power of*** y.)

Now, here are two options. Pick the one you think will result in the larger number:

1. Add another *x*, and here's what you'll get:

$$(x*2)^y$$

2. Add another *y* instead, and now here's what you have:

    x^(y*2)

Option two is the winner, right?

Not so fast. I want you to be absolutely certain, so I'll elaborate:

- Let's say *x* is your invites sent per user (*i*), or how many new users an existing user will spread your product to per cycle.

- Let's then say *y* is the number of cycles that take place within a certain time period, which is your viral cycle time (*ct*).

If you work hard to increase *x*, and your viral cycle spreads to ten people ($x = 10$) but takes seven days to replicate, in four weeks ($y = 4$) you'll have **10^4**, which equals **10,000**.

If you *instead* focus on cycle time, and your product spreads only to three people (x = 3) but only takes one day to replicate, in four weeks (y = 28) you'll have **3^28**, which equals ***22.8 trillion***!

That's some impressive exponential growth.

Here's what it looks like in exciting graph form:

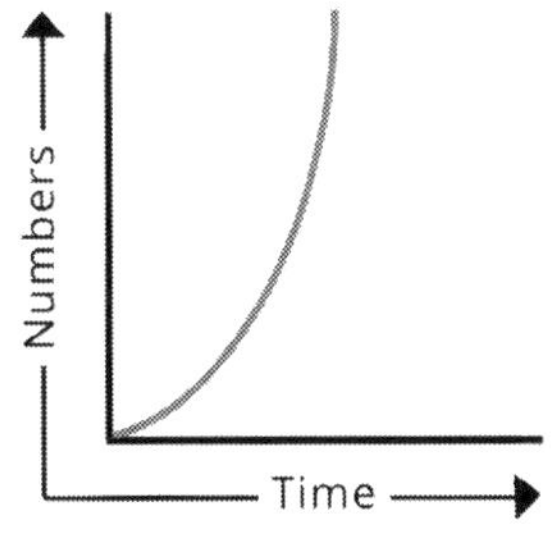

What's the takeaway here? Trying to achieve a faster cycle time (*ct)* is a *far* more impactful change than increasing how many invites your users send (*i)*.

Rabbits Are Fluffy and Cute and Reproduce a Lot, but . . .

So, now that we've heard all about rabbit reproduction and established the power of a short cycle time, what are some ways we can influence our company's viral cycle time? Let's look at another example—it'll start out very similar to a use case we looked at earlier, but stick with me.

Let's say you launch a web application, and you invite ten of your closest friends, who all join: $u(0) = 10$.

Easy enough.

> Now let's assume you're doing things like adding the following:

- Substantial core and viral value
- High-arousal emotion-evoking headlines, imagery, and copy
- Appealing viral incentives
- Tactics that lead to a decent branching factor

The above is obviously a *huge* leap, since we're assuming you're doing all of this already at launch. But hey, let's assume you've read *Viral Hero* already, and you're building your application with virality in mind.

Given that, let's say you reach a ***K* factor of 2.0**, which is massively awesome. Congratulations. You've hypothetically achieved true viral growth.

Now **twenty days** go by. How many users do you have?

Coming up blank, huh? You'd better wait to cash in all those hypothetical checks rolling in. We forgot what we've just been talking about: **we cannot calculate viral growth over time if we don't set our viral cycle time.** After all, if we don't know how long it takes for users to go through our viral loops, how do we know how many loops can occur within a fixed time period?

Adding Viral Cycle Time to the Mix

So let's assume our entire viral loop takes an average of exactly **five days** from start (initial awareness) to finish (sending an invite).

Here's what we have now:

- $u(0) = 10$
- $K = 2.0$
- $ct = 5.0$ days

(*Note: Notice I assigned a cycle-time value of 5.0 days. As I mentioned earlier, for the sake of projection equations we'll be using shortly, we'll need to convert our viral cycle time to days and represent it in decimal form. This means that even if it's only a few minutes long, we'll have to convert it to a decimal fraction of a day to make sure the equations we use remain accurate.*)

We can now accurately answer the question we raised earlier. So, assuming all the above metrics are true, **after twenty days go by,** how many users will you have?

Here's how we calculate that:

$$u(t) = u(0)*(K^(t/ct + 1) - 1) / (K - 1)$$

$$u(20) = 10*(2.0^(20/5.0 + 1) - 1) / (2.0 - 1)$$

$$u(20) = 10*(2.0^5 - 1) / (1.0)$$

$$u(20) = 10 * 31$$

$$\mathbf{u(20) = 310}$$

Wow!

We started with 10 users, and twenty days later, we now have **310** users. Not too shabby, right? Especially since we didn't spend *any* money to acquire those users (aside from the engineering costs to build the viral loops).

The Snail and the Hare

Ever hear the fable about the snail and the hare? You're about to.

Our cycle time seems a bit long in the example above, doesn't it? Why is it taking **five whole days** to execute one loop? Is there anything we can do to speed this up? Onboard users more quickly? Get them to the moment of value faster?

Upon a bit of careful examination, we realize we've got our friendly pet snail hand writing all our viral invites and taking them to our users' friends. He means well, but we need to make some changes to try to reduce our viral cycle time a bit more.

We move our snail pal over to our business-development department and replace him with our pet rabbit, who can run a lot faster.

Making that one change reduces our viral cycle time from five days to two days.

Here's our formula again, but with **a faster cycle time**:

$$u(t) = u(0)*(K\hat{}(t/ct + 1) - 1) / (K - 1)$$

$$u(20) = 10*(2.0\hat{}(20/2.0 + 1) - 1) / (2.0 - 1)$$

$$\mathbf{u(t) = 20{,}470}$$

Holy moly! Over twenty thousand users in the *same* time period . . . **because of one little change**? Yes, it's sometimes as simple as replacing a snail with a hare.

But wait—something still isn't right.

Get with the Times

Why is our pet rabbit still hand delivering all our user invites?

Umm, *helloooo*! That is so 1994. Why wouldn't he use email instead? That would be far faster (and adorable) and should reduce our cycle time even further.

Making that change (going from hand delivery to digital delivery) reduces our cycle time from 2.0 to 1.0. Now it only takes one full day on average for a new user to complete a full viral cycle.

Here's our formula again, but with an **even faster cycle time**:

u(t) = u(0)*(K^(t/ct + 1) - 1) / (K - 1)

u(20) = 10*(2.0^(20/1.0 + 1) - 1) / (2.0 - 1)

u(20) = 20,971,510

Over twenty million users in the same time period—all because we made our pet rabbit use email? *That's incredible!*

I know, you're speechless. It happens when your mind gets virally blown.

Three Key Things to Remember about Cycle Time

Snails and rabbits aside, this is all actually just simple math. Since our viral cycle time functions as the exponent in our projection equation, reducing it results in **exponential improvements** to our user base.

Given cycle time's exponential nature, the more viral cycles that occur, the more users will start going through additional cycles. The more cycles that can take place for more users in a set period of time, the better. However, it's not always obvious at a glance just *how* much better it can be.

To **make *ct* as short as possible**, look at three things:

- What are users' main motivations as they move through the viral cycle?
- What are users' most common negative reactions as they move through the viral cycle?
- What is your "viral snail" (or the one factor that's prolonging your viral cycle time the most)?

If you succeed in massively reducing cycle time *and* the rest of your metrics hold steady, be prepared for what may happen. Specifically . . .

That's right—baby-rabbit levels of growth.

Starting to grow like crazy has a price. It has its own set of problems, and if your churn is too high, you may be in for a rude awakening. We'll talk more about this catastrophic crazy avalanche of terribleness later, but for now, let's avert our eyes from all those horny rabbits getting it on and refocus our attention on our viral marketing engine.

What's Next?

I know what you're thinking. Didn't I say at the start of this section that we were at the end of creating your viral marketing engine? That's true. But just like any good viral loop, to keep growing, we need to end with a new beginning.

Over the past few chapters, we've explored various methods of gathering viral data about your marketing campaign. This was to ensure the viral engine you created was working properly.

But that was just a primer. Now that your viral marketing engine is going full speed ahead, it's time we put it to the test and pit it up against the best of the best in the viral game.

Fasten your seat belts. It's going to be a virally ride.

You won't grow as fast as you could if you don't measure things effectively. Viral analytics can be tricky, but going through the process in the *Viral Hero* Workbook (available free at viralhero.com/workbook), you'll be well on your way to getting yours nailed.

Part 3: Making Your Viral Engine Run

Chapter 9: Tips from the Pros

YouTube's Viral Marketing Machine: How It Created a Perfect Storm of Rapid Growth

We just spent the past four chapters establishing your viral marketing engine for your website or app and learning what you can do to make it more successful. But what makes your viral engine *run*?

Before we get to the actual fuel of your viral engine, let's explore how some other companies built and power their own viral engines and learn some important things to keep in mind about your product's potential for viral success.

YouTube Changes the Viral Game

What made YouTube viral?

When did this happen? Why do people immediately think of YouTube when they hear the word *viral*? Why does this one application have such a powerful reputation as a viral site, even though most people don't know what viral growth really is?

The answers to all these questions lie in YouTube's own growth story.

The Perfect Viral Storm

The term ***perfect storm*** refers to a situation in which several independent factors, which would be manageable by themselves, all occur at the same time and build off each other to create a never-before-seen maelstrom of insanity.

While relatively common in overdramatized movies starring George Clooney, these are incredibly rare events in real life.

That said, against all odds, three former PayPal employees (Chad Hurley, Steve Chen, and Jawed Karim) **engineered the perfect storm of virality** when they founded YouTube.

But let's back up.

We've already talked about various viral engines and the high-level ways to optimize them. I've also stressed how all virality stems from value and how **virality must be built deep into the bones of your product** for it to really work well.

Well, YouTube took my advice and satisfied every ounce of the requirements for creating viral growth.

Fusing Core Value with Viral Value

Founded in 2005 by Chad, Steve, and Jawed, YouTube started out wanting to make playing and sharing videos online easy, fast, and cheap.

Before YouTube, in an era jam-packed with huge file sizes, slow connection speeds, and low processing power (at least compared to our experiences today), **video was a huge pain**. It often took roughly ten years to download a short, low-quality clip. So the founders sought to provide users with a better way to upload and play videos, focusing on making that experience their product's core value.

This one solution was valuable enough and would have been a hit by itself. However, **they didn't stop there**.

It wasn't just the upload and playback problems they were trying to solve; they also wanted to crack the issue of **online video distribution**, which became their viral value.

So, at the end of each video, the founders added calls to action for two different methods of user-driven video distribution:

- A **direct link** to the video on YouTube's site, which users could send to others (a.k.a. online viral word-of-mouth marketing).
- The **embed code** to display the YouTube video player containing that video on any other site (a.k.a. embeddable viral marketing).

This was not only a new solution to a widely experienced problem at the time, but the viral calls to action emphasized the viral value ("share this video so others can enjoy without downloading") without over-emphasizing the core value ("share YouTube because we're awesome").

In other words, YouTube successfully mastered the viral one-two punch.

Amazingly, this perfect synthesis of core and viral value was not what made YouTube viral on a scale greater than anyone had ever seen. That explosive growth came down to its incredibly short **viral cycle time**.

How YouTube Became the King of Viral

As we've discussed, **a full viral loop (or cycle) has several steps:**

- Prospective user becomes aware of your product.
- Prospective user tries your product and thereby becomes a user.
- User's experience is good enough to invite his or her friends.
- User sends invite(s).
- Friends of User receive invites, become aware of your product, and start their own viral loops.

As we've already covered, viral cycle time (*ct*) is the amount of time it takes for one full viral loop or cycle to take place. YouTube's cycle time was extremely short. Users would come to the site, watch a video, see a few ways to share it with others, and immediately do so. This entire process took just a little over **two minutes**, making YouTube's overall cycle time 0.0013889 (there are 1440 minutes in a day, and 2 / 1440 = 0.0013889).

With each passing loop, more and more people were exposed to YouTube. And with every cycle, more and more people were sending invites during the next cycle. As YouTube then began to aggregate stronger and stronger viral media from users, things took off faster than a herd of horny rabbits.

Virality for Reactivation

Another amazing achievement by YouTube is that its virality is long lasting, even among users who have been active for years (which is incredibly rare, and which we'll cover in a later chapter).

In most cases, users start using an application and see the value, virality spikes as they send a big batch of invites, and then virality drops to a slow crawl. However, one of the most prominent forms of value in YouTube's application is in the **distribution of videos through its video player**.

In other words, every time somebody uploads new, noteworthy media to YouTube, even users who have been on the site since the beginning send it out. It doesn't feel spammy because the player is just the vessel for the media, **which is always new**.

If, from the start, YouTube had opted to build its viral engine around sharing how awesome YouTube is as a tool (**a mistake most products make**), it wouldn't have seen nearly as sharp a growth curve.

YouTube's Viral Volley Pays Off

In hindsight, it's not hard to imagine that three early employees of an engineered viral sensation like PayPal would start an engineered viral sensation themselves afterward. But nobody predicted what happened next.

By July 2006, a single year after the company was founded, YouTube had already raised over $11 million in venture funding, had over twenty million visitors per month, and was the **fifth most visited website on the entire internet**.

This earth-shattering growth was driven by a few smart people trying to solve a widely experienced problem in a simple way. **The virality was part of the solution to the problem.** That, combined with a well-executed approach, resulted in YouTube's acquisition by Google in November 2016 for $1.65 billion.

What You Can Learn from YouTube's Viral Success

So what's the moral of the story?

Don't expect to be the next YouTube. It was an outlier among outliers, the ever-elusive "perfect storm."

> That said, you *can* learn from YouTube's success in the following ways:

- Build viral value into the core of your product.
- Build enough of it to ensure users keep inviting others over time and not just in one big batch at the beginning.
- Pay attention to viral cycle time above all else.
- Sell the benefits of sharing and inviting others. Nobody cares about promoting you, but people *do* want something for themselves.

Do these four things, and you're going to grow a lot faster.

YouTube's Viral Growth: The Battle for Viral Dominance It Didn't Even Know It Was Fighting

While you were reading that last section, you may have thought all the decisions YouTube made seem sensible enough to support the belief that, with good engineering, virality is a slam dunk.

The truth is that **it's incredibly difficult to create**.

With the right education, effort, and implementation, there's no reason you can't create a satisfyingly viral product. But there's a reason I said in the last section that you shouldn't expect to be the next YouTube. That's because there's one other element that played a major role in YouTube's momentous success. And while you can't always control it, knowing why this factor occurs could help you find the perfect time to try your hand at virality.

A Few Reminders

As we learned from YouTube's success story, virality requires things like the following:

- An incredibly smart and capable team

- Ultrastrategic architecture, UX design, and engineering
- A truly valuable product that solves a **clear and present problem** for a large population of people

These are the obvious requirements. The not-so-obvious one—and the really tricky one—is **timing.**

To achieve true viral growth on the scale of YouTube, the product you're working with must be introduced at the perfect moment and accepted with open arms—both of which depend on your competitors and **what the market is positioned to accept** based on other factors in their lives.

To explain more clearly, let's look at a little-known startup called Tabblo.

A Brief History of Tabblo

Ever hear of it? If not, you're not alone.

Founded in 2005 (right around the same time as YouTube), Tabblo was a solid photo-sharing platform with early potential to be a viral sensation. Users posted their photos on Tabblo and sent a link to their friends so they could share in the experience by viewing and "liking" the photos.

Pretty cool, right?

Overall, Tabblo was a well-executed concept with solid theoretical value. So why hasn't anyone ever heard of it?

There was a big problem: **the market wasn't ready for it yet.**

Camera phones had not yet become prolific. Mobile apps were still conceptual. Photo-editing software was still only a tool for professional photographers, and most cameras were still producing hard copies. Basically, 2005 might as well have been the Stone Age.

This was the landscape of the market, and it was all anyone knew or wanted to know. Thanks to years of accepting "it's just the way things are," most people couldn't even imagine anything different. Probably because they didn't have to.

Okay, cameras weren't *quite* this old timey, but they may as well have been from Tabblo's perspective.

So, the main issue that Tabblo experienced was *not* poor execution. It was bad timing. The world just had not yet adopted photography into the mass-market digital age. And Tabblo was virally squandered as a result.

Comparing YouTube and Tabblo

When a YouTube user uploads a video and shares it, YouTube has an opportunity to **demo** the ease of use of its video player and uploading and sharing features.

However, YouTube doesn't have to actually create the viral media displayed inside its application. Instead, it relies on **user-generated content** for its viral media.

In contrast, since Tabblo's core value was more about users uploading their own photos and sharing those memories with friends, it was inhibited in its viral potential. YouTube did not require users to *make* the content. Tabblo did.

That's a big difference. But it's not the only one.

Key Differences in Cycle Time

YouTube's blend of user-generated content search, combined with all its other features, makes its viral cycle time last only minutes.

Alternatively, Tabblo's experience was much different. When users uploaded photos, only a few would actually email those photos to friends. Some users merely used Tabblo for file storage, which was basically where virality went to die. In addition, social media was nowhere near as mainstream, and integrations with third-party tools had yet to be a thing. So overall there were far fewer viral engines for Tabblo to work with—and it lacked the YouTube-esque features to compensate.

I should note that those friends who did receive photos from Tabblo users *would* sign up for Tabblo relatively frequently. However, it unfortunately often took months for those new users to come back and upload their own photos.

Cameras at that time were still large, nonnetworked devices, and the photo-upload process was far lengthier and more tedious. (Remember having to plug in your point-and-shoot camera, upload its photos to your computer, and then upload them again to your social media accounts? Seriously, how did we even survive?)

In hindsight, there were many factors working against Tabblo. Of course, at that time, none of them were obvious on the surface.

Winning the Waiting Game

I know what you're probably thinking: *Isn't Tabblo basically Instagram, but before Instagram was Instagram?*

You're basically correct. Instagram is definitely similar to what Tabblo wanted to create, but Instagram had something crucial on its side that Tabblo did not—namely, Instagram arrived on the scene over a decade later, when a quality camera was in everyone's pocket and the upload process was next to instant (hence the "Insta" part).

In other words, Instagram worked where Tabblo failed partly because it had timing on its side.

Timing Is Everything

Because Tabblo was ahead of its time, it couldn't become the viral sensation it may have become today. As I emphasized, this was *not* due to poor execution by its team. The product by all accounts was pretty solid. In fact, it was so well executed that it was acquired by HP in 2007.

However, the consensus was that the acquisition was more of a future-minded "acquihire" (i.e., Tabblo was purchased for the talented people working on it) by a publicly traded entity looking for a stock boost.

The takeaway?

A major reason YouTube, Tabblo, *and* Instagram ended up the way they did—good, bad, or viral—was market timing. At the end of the day, you might do everything right on the engineering front, but if you haven't yet hit product-market fit in the *current* landscape, **you've got no shot at virality**.

So when you're planning on creating the next greatest viral sensation the world has ever seen, take a look around first, and decide whether the time is right.

So what can you learn from some of the lessons others have had to learn the hard way? Explore this and more in the *Viral Hero* Workbook - available now for free at viralhero.com/workbook.

Chapter 10: Sparking Initial Virality with Inbound Marketing

Nonviral Marketing: The Surprising Fuel for Your Viral Engine

Now that we've learned how to build your viral engine and looked at some real-world examples of powerful viral engines in action, you hopefully have a more practical sense of how to achieve viral success. Let's roll up our sleeves and get back to the mechanics of making it happen for your business.

Because although we've done everything right in creating your viral marketing engine, unless you have a $K > 1.0$ from day one (which you won't), to continue to see new traffic and growth, you'll need to feed your viral machine. You can't just send your product to a few friends, pat yourself on the back for a job well done, and expect it to take off like a rocket ship (unless maybe your name is Elon Musk or Iron Man).

So now that we've successfully created your viral marketing engine, let's get it pumping.

But where do we begin? What should we use for fuel? And how long until you become a genius billionaire playboy (or playgirl) philanthropist?

We're about to find out—hold on tight for takeoff.

Every Engine Needs Fuel

The fuel you need to feed your viral engine is none other than . . . *drumroll please* . . . **nonviral marketing.**

I know what you're thinking: *Travis, how can you go viral by being nonviral? That just doesn't make sense.*

Put the pitchforks down—let me explain.

Nonviral marketing tactics, such as digital advertising, content marketing, and SEO—plus many others—serve as additional on-ramps bringing new leads into your viral loop. Nonviral marketing doesn't *replace* viral; it just ensures no growth potential gets left on the table. Even if you achieve an absurd amount of success through virality, you should always search for **new sources of traffic to feed your viral loop** (as long as it continues to make sound business sense, of course).

Profiting from Nonviral Marketing

We'll go over more explanation of what nonviral marketing is in a bit, but first, here's a quick note about what I mean by nonviral marketing making sound business sense.

Here's an example. Let's say you have a solid viral collaboration marketing engine. On top of that, you add a viral incentive that costs you the equivalent of five dollars. Assuming you can continue to acquire new users through other, nonviral methods for an amount less than or equal to the cost of your viral incentive, it makes sense to keep those additional nonviral engines active.

However, if you find that your nonviral marketing techniques are costing you *seven* dollars per acquired user, you should reevaluate.

Of course, if you're earning a good ROI from those nonviral users who cost seven dollars, you still may want to keep that engine alive. Even if your ROI isn't positive, if the user segment for which you're paying a bit more to acquire is driving strong viral growth, it *still* may be worth keeping that engine active, since it's still bringing you user growth.

Basically, you should only shut off a nonviral engine when sustaining it requires you to give up more of your margin than makes sense.

This is the embodiment of *A*, which you now know is your amplification factor. Remember what we discussed in chapter 9 about getting the most out of your amplification factor? Here's where viral and nonviral marketing meet: though your viral marketing engine likely won't drive self-sustaining growth forever (if at all), if it's done well, it will *always* get you a deep discount on your nonviral marketing spend; then, the virally acquired users driven by those nonvirally acquired users will bring **the average cost per acquisition** down considerably.

Which means in no time at all you'll be a viral hero and undoubtedly asked to join the Avengers.

What's Next?

In the next few sections, I'm going to walk you through the different forms of nonviral marketing that exist and teach you how each can be implemented more effectively by adding virality into the mix.

By feeding your viral engine the right grade of fuel, you'll have it running as smooth as a Porsche in no time (or a Tesla if you're trying to go green).

But first, it's important to know that most marketing channels can be broken down into two categories:

- **Outbound marketing,** in which you proactively embark out into the world to grab people by the hand and lead them back to your product. This typically entails some kind of advertising. With ads, you're placing miniature exposures to your product in other places where people are.

- **Inbound marketing,** in which you create a lead magnet to allow those people to come to you of their own volition without interrupting their experiences elsewhere.

In this chapter, we're going to look at several types of inbound marketing you can use to draw people to your product.

Ready? Let's learn what types of inbound-marketing fuel we've got to choose from.

Stop the Presses: Using Press and PR to Fuel Your Viral Loop

Now that we've learned how nonviral marketing is the fuel that will drive your viral engine toward success (and profit), we're going to look at the first, and oldest, form of nonviral marketing that can get us there.

Put on your newsies cap—we're joining the fray with some good old-fashioned **press and PR**.

Using Press and PR to Fuel Virality

These days, we all read and consume content online (unless you're a hermit with no internet connection).

Given that, it's worth mentioning that the unfortunate part about the fact that anyone can create content online is that—*anyone* can create content online. This guarantees that all of us, without fail, have consumed content created by folks who either aren't anywhere close to the experts they've positioned themselves to be or have some sort of agenda in getting you to believe their short-sighted perspectives.

Since this section is clearly about the press, you could jump to the conclusion that I'm bad-mouthing the press here. On the contrary, I see press and PR as an incredibly viable short-term and early-stage growth lever.

Just like every single other marketing channel (yes, *all* of them), you can transform press and PR into a solid needle mover *if* you take a strategic, well-timed, and carefully planned approach.

Using the Press as an On-Ramp

Once you've engineered and optimized your viral loops (which we've already talked about and will continue to cover in later sections), your goal with all nonviral marketing channels becomes adding fuel into your viral engine.

Here are **a few key points to remember about using PR** to accomplish this goal:

- Just because you hire a great PR firm or an in-house PR specialist does not mean you'll get great coverage. Regardless of who's trying to spread the news on your behalf, **you won't get written about unless you're doing something newsworthy**. Be honest with yourself: if you, as an objective observer, read about your company today, would you find what you're doing unique and interesting? I made this mistake personally with one of my companies back in 2012. We wasted at least thirty thousand dollars trying to get coverage until we realized that while we had a good business, we just weren't doing anything innovative or newsworthy.

- If you do happen to get covered in the press, **do not assume readers will care**. You've effectively sold yourself to that reporter as a potential story, but that doesn't mean the reporter's readers will be interested in reading it or will care enough to check out your site even if they are. Target publications that your real customers are likely to read, and offer readers a clear, frictionless path to getting more info. Also offer those readers an exclusive incentive to take action.

- Press and PR can be **a short-term direct win**. Any traffic you get from it will spike quickly and then drop dramatically soon after. You should not only be confident in your viral loop optimization before going to press but also have retention initiatives in place to retain the new users from the resulting traffic. Do *not* try to get in the media before either of these are done. You'll just waste your moment in the sun.

- Press and PR is also a unique marketing channel because of the **long-term social proof** it can grant you. How many times have you seen media logos on a website showcasing the media coverage that site has garnered? Leads know and trust those logos. As a result, they'll often transfer that trust to your brand if you showcase them at the right times.

Adhering to these four guidelines should allow you to make the most of press and PR to feed your viral engine.

Making Your Story Spread Faster

When dealing with press and PR, keep in mind that you're providing these media sites with content that they're hoping will drive page views and, therefore, ad clicks. Because of this, you aren't the only one who wants your piece to be successful. They want the same thing because it is in their direct financial interest.

More often than not, media sites are driven by online viral word-of-mouth marketing. You can use this to your advantage.

Rather than releasing just a plain old boring press release about your product, funding, and market size, try creating something eye catching and engaging. Try guiding the piece in a direction that sparks the high-arousal emotions that will drive a media site's audience to share and talk about your product with others.

Stop the Presses with Your Product

Have you ever heard the phrase "stop the presses"?

You often hear it in older movies when something so major happens that no other news matters in that moment. In such an instance, the shot caller at a publication makes the decision to physically stop their presses from printing, recraft their next-day publication, and distribute something reporting on that momentous event.

There aren't nearly as many "presses" to stop these days, but your goal is to spark that same sense of urgency. Media outlets *want* to feature stories that spark high-arousal emotions in their readers. So it's your job to give it to them. How? By providing eye-catching, engaging, newsworthy narrative surrounding your product that makes readers feel something strong. Remember, it's not about you—**it's about readers and how they feel**. Make them feel as though they want to talk about your story with others. That's the key to good press and PR.

In other words, use your press and PR nonviral marketing to seize the day.

(If you get that *Newsies* reference, we are definitely friends.)

Publicity Stunts: When One Person's Nonviral Marketing Is Another's Viral Media

In the last section, we saw how you can help fuel virality by using the tried-and-true nonviral marketing method of press and PR. But doing so has its limitations—namely, this channel doesn't typically generate user spikes on par with its more explosive viral engine counterparts. Getting a bigger surge of nonviral traffic from news and media outlets often calls for something a little more extreme than merely releasing a press release or doing an interview.

In other words, you have to go a little crazy.

Publicity Stunts: Do Somethin' Crazy

A **publicity stunt** is a unique piece of content you release that draws attention from the media. (Some call it "unconventional PR," but let's call it like it is, shall we?)

Unlike traditional PR, where you create a narrative about your company to be carried by the press that will hopefully elicit a high-arousal emotion in their readers, publicity stunts involve creating a high-arousal emotion for the press and media outlets themselves to capture their attention. Basically, *they* write the story instead of you.

You know the saying "There's no such thing as bad publicity." Publicity stunts are based on this idea, but they take it one step further by incorporating the belief that the more outrageous or bombastic the action, the more attention it will receive.

Hijack the Media

In essence, publicity stunts can be considered a form of curated viral media. They're created for various press outlets to use as "carrots" to draw users to their sites. In other words, you provide these organizations the ammo to form opinions about you, create their own narratives, and then share them with their followers.

And because it's coming straight from the horse's mouth, as opposed to, say, a press release you wrote yourself, the story will likely have far more prominence.

Some press outlets will love what you're doing. Some will not. Regardless, you *must* create something around which each outlet will form some sort of strong opinion. This is what forces them to start dialogues, which allows you to effectively hijack their audiences.

Publicity Stunts That Don't Look Like Publicity Stunts

When famed stuntman Evel Knievel was in his prime, he became famous for doing crazy stunts, like jumping over things on his motorcycle. The media always covered these stunts. Quite simply, they knew what he was doing would capture their audience's attention, and as a result, they would get more impressions on their ads. This obviously made them more money, so they were all-in.

Knievel knew this too. In fact, that's why he did the stunts in the first place.

Doing these stunts garnered Knievel media coverage, which made him famous. He hijacked the collective viewing audience of the media outlets, and many of those people went on to become his fans and put money in his pockets.

The point? **Evel Knievel's stunts were nonviral marketing masquerading as entertainment.**

Zappos Lets Their Puppets Do the Talking

Remember when we talked about Zappos's decision to include real recordings of customer-support calls in its advertising campaign? It was a stroke of marketing genius. After all, it had built a fiercely loyal following because of its customer service (thanks to some expertly executed satisfaction viral marketing), so why not promote it?

The ads reenacted those phone calls with puppets—which you have to admit is hard not to smile at. To all appearances, Zappos was just creating some simple, enjoyable ad spots.

However, the campaign had an ulterior motive, which was to showcase to the press how much Zappos's customers loved something it provided that usually people hate (i.e., calling customer service). As a result, members of the press formed opinions and wrote about the spot.

The Press Can Be a Fickle Beast

Zappos is not the only company to use TV ads to its nonviral marketing advantage. Think of Super Bowl commercials. It almost seems more people tune in to watch those than the game itself. This is why ad spots during that time are so coveted (and pricey)—whether they're comedic or tearjerkers, these commercials are not just highly viewed during the game; they're also highly covered by the media afterward—meaning they double as publicity stunts as well.

But if you're thinking about creating some sort of publicity stunt to get the press talking, the main thing to keep in mind is that they're undoubtedly going to drum up opinions on both sides. So whether that coverage is good, bad, or downright nasty, make sure you're creating content that sways your ideal customers to the opinion that convinces them to do business with you. That way, if your crazy stunt ends up with you slamming headfirst into a tree (as it did for Red in the image that kicked off this section), at least you'll come away with a few new users.

Organic Search Optimization: Customizing Your Viral Loop Based on User Desire

Now that we've got your viral engine revving after fueling it up with traditional PR and unconventional publicity stunts, let's broaden our horizons by searching elsewhere (quite literally).

Get ready to fight for your spot atop the rankings.

Organic Search Optimization: The Ultimate Open Virality Example

When we talked about open virality back in our section covering the twelve types of viral marketing, most of our minds went to the "marketplace" model and not to, say, organic search optimization. For example,

- if you want to sell a physical product, most people eventually put it on **Amazon**;
- if you want to find a new app, you usually search for it on the **App Store or Google Play**.

  However, this is just as relevant:

- If you want to find information of some kind, you'll search for it on **Google**.

When you think about it, Google is essentially a marketplace for information. Most people call it a search engine, and they're right, but its mechanics are similar to the search function in any other marketplace, in that it's a singular source where you search for (and find) something specific.

In other words, by telling somebody to "Google" something, you're feeding traffic into Google's own open virality loop. This means using that term instantly activates two separate viral engines: offline viral word-of-mouth marketing and the aforementioned open viral model.

We don't often think of Google as a viral sensation, but in fact, it's **the ultimate viral sensation**. It's so prolific that we don't even think about how awesome it is. We just assume Google *is* the internet.

Kind of crazy when you zoom out like that, isn't it?

Fighting for That Top Spot

The interesting thing about marketplaces is that they can become *so big* that strategically crafting your product to appear higher in their organic search results becomes of significant value.

For example, once upon a time, I owned an online fitness company called WorkoutBOX. To its credit, we crushed most of the industry juggernauts in organic search results. We were number one for terms like *workouts* and *exercises*, among dozens of other major keywords. As a result, we got nearly half a million people on the site every month for free—all of whom were proactively searching for exactly what we had.

This is the kind of value that has companies battling one another in a heated game of King of the Digital Hill. This in turn sparks thousands of agencies to spring up and offer their help in getting you to the top.

- For organic search on Google, this is called search engine optimization (**SEO**).

- As the App Store and Google Play grew, they introduced similar organic search algorithms, which birthed app store optimization (**ASO**).

These aren't the only examples of optimization for search, just the most well known. For my last startup, we gamed the search function of the WordPress plugin marketplace using the same organic-search optimization tactics one would for search engines. Similarly, I'd be incredibly surprised if there aren't businesses already doing very well optimizing physical products for search on Amazon as well.

The best part?

If you educate yourself and do the legwork required to optimize your product for organic discovery, this traffic source can be ***tremendously* cost effective**. While it isn't completely free (you have to factor in the costs to produce content as well as the blood, sweat, and tears spent in wowing search relevancy algorithms), it can be a hell of a lot cheaper than paid marketing channels.

Organic Search and Virality

Organic search is a dynamically different source of traffic than others. To make search traffic a viable on-ramp into your viral loop, you must examine the context through which users are discovering your product, specifically compared to how other users from other sources are becoming exposed to you.

For example, let's say Dropbox decided early on to make SEO a primary method to feed its viral loop. As such, it optimized content and pages around two terms (a.k.a. keyword phrases):

- Better file storage
- Easier document sharing

These are both massive elements of the core value Dropbox offers to its users. However, users who search for only one of those terms are clearly indicating where their interests lie. So the right move would be to **highlight the core value** provided by that specific term throughout the entire viral loop.

How would Dropbox achieve this?

Say a user reaches Dropbox's site by searching for "better file storage." That user's subsequent journey through Dropbox's viral loop should then emphasize the fact that by inviting friends, the user will unlock even more file storage space (as we've discussed, this tactic is known as the viral hook). When Dropbox makes this clear, the user realizes that inviting friends delivers even *more* of the core value he or she wants, which was demonstrated by the original search.

In essence, Dropbox is using organic search to tap into viral incentive marketing.

Get extra space free!
Complete these simple tasks and instantly boost your Dropbox space!
Like Dropbox? Tell your friends on Facebook
128MB
Tell your friends on Facebook why they would like Dropbox and get some extra free space!
I love Dropbox because it's so easy to use, and I never have to carry my flashdrive around.
Post on Facebook
Tweet about Dropbox for more free space!
128MB
Tell your friends on Twitter why you love Dropbox and get some more free space!
I love Dropbox because it's so easy to use, and I never have to carry my flashdrive around.
Post on Twitter

However, if a different user reaches the site by searching for "easier document sharing," that user's journey through the viral loop should be different. Instead of highlighting better file storage, this loop should show how easy sharing files with friends can be. By entering a friend's email address into a field, the user can easily share a folder with that friend. Then the friend, who has now become a potential new Dropbox user, can see and collaborate on every document within that folder.

In other words, Dropbox is using organic search to tap into viral collaboration marketing.

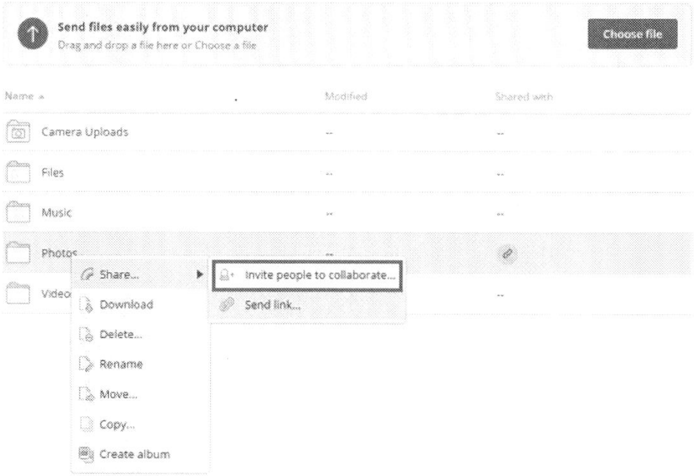

Two different organic searches; two amazing opportunities for virality.

Scaling Your Viral Growth with Organic Search

As we've seen, organic search optimization is a powerful, scalable marketing channel.

However, SEO is increasingly competitive and typically not a low-hanging fruit for new companies. Unlike four or five years ago when my fitness startup was the champion of all fitness-related search, today you need considerable time, research, effort, and resources to rank well for a major keyword.

What's more, you should not be subversive or "game the system" in any way. Even if you do rank for a brief period of time, it won't last. Google, Apple, Amazon, and the other major marketplaces you're trying to optimize for are smarter than you. They'll build systems to combat any black- or gray-hat tactics you try to use. Your best bet is to **invest your time in *becoming* what people really want to see** when conducting a search for specific keywords or phrases.

If you do that, your rankings will have nowhere to go but up!

Niche Search: Shelf Placement for Virtual Window Shopping

As you've probably realized by now, not every form of marketing works with every type of product. That's why it's so important to know what your options are and pick the ones that fit best with your business. That being said, there are several forms of nonviral marketing that you might not immediately think of when you hear the term *nonviral marketing* but that can be just as conducive for your business, if you know how they work.

This brings us conveniently to our next nonviral marketing tactic: **niche search**.

Virality is all about getting in front of the right people at the right time. While this might seem reliant on chance, you'd be surprised at how effectively some companies can veer destiny in the right direction using the right type of optimization.

Remember our discussion about open virality?

This type of viral marketing essentially describes the virality involved in creating a marketplace-type product that houses smaller products within it. (Think the App Store.)

Open virality ensures that the developers producing the products within the marketplace all have a vested interest in bringing users to that product. This in turn inadvertently exposes those products' customers to your marketplace.

To clarify, if you're the one who builds the marketplace (e.g., Apple building the App Store), you'll experience this sort of virality directly. It would be like being the owner of a department store selling other people's goods.

If you've instead created a product that can be distributed *within* a marketplace, you're a prime candidate for the **niche search marketing channel.**

Niche Search: It's All about Direct Line of Sight

Niche search marketing is like creating a product that's sold in somebody else's department store and then working hard to get it placed on the shelf in the direct line of sight of your ideal prospect.

Or to put it another way, say you produce a sugary cereal. Niche search marketing is like going into every single grocery store that sells your brand of cereal and physically moving your boxes to the best-possible position on the shelves: in front of the competition and right at the eye level of sugar-crazed eight-year-olds. (*Note: Probably not a cool thing to do in the world of cereals, but it's a totally legit practice in online marketplaces.*)

The key is to **place your product in the most successful marketplaces**—specifically, ones that already see significant traffic from open virality, in addition to their own nonviral marketing efforts.

By placing your product in those high-traffic marketplaces and then optimizing your product listing so it's more frequently seen by those looking for a product like yours (which is called niche search optimization), you'll be able to temporarily **hijack the marketplaces' audiences** for your benefit.

In other words, sugary cereal for everyone!

Niche Search in Action

Here's are some examples:

- Apple's App Store is a niche search marketplace that lists apps for the iPhone and iPad. Optimizing your app's listing (a process called ASO) can yield significant traffic for you that you don't pay a nickel for.

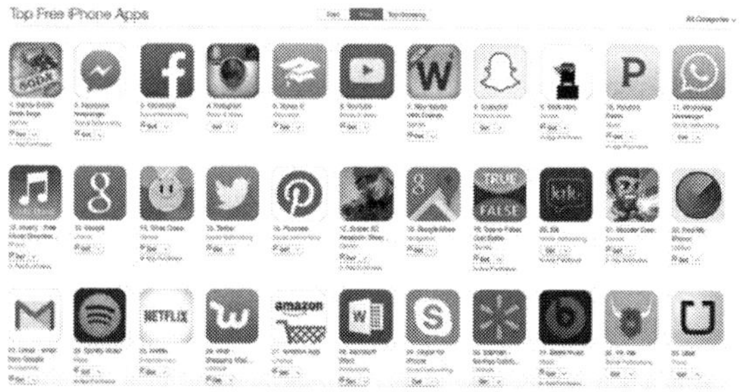

- WordPress's plugin store is similar to the App Store. It lists various "plugins" that can augment a blog or WordPress website in a one-click format that's extremely user friendly. Optimizing your plugin's listing can be very lucrative when you have a way to monetize it.

- Udemy's online course marketplace allows users to find and learn from courses created by other users on a variety of topics ranging from coding to music to learning new languages.

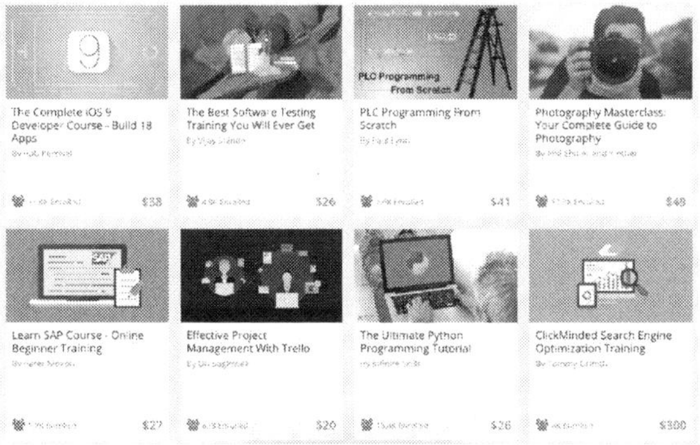

Utilizing a marketplace where tons of users already flock can help tie your product's growth to that marketplace's viral engine, which can be a very good move on your part.

Imagine Apple giving you a piggyback ride. Sounds kind of nice, doesn't it?

Niche Search and Virality

Unlike most other marketing channels we've discussed, you have to **be careful** when encouraging virality using a niche search marketing channel.

One reason is you don't want to work hard to drive traffic to your product through customers who are sharing and inviting others only to watch those new viral leads get sidetracked by other items in that larger marketplace.

For example, if you're an app in the App Store, I recommend you consider deep linking. This will send existing users directly into your app while directing new prospects straight to the download page for your app.

You also need to pay close attention to the economics of the marketplace itself by crunching the numbers. For example, say a marketplace takes a decent chunk of your sales every time a sale of your product is made in that marketplace, and you make far more when you sell the same product from your own website. In such an instance, consider routing your viral traffic to your own internal sales page rather than the sales page on the marketplace itself.

Know Who You're Doing Business For

Remember, the marketplace is a business that encapsulates your business. They need their own margins, and if they can get their users to grab other products that make *them* more money, even though you sent the traffic their way to buy *your* product, they will always act in their own self-interest.

Expect this behavior, and look for a way you can even potentially use it to your advantage, such as increasing your conversion rate and reducing your return rate so much that marketplaces feature your product more prominently.

They'd be fools not to, since they'll make more money by doing so.

Engineering as Marketing: Building and Growing a Product to Build and Grow Your Product

Everyone is well aware of the concept of marketing through the press and search engines. So as we make our way through the sixteen nonviral marketing methods to fuel your viral engine, there's a good chance you're thinking this to yourself: *Travis, tell me something I don't know.*

All right, how about this:

- There is a breed of fruit fly that cannot get drunk.
- Buzz Aldrin was the first human to pee on the moon.
- You have a tongue print that is just as unique as your fingerprint.

Bet you didn't know those. Here's another:

- One of the best ways to achieve viral growth is to turn your engineering into marketing.

Confused? Let me enlighten you.

Back in the day when the SaaS company Moz was still SEOmoz, it embarked on a strategy now called **engineering as marketing.** This is essentially the process of building smaller niche products with the sole purpose of pushing their users into your main product.

For example, SEOmoz built a free tool called Open Site Explorer. This tool offered a small but valuable amount of backlink information to its users in exchange for their contact information. It was a helpful tool at a time when most similar tools either sucked or were only available for a premium price.

Engineer a Better Way

SEOmoz knew that those using the tool would only be doing so if they were trying to get their sites to rank well for search engines. So, little by little, the company marketed other SEOmoz products to the leads it generated through Open Site Explorer. Sure enough, those users began to convert.

Inevitably, as the market landscape changed, SEOmoz became Moz and rolled Open Site Explorer into its main product offering. However, engineering as marketing is still viable in many cases. Often, large brands will build "microsites" for promoting certain offers or events. Large premium apps will build smaller utility apps or games and then serve ads to the organic users of those apps.

In short, under certain circumstances and provided you have the resources available to do so, you might want to think about building other smaller products that cater to the same audience you want using your main product.

Engineering as Marketing and Virality

The nice part about engineering as marketing is that **it's flexible.** Unlike blogging, there is no predefined format expected by users. Unlike advertising, there is no predefined asset format or size that you're confined to. In other words, the possibilities are endless.

For example, let's go back to the Moz example above. Had Moz opted to promote Open Site Explorer virally, such as by providing some sort of collaborative functionality and value for inviting other team members to OSE, it's highly likely that its lead-generation strategy would have been amplified. This would then have provided Moz with more warm leads to market its paid products to, ultimately providing more bang for its buck.

The rule of thumb here is to ensure you're thinking about your microproduct in the same way you would think about any product. Focus on providing **value first and foremost.** This is how you get those leads to warm up and trust you. It's also how you get those users to convert and then stick around for months or even years afterward.

Content Marketing: How Blogs, Videos, and Podcasts Can Steadily Feed Your Viral Engine

We're fast on our way to filling up your viral engine with the best of the best nonviral marketing tactics. But pursing traffic with PR, publicity stunts, and search engines can be draining. So why not kick back and let the people come to you?

Put on your leisure pants—it's time to get creative.

Content Marketing: Inbound Awesomeness

Content marketing is a form of inbound marketing that focuses on creating and sharing materials for a targeted audience online. This generated content can include videos, blogs, social media posts, graphics, podcasts, and more.

The key is that the content does not explicitly promote your brand but **implicitly arouses interest** in your product.

When potential users are exposed to your content, they consciously choose to check it out. That's because your content (which you've crafted so well) adds to or augments what they're already experiencing and consuming online. (This initial exposure could result from anything from backlinking to organic searching to online viral word of mouth.)

Then, little by little, you begin nibbling at those potential users. Eventually, through exposing them to enough of your content, you can craft a narrative in their minds that leads them to become users of your product. The best part? They think this has happened of their own volition. Because it has.

In this way, content marketing is kind of like the movie *Inception*, only without Leonardo DiCaprio trying to rob you blind and murder your dreams.

Content Marketing and Virality

If you want your content-marketing efforts to help spread your product virally, the first and most obvious strategy would be to mirror the efforts of media sites whose content spreads like wildfire. Especially those benefiting from online viral word-of-mouth marketing (think BuzzFeed or Uproxx).

Proactively eliciting high-arousal emotions in readers and then prompting them to share your content with others who have similar interests is a winning strategy. Beyond that, viral transaction marketing is another solid content-marketing strategy, but not in the way it's normally used.

You know those "click to tweet" widgets you see so often on blogs and online news articles? They prompt viral transaction marketing. Those tweet prompts aren't asking you to share how awesome the content provider is; they're giving you an opportunity to share a piece of valuable wisdom to your network. This allows you to elevate your own status and be considered smart and insightful by your peers.

To take advantage of this specific method, you can use an online service like the aptly named Click to Tweet, or if you're using a self-hosted WordPress site, install the Better Click to Tweet plugin.

Don't Lose Sight of Your Product

Those are just two examples of ways you can make your content-marketing efforts more effective using viral concepts. Additionally, if you work hard to optimize your content for organic search and you promote it with a few native-content ad engines that make it appear as if other sites are promoting *your* content (e.g., Outbrain), you can blend a few of these channels together pretty effectively.

However, no matter whether you use a blog, videos, or podcasts as your chosen form of content marketing, don't forget that at the end of the day, **the goal is to get new leads** and do so in a cost-effective way.

Don't lose the ability to convert leads with your content because you're solely focusing on spreading your content. In other words, don't just create stuff to create it and then get off when people start sharing it. There's already enough crap like that on the internet already.

Instead, focus on creating high-quality, relevant content that converts leads when it reaches them.

Chapter 11: Fueling Your Viral Engine with Outbound Marketing

Social Media Ads: How Absurdly Granular Ad Targeting Can Increase Your Viral KPIs

In the previous chapter, we covered several types of inbound marketing you can use to draw people to your product. Remember the definition of outbound marketing? It's types of marketing that involve you going out into the world and leading people back to your product rather than letting them come to you on their own. Depending on your product, these next few types can be just as viable for your viral success as inbound marketing.

We'll start with an outbound-marketing type everyone has likely encountered in daily life.

Social Media Ads and Banners: The Resurgence of Display Marketing

Thanks to the proliferation of social media platforms like Facebook, Twitter, and Instagram, **social media ads** are now a thing. A really, really big thing. As a result, display advertising, which briefly took a hit in favor of search engine marketing, is now back in a major way.

(*For those of you who don't know, display ads are advertising done through banners or other ad formats made of text, images, video, and audio that are displayed on websites and in apps.*)

In fact, now that the Google Display Network and the hundreds of other smaller web and mobile display-advertising networks are on the rise, display advertising is the primary form of advertising on the internet today.

Get Granular with Your Targeting

The real magic in social media and display advertising is in the specificity of its targeting.

For better or worse (though for us marketers and growth engineers, it's definitely for the better), this magic is possible in no small part because of the mass amounts of data social media platforms collect from users.

As a result, no matter what audience segment you want to target, you can expose ads to those people. Want to reach men between the ages of nineteen and thirty-one who like carving *Lord of the Rings* figurines out of carrots and live in Cincinnati? Done.

If you gather even one piece of information from those folks, you can then target and retarget them even more specifically based on what they've done while interacting with your product. The resulting potential for increased growth and conversions is truly astounding.

Display Advertising and Virality

Thanks to absurdly granular targeting and the slightly newer "custom audience" functionality that various social media ad platforms now offer, there are **three main ways** social media and display advertising can tie directly into your viral loop:

- The ad itself can spark **online viral word of mouth**. For example, Teespring has become famous for its "name segmentation." Since it has a product that's ultrapersonalized to the user (think T-shirts with people's names on them), its team regularly creates hundreds of targeted ads that display certain first and last names. When prospective customers see these ads, they're often a bit spooked because they've never seen an ad with their name in it before, **and they tell others about it**.

- You can retarget users who have gone through most of your viral loop but haven't finished the final step by **showing them an ad meant to specifically showcase your viral value**. For many of those users, they simply didn't send invites because something else came up. They meant to get back to it but just never did. By giving them another on-ramp, you can ensure more of those users complete the process. This will increase your *i* value and possibly even improve your average viral cycle time.

- With social media ads, you can **target users who have been invited** to your product by friends **but haven't yet accepted the invite.** (Crazy, right?) By saving the emails or phone numbers a user enters into your application when inviting friends, you can begin showing highly targeted ads to those prospective users. Remember, these people have not yet granted you enough trust for you to actually message them—it was their friends who did the direct inviting. However, that doesn't mean you can't show them ads where other companies would show their own ads anyway. Some may contest this, but I personally don't view it as a breach in privacy, just another form of awesome targeting. If done well, this will help you increase your *conv%* value, thereby increasing your K value.

At the end of the day, social media ads and display advertising offer so much power because of the targeting options they offer.

Getting your ads in front of people is never hard. Getting your ads in front of the *right* people is far more difficult. This is the primary puzzle most digital marketers are always trying to solve. And it's something your viral engine can greatly benefit from by mastering social media ads.

Search Engine Marketing: Four Ways It Can Be the Viral Growth Engineer's Best Friend

As we learned in our discussion of organic search optimization, these days, the top search results for major high-traffic keywords can be pretty coveted real estate. Achieving a high page rank can take a lot of time and effort, some tremendously strategic architecture, quite a bit of writing, and tons of caffeine.

But what if you could just *pay* to show up in search results?

Enter SEM. It's expensive, but the payoffs can be extremely lucrative—so don't make the mistake of assuming it's *too* expensive to try.

SEM: You've Gotta Pay to Play

Search engine real estate is *so* coveted that Google and other smaller search engines started to make nearly all their money by selling ads above and alongside their organic results. This created a new marketing channel called search engine marketing (SEM).

These days, those ads get quite a bit more priority on a search page—specifically because it's in the search engine's direct financial interest—though admittedly these ads are actually pretty solid by themselves in most cases and not just wasted real estate. As more users click on those ads, the search engines see those ads as more relevant to the users searching for those terms, and they serve that ad more frequently.

In this way, the saying "You've gotta pay to play" runs the show in today's world of search engine marketing.

"Steal" Your Place at the Table

By paying either a fixed or fluid amount of money per click on those search ads, advertisers can "steal" traffic away from the folks who have done a lot more work to get there organically.

Before you start saying "that's unfair" and throwing tomatoes at me, relax for a moment. It's not only fair, since one person is paying for those clicks and the other one isn't, but search engines have bills just like every other company. Ads are one excellent way to pay them.

That's just business. And SEM not only powers the search engine's business but can power yours as well.

SEM and Virality

There are four ways that SEM can be a great asset for feeding your viral loop:

- Organic or not, showing up as an option for users searching for a solution to their problems is incredibly powerful, specifically because it allows you to **segment your audience** into the users you want to target. For example, if I do SEM for key phrases like *viral marketing* to promote *Viral Hero*,

I only pay for the clicks of people who are proactively searching for information on viral marketing. Which is exactly who I want landing on my site and entering my own viral loop.

- Your brand appearing next to other major brands or in the top spot of search results can **boost your perceived "social proof"** in the minds of visitors. This lends trust. The more those visitors trust you, the more likely they will do what you want them to.

- If your organization has room in the budget, **SEM is a far bigger win than SEO** (i.e., the process of ranking for keywords organically), especially if you lack the time or expertise to implement the latter. Even if you rank well for many keywords, you likely don't have full coverage over all the relevant keywords you want. SEM can help get you that coverage—for a price.

- Search engine marketing **scales very well**. So many people use Google, brands like eBay spend over $250 million each year on SEM. Since eBay is obviously a diverse marketplace, it has the luxury of casting an incredibly wide net without oversaturating. You likely won't be able to scale to this level, but very few companies on Earth really need to.

In a nutshell, search engine marketing can help throw gas on your nonviral marketing fire and become the catalyst for your early growth.

Email Marketing: How Unused Email Notifications Can Result in Viral Alchemy

Most people view **email marketing** as the process of marketing to a list of email addresses you acquire. However, that's not exactly right. These people are mistakenly assuming that the conversion tactic (important, but not what we want here) is the same thing as the acquisition tactic (what we want here).

Let me show you the difference.

Email conversion:

- Using permission-based tactics to market a product to a list you generate, such as offering a "lead magnet" in exchange for a user's contact information. The goal is to convert that user into a customer via an autoresponder.

Implementing email as a conversion tool is obviously important. But it's not so much a method of viral feeding as it is something you use once a lead has already been acquired.

Email acquisition:

- Acquiring a new list from a source, such as an information broker or another company, to market directly to that list in a non-permission-based way (which could be seen as spam).
- Marketing a new product to existing contacts who opted into your list for something different.
- Collaborating with a complementary product or service and cross marketing to each other's list with the idea of providing an extension of the same value both sets of your subscribers opted in for.

The third acquisition tactic listed above is the one I advise pursuing the most.

Email Marketing: To Feed, or Not to Feed

It takes quite a bit of time and effort to build up an email list of subscribers who trust you and engage with what you send them. Marketing to an existing list of engaged subscribers through a partnership (whether paid or cross promotional in nature) usually gives you the most bang for your buck.

This engine can scale pretty well, and it can also be incredibly personalized in its best form. Strive for as personalized and as valuable a campaign as possible, whether it's email being sent out by you or by somebody else on your behalf.

Email Marketing and Virality

By this point you're hopefully aware that email often serves as a logical viral carrier for your viral loop, so I won't elaborate.

However, if we take this one step further, we can use email marketing as gasoline for your viral fire. How? By leveraging your transactional emails that **currently contain no call to action**.

For example, let's say you just purchased some scuba-diving equipment online from Scuba Steve's Scuba Shop (which isn't a real store that I'm aware of). You instantly get a receipt for your purchase. This is a transactional email. You received it based on an action you took within Scuba Steve's application.

Normally, this is just an informational email for your records. However, if Scuba Steve is a certified viral hero black belt, this email likely **will also contain a call to action**. This call to action would say something like this: "Unlock a promo code for 50 percent off a Scuba Steve Snorkel when you share your purchase on social media using this link!" Scuba Steve would also have a similar call to action prompting his customers to share his shop with their friends in all the other emails he sends out. This ensures all emails serve a purpose and share unique viral value for the customers receiving them.

Become a Viral Alchemist

As Scuba Steve's email shows, viral engineering can transform lumps of coal (i.e., email notifications with no existing calls to action) into **lumps of gold** (i.e., emails that can drive business value and additional traffic). With enough lumps of gold in your safe, you could become very rich.

And buy a whole lot more scuba gear.

Here's a helpful tip: Be sure to craft the language communicating your viral value, and even your viral incentive itself, around the past and current behavior of the user. For example, if a user just purchased a product, make sure your viral incentive is something related to that purchase, like a promo code for a future complimentary purchase, two free months of your subscription offering, or something equally as pertinent.

Basically, if the value you're sharing doesn't make sense to the user in the context of the situation at that moment, it won't be nearly as effective for you.

Direct Sales: Using Targeted Cold Outreach to Fuel Growth and Feed Virality

Sometimes when you're trying to ignite your viral engine (as we've been doing throughout this section), you need to give it an extra-firm push in the right direction to get it going. That means getting your hands dirty (figuratively). With nonviral marketing, the best way to do this is direct sales.

Direct sales is a niche marketing channel that isn't appropriate for everyone, as it involves real human beings reaching out to other real human beings and getting the occasional "door" slammed in their faces. But it can be effective in driving new traffic to your product, as long as you're committed and enact it in the right way.

But which way is the right way, you ask?

Let's meet our contenders!

Direct Sales: Feed Your Virality Engine by Hand
Direct sales takes a variety of forms, such as the following:

- **Cold Calling:** Calling actual prospects on the phone to try to have conversations. (This also includes going door to door, which isn't often done today but happened a lot more frequently back when vacuum cleaners were a hot-ticket item.) This ideally begins with a targeted list that ensures the calls you make aren't to just random people but to your ideal customers who would theoretically benefit from your product based on who they are and what they do. The speed at which those calls happen and the economics of paying good people to make them is what limits growth most for this channel.

- **Automated Cold Calling:** This is similar to cold calling but done with robots and prerecorded messages. This channel converts at a far, far lower rate, but the economics are more favorable in that you don't need to employ a large sales force to make it happen. The lack of personalization or permission to contact prospects is what limits this channel.

- **Cold Email:** This is similar to the first two channels but is done via email. Cold email can actually convert better than automated cold calling if you craft the subject line and copy well. But it can also be flagged as spam and filtered out of prospects' inboxes. The risk of appearing as spam can be a serious limiting factor, so I don't recommend cold email.

- **Direct Mail:** An effective yet undervalued channel, if done well. What you don't want to do is send direct mail that looks like junk mail. Instead, send direct mail that looks like a real person sent it and spent time on it. Make sure you let prospects know how you got their contact information.

These are just four of the most common direct-sales examples out of dozens. But the basic pattern of all of them is your team proactively reaching out and initiating a conversation with a prospect who has granted you little or no permission to do so.

What could go wrong?

Stand Out from the Crowd

Direct sales is a unique marketing channel because if it becomes saturated by other marketers from completely different industries, you can become negatively associated with them. If prospects are getting pummeled with direct-sales offers by other marketers that they deem aren't relevant, they often develop blindness to other direct-sales efforts as well.

How often have you answered a call, heard an automated voice on the other end, and promptly hung up without learning what the voice had to say or who it was? We've all been there.

It's therefore important that your **direct-sales marketing efforts do not follow the same old templated approach**. Prospects will ignore your efforts completely if you try to blend in. Take the initiative to offer something new that's worth their time. That's how to avoid getting the phone slammed in your face.

Direct Sales and Virality

The most obvious, and therefore most overlooked, method of eliciting viral invites from this channel is **asking for referrals**.

Yes, I'm being serious. Just asking. Plain and simple.

That said, this ask must come later in the process—ideally, after you've sold the prospect on your product. When the prospect fully believes in what you're selling and is ready to buy, **that's the perfect moment to ask something like this**:

I'm excited to get you started using [product]! Before we get started, I wanted to let you know that most of our growth comes from referrals. This means our satisfied customers are really happy with their experiences, and they want to introduce their friends and colleagues to the same great experience. Now, this is totally optional, but if [product] exceeds your expectations and we make sure you get a great experience from it, would you be willing to introduce us to two people you think would enjoy the same great experience?

This does a few things:

- It ensures prospects understand that this ask will *only* occur if they love their experience.
- The fact that you're saying most of your growth happens in this way increases prospects' expectations that they'll like their experience.
- If they do say yes, it makes it much more likely that they'll send you additional referrals both during the process and after you deliver the value you're promising—especially if you

call them again later on, ask them about their experience, and then ask for the referrals.

This is a great example of how, in marketing, you'll get something way more often if you simply ask for it than if you just hope and pray somebody will give it to you.

So don't be shy—virality waits for no one.

Affiliate Marketing: The Confusing, Powerful System of External Sales Reps

When most people hear *affiliate marketing*, they think of skeevy internet marketing products. Many of these products have a small army of affiliates running various microsites like the ones that mask themselves as unbiased product reviews. Not cool.

Because we have strong (usually negative) opinions about these tactics, we assume these distasteful examples define this marketing channel. In reality, this is pretty far from the truth.

The Truth about Affiliate Marketing

The majority of affiliates market the products of others to you without *you* even realizing they're doing it. They either look like normal ads, or they appear to be someone else's products, and you never think twice about it.

In the few cases where you *do* recognize that a product might be an affiliate promotion, it often seems like a complement of the core offering of the person or brand you're following. And once again, you don't think twice about it.

We don't remember these positive scenarios when we hear the term *affiliate marketing* because they don't stir up any high-arousal emotions within us. They seem like typical, acceptable forms of marketing, and they don't register as worth remembering. Which, in this case, is a good thing—it means you're doing affiliate marketing right.

But we're getting ahead of ourselves. Let's back up first.

Affiliate Marketing: Sales Reps You Don't Hire

In a nutshell, an "affiliate" is essentially an external sales rep. If you were to become an affiliate for my product, I would typically **pay you a fee** for every product of mine that you sell to your (or any) customers.

That's it. Plain and simple.

This engine can actually help you scale quite a bit—for instance, if you've saturated another marketing channel (i.e., hit a brick wall) or reached a ceiling in the performance of your internal digital marketing efforts. (However, note that a common mistake is starting to use affiliate marketing too early and paying a fee higher than the cost to market to customers internally.)

Have you ever visited your favorite blog and noticed a widget box showcasing a recommended product from Amazon? More than likely, if you click the box, go to Amazon, and buy that product (or any other), the owner of your favorite blog will get a cut of your purchase. That's affiliate marketing, and that blog owner is an affiliate marketer.

But many of us assume affiliate marketing only takes place on smaller websites pushing Amazon products, or when internet marketers push digital products for other internet marketers.

This is only a fraction of what affiliate marketing actually is.

An Affiliate Marketing Use Case
Take the Southwest Airlines Visa card.

Patrons of Southwest Airlines know the value they receive from the airline. They pay Southwest to travel to and from destinations because of the things Southwest does differently than other airlines (e.g., open seating, better customer service, no charge for bags, no change fees, etc.). Because of this, Southwest has grown into a large, popular brand (rightfully so; baggage fees are the worst).

Visa marketers recognized this growth. Concurrently, they realized that their own marketing for a normal, everyday Visa card could only take the company so far. However, if Visa brought on other brands as affiliates to market its cards as well, the sky would be the limit (pun intended). Visa would not only gain a portion of the revenue from the sale of those cards but also would drive some serious customer loyalty, as card users would drum up free "miles" they could use on flights.

So Visa pitched those brands on selling their own branded Visa cards that they could then market to their own customers. In this way, **Visa made Southwest an affiliate**.

Every time you sign up for a Southwest Airlines Visa card, you become a Visa user. Southwest gets some great benefits from it, but the bottom line is that Visa is leveraging Southwest's audience to promote its own product.

Is Affiliate Marketing Technically Viral Marketing?

If we're currently trying to find nonviral means to ignite virality, why are we talking about something that looks blatantly like *viral* marketing?

I've fielded this question before, and it's a valid one. It usually goes something like this: *Company A is asking company B to join its affiliate program, and then company B exposes company A to its customers for an incentive. Isn't this just viral incentive marketing?*

Great question, and I'm glad you're thinking about things this way, but *no*, it's not viral incentive marketing; if it were, you could make the argument that all advertising is technically viral incentive marketing, which it isn't.

Affiliate Marketing and Virality

There is one and only one difference between affiliate marketing and viral incentive marketing:

- The promoter of the product is **not a user** who signed up to gain core value and then recognized the viral value and began sending invites.

An easier way to look at it is the way a virus spreads. (Gross, but true.)

One person is exposed to the virus by somebody else who has the virus. That person then becomes infected and exposes another person. Both, at one time, were normal people who came into contact with a carrier of the virus. But because of those interactions, they each became a carrier of the virus as well.

Southwest Airlines wasn't simply a Visa user who saw so much value in Visa that they decided to invite their network. Southwest and Visa working together was a dynamically different process involving many hours of purposeful negotiation, planning, engineering, and promotion, which is why we categorize affiliate marketing differently than viral incentive marketing.

That said, it's worth considering that an affiliate program itself can be considered its own product. Which means it **can spread virally if it's engineered correctly**.

Engineering Virality Using Affiliations

The following is an example of how a company could use affiliate marketing to fuel its viral engine.

Many great affiliate programs have "tiers" of affiliates. This means that if Company A starts an affiliate program and Company B joins, then Company B would get "tier one" incentives by promoting Company A directly to consumers. Additionally, if Company B recruits

Company C as an affiliate of Company A as well, Company B would get "tier two" incentives for every sale that Company C makes for Company A. Of course, Company C would still get the same "tier one" incentives.

With an affiliate-marketing-program structure like this, one could theoretically engineer many forms of viral marketing, in addition to viral incentive marketing.

I'll leave the possibilities up to you!

Virality doesn't begin on its own. Every viral engine needs to be fed traffic from other sources, and inbound marketing is a great, scalable way to do just that. Explore how you might be able to utilize it in the *Viral Hero* Workbook. Get your free copy at viralhero.com/workbook.

Chapter 12: Using Offline Marketing and Other Methods to Feed Your Viral Fire

Offline Advertising: A Tough Nut to Crack but a Surprising Viral Weapon

We've now covered twelve effective forms of both inbound and outbound nonviral marketing for fueling your virality—most of which occur online. However, not all your nonviral marketing *needs* to be done online. In fact, there's a whole world of people out there who aren't whiling away their days staring at screens but who would be just as eager to hear about your awesome new product.

In this chapter, I'll show you how to get their attention using a little creativity and provocativeness.

The History of Offline Advertising

Back in the glory days of advertising (think the Don Draper and *Mad Men* days), offline advertising wasn't called offline advertising. It was just called advertising. There were no online options, and there were no forms of attribution or analytics other than estimates. In those days, execs went with their gut on what they felt the most appealing ad spot would be. They then downed a glass of scotch and went out for lunch.

It was pure opinion, and if you were good at pitching, your advertising firm would win contracts because of how well you could speak to (or party with) the advertiser who was purchasing your services. Essentially, the customers were just along for the ride.

Today, things have changed.

The age of digital advertising has elevated the quantitative standard that marketers and growth engineers adhere to, particularly in the tracking and experimentation practices they bring to their advertising campaigns. As a result, many will choose to speak negatively about the world of offline marketing—though whether they really believe that or are just trying to sell you on their digitally based services is tough to say.

Either way, offline advertising isn't the grand ol' time it was in *Mad Men*, at least not anymore. But that doesn't mean there isn't still strong value to be gained from this nonviral marketing method.

Offline Advertising: A Tough Nut to Crack—and Track

The idea that traditional **offline marketing methods** are dead is just plain wrong.

To clarify, there's *no* form of marketing that's "dead" unless it fails to get your message in front of your audience in some way. And even then, that's more on you than on the method. Some marketing channels may not favor your economics or cater to your specific audience, but your circumstances won't be the same circumstances for everyone.

Print ads, billboards—heck, even the planes flying around with giant banners behind them—all of these *can* work if done by the right company and presented to the right audience.

However, none of these are as easy to track as digital marketing channels. So you must have a plan for attribution in place so you can learn what leads and users are driven from which sources, at least with reasonable accuracy.

So, what does all this have to do with virality?

Offline Advertising and Virality

It turns out that in life, people are often around other people. Go figure. But if those people are not psychically around other people, there's a good chance they're either currently or very soon will be interacting with others on the internet via their mobile devices.

If you strategically craft your offline advertising efforts to help drive offline viral word-of-mouth marketing (i.e., create ads that people talk about), you can become the topic of conversation for people who see your ad spots—that is, as long as it evokes a high-arousal emotion. (No, we're not talking about that kind of arousal. Get your mind out of the gutter.)

In a nutshell, the purpose of your offline ads is not just to acquire new leads; it's to curate your touch point with those leads. The endgame then becomes strategically encouraging those leads to expose your message to other potential leads.

I know what you're thinking: *Wow, Travis, offline advertising totally reminds me of dengue fever.*

No? Well, guess what? It's about to.

Learning from Dengue Fever

Since it first appeared back in the fifties, the dengue virus has primarily spread in tropical and subtropical regions. This might seem isolated, but about 40 percent of the world's population currently lives in areas where dengue is regularly found. Up to one hundred million people are infected with dengue every year, and if they have the strain that results in hemorrhagic fever, 20 percent of those infected people will die.

Dengue's unique aspect is that it spreads primarily through infected mosquitoes. Being somewhere that a dengue-carrying mosquito might be is all it takes for a person to be susceptible to the disease. That person doesn't even have to interact with a sick person (although this does spread dengue as well); he or she just has to be somewhere topical or subtropical.

So what can we learn from dengue?

1. First and most importantly, our offline marketing materials

will not be as effective if prospects have to go out of their way to be exposed to them. Remember, they have no intention of seeing your ads. You have to place your materials where prospects are already going to be—either in their line of sight or somewhere they can hear your message.

2. Next, keep in mind that without new "strains" (in our case, new messaging and media), prospects who are exposed to our offline marketing materials will soon develop "ad blindness," meaning they've seen our ads so often that the ads will blend into the environment for them. Keep refreshing the ads regularly.

3. Lastly, we should attempt to make the content of our offline ads so different or unique that prospects don't just *see* them; we want them to *talk* about the ads with others. We want them to ask others if they've seen our ads, what they think of them, and what their own opinions are. This expands the reach of each ad, reducing the cost per impression.

Expose Yourself (Sometimes Literally)

Consider American Apparel.

This company, which primarily just sells comfy yet blank apparel, is famous for effectively leveraging offline viral word of mouth (and sometimes online viral word of mouth) through its offline advertisements.

Here's one of them. See if you can come up with why it works:

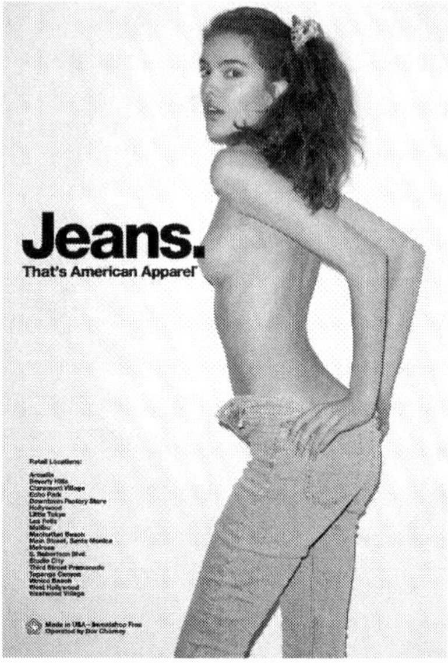

(Okay, so maybe we are talking about *that* kind of arousal.)

Not feeling it? Here's another example:

Spotting the trend? Wait, here's one more:

Threw a monkey wrench at you with that last one, didn't I? American Apparel's ads aren't only good-looking women in provocative attire (though most of them are). But regardless of who's flexing or cupping, there's no denying they are eye catching.

But *many* brands advertise using good-looking women (and men) in provocative poses. What makes American Apparel so special? Well, American Apparel just does it a bit differently.

> **You look at American Apparel's ads, and you think one (or all) of these things:**

- *Holy shit—I can almost see her nipple!*
- *She looks pretty young—is she over eighteen?*
- *Whoa, she's about to take off her pants!*

- *Is that girl going to fall over backward?*
- *I can almost see her boobs.*
- *What the hell is up with those random reindeer statues?*
- *That dude is buff as hell. I wonder if he's a bodybuilder?*
- *Is his shirt in Spanish? Is this an outsourced factory? No . . . it's in LA. Wait, what?*

These are questions I ask myself as I look at these. Similarly, each photo does something to the person viewing it. People love it, are entertained by it, are aroused by it, or absolutely hate it—all high-arousal emotions.

The point is, **almost *nobody* will look at these ads and feel nothing.**

You see these ads and talk to people about them. Your friends all have opinions about them. The internet loses its collective mind because of them. And American Apparel gets free press along with some pretty sweet online and offline word-of-mouth marketing. Which is what it was going for the whole time.

Get People Talking like American Apparel

American Apparel's products might not be newsworthy, but its branding decisions sure are. And don't think for a second that it's not all on purpose.

Even the above non-naked-woman ad accomplishes this goal. People who see it and are "in the know" will start to explain American Apparel's controversial ad choices to those around them who don't get it or have never seen one of American Apparel's more risqué ads. Those people will then start hitting up Google Images to see the ads for themselves (most likely right on the spot, since smartphones are awesome). American Apparel will then be the topic of conversation for the next fifteen minutes, and when that newly exposed person visits that same spot with another clueless friend, guess what happens?

Virality all the way.

Live Events: Your Opportunity to Flex Your Creative Viral Muscles

If offline advertising works well, what else can we do that's not exclusively online? Let's find out.

A few chapters back, we got a little more imaginative using content marketing. Now let's look at another great opportunity for all of us to flex our creative viral muscles, no matter what industry we're in.

This is a fun one.

Live Events: The Hidden Treasure for Creative Virality

The term *live events* encapsulates such a wide range of opportunities with which you can get creative there's no reason you *shouldn't* brainstorm some of them.

Here are some examples of live events:

- An **industry trade** show that you sponsor or where you set up a booth
- A **public-speaking gig** where you or one of your team members gives a talk
- An **athletic, musical, or community-related event** your company sponsors or publicly participates in
- A "**meetup**" you organize for users of your product in a specific area
- An **event or festival** that your company organizes
- A **free event** that you also stream as a webinar teaching prospects a valuable skill that also provides insight into why your product is valuable

As you can see, there are many possibilities—but not nearly as many as ideas of what you can *do* at these events. That's where you can really flex your creative muscles and try something unique, valuable, or interesting to evoke high-arousal emotions in others.

In addition, since you're able to interact with potential customers in a live environment, this marketing channel doubles as a method of incredibly powerful market research and product testing. Just make sure you have everyone who's in charge of designing your product at the event if possible. That way, these people will be able to ask customers questions directly and really see them interacting with the product in person.

Live Events and Virality

As we just discussed, one of the obvious benefits of live events is spreading the word about your product in an environment where you can directly interact with potential customers. But it's also a perfect place to inject some virality.

Here are a few creative ways of doing this:

- Set up a photo booth with funny props and your brand's step and repeat in the background. Grab prospects' emails and Twitter handles after their photos are taken so you can email those photos to each of them individually. That way, you can not only build your contact list but also tweet each photo out and tag the people in it (which is one of the best ways to generate retweets).

- Create some sort of funny theme for your speaking engagement, and come out in costume. Encourage attendees to take photos and live tweet them or post them on Facebook or Instagram. Just make sure they tag your brand on each. (Place a sign with your social media handles in the audience's view.)

- Create some sort of event experience that's collaborative or competitive in nature, and encourage those experiencing your event to bring friends to participate. Gather an email address from each person, and offer everyone some free swag to take photos and tag your brand. Who doesn't love free swag?

These are just a few ideas that come to mind, but the possibilities are endless.

Remember, **focus on offering value** to those experiencing your event. Show them a good time, go above and beyond to make them happy, and provide numerous opportunities and reminders to share their experiences with others (as long as these opportunities makes sense—i.e., don't make the most ridiculously amateur mistake possible by just randomly asking people to follow you on Twitter).

Community Creation: How It's Simultaneously Every Marketing Channel and None of Them

With live events, what are you creating for your brand or product (besides awareness)? That's right—a community of people who share at least one thing in common: interest in your brand or product. This is the essence of our next type of nonviral marketing.

Community creation is a unique marketing channel. Through one lens, it's not a marketing channel at all. Through another, it's several marketing channels at once. It can also be considered a combination of several forms of virality.

Sound confusing? Just wait—quite to the contrary, it's awesome.

Since this multiplicitous viral nonviral marketing channel is so difficult to define, we're going to give it its own category and name.

Community Creation: The Eclectic Hybrid of Marketing Channels

In a nutshell, community creation is exactly what it sounds like—the act of **creating an engaged community around a specific topic**. Ideally, this community will either directly or indirectly relate back to your product or service. The resulting promotion that occurs as that community grows is collectively what makes it its own channel.

Here are a few examples of how this can happen:

- You create a local community rallying users around a specific interest, such as a running club. You advertise this community, the membership base, and the benefits of joining at local gyms (this is offline advertising, which we'll discussed in a bit). Early users invite their friends to join the club as well (viral collaboration marketing).

- You create a user-generated-content site based around baking and dessert recipes. One recipe gets one hundred "upvotes" in the first two days, so you decide to place an ad promoting it on Facebook (social and display advertising). While readers are consuming the content, you encourage them to become contributors to promote their own recipes (open virality).

- You create an online forum to build a discussion around a specific topic—in this case, professional wrestling. You launch your forum through a featured piece in a professional wrestling magazine (press and PR). You then convince the number-one contender for the professional-wrestling world title to create an "ask me anything" (a.k.a. AMA) thread. This AMA gets a lot of traction on Twitter (online viral word of mouth) and gets promoted on a handful of professional wrestling blogs (unconventional PR).

And these are just a few examples that come to mind!

Community Creation and Virality

Since this specific marketing channel is so flexible and often acts as a hybrid of numerous nonviral *and* viral marketing channels, it deserves its own category. And since we've covered all those channels in previous chapters, I suspect the examples above already provide you with enough insight into how community creation can connect with virality—which is to say, quite a bit.

The thing to remember above all else here is that the value of a community comes from how well it **facilitates members interacting with other members.** The more frequently this happens and the more valuable those interaction are, the more value of an incentive community members will have to invite other community members.

Promotional Partnerships: Giving Complementary Brands a Financial Interest in Your Growth

There are plenty of nonviral marketing methods out there to fuel your viral engine, but a lot of them require you (and your company) to go it alone. This is usually how most people approach business ventures, especially in the highly competitive sandbox that is the internet. But don't make the mistake of discounting one of the juiciest marketing channels of all: teamwork.

Are you ready to do some back scratching?

Let's face it: cold calling and cold emailing is hard (not to mention often boring as heck). So as the saying goes, when the going gets tough, get someone else to do the work for you.

Not always, of course. That would be irresponsible and too enjoyable. But outsourcing the selling (or promoting) of your product can be very lucrative and another great way to boost virality, as long as you do it correctly.

Think that business development, joint ventures, and strategic partnerships are not marketing channels? Think again.

In the past I've discredited this channel a bit myself, not because I didn't think it could work but because I didn't realize just *how well* it could work.

I'll show you what I mean with an example.

A Partnership Use Case

Say you started a company that sells ski hats. Your company does not manufacture or sell *skis*. You just make the hats, and you're awesome at it. Your hats are the warmest hats on the planet. They're super soft and fit perfectly. What's more, both professionals and hipsters alike want them. In other words, you're the king of ski hats.

Well done.

But *wait*. You just realized that your product's audience is the same audience that Skis.com caters to. If you could only expose your product to Skis.com's audience, you'd likely significantly **increase your market exposure very quickly**. So you decide to try to partner with Skis.com in some way.

You head out from your ski-hat kingdom and attend a regional tradeshow. You visit the Skis.com booth and offer to take one of the execs out for a beer to chat. We're assuming the Skis.com executives love beer (who *doesn't* love free beer?), so they accept.

During that initial conversation, you realize that a company of this magnitude won't rush to promote a new brand out of the blue. They instead want to feature brands that their audience already knows and trusts because it increases their conversion rates. Recognizing that every company must operate first and foremost in its own best interests and the best interests of its investors, you realize you need to sweeten the pot.

So you **offer Skis.com equity**. It's not a significant piece, but it's something, and it's enough to ensure that Skis.com recognizes it would benefit substantially by promoting your brand. What's more, you become an affiliate for its skis and market those to the contact lists you acquire through other sources. This ensures Skis.com knows it's not just bleeding traffic to you. As you grow, you push even more value to Skis.com as well.

In short, Skis.com is taking a risk on you, so you make it worth the company's while by giving it **a vested interest in your success**. In return, Skis.com promotes your product on its homepage, to its list, on its social media channels, and through any other means by which it reaches its audience—all of whom are clearly die-hard skiers and love wearing awesome ski hats.

Promotional Partnerships: One of the Juiciest Channels Out There

Obviously the example above is fictitious, but it's a good one to illustrate just how powerful promotional partnerships can be as a marketing channel if you strike the right deals with the right partners.

And you don't always *need* to give up equity to make it happen.

Mint.com paid $500 to a dozen or so large and midsized financial-instruction blogs to help promote Mint's launch. As a free budgeting tool, Mint knew that these blogs catered to a large audience of the exact users it was trying to acquire.

As a result, Mint reached ten times its user-acquisition goals in year one.

Promotional Partnerships and Virality

If your partners have physical products, one of the best ways to work virality into your partnerships is to provide them with free stickers for your brand. Better yet, also throw in a small flyer with a promo code that they can slip into every order. This adds more value to their customers, as it's often a nice surprise bonus. It also adds value to you because those customers who have already demonstrated both ability and willingness to purchase complementary products are getting exposed to your brand.

What's more, if those customers stick your sticker somewhere that's even remotely visible, they'll indirectly expose your brand to their friends, who are often likely to also be your target audience.

This concept can be applied in emails as well—for example, offering a digital promo code for a product. However, it's unlikely you'll get the same offline visibility and exposure as you would with something like a sticker. It's also more appreciated—it's a small bonus gift, rather than just a section of an email that gets ignored.

Niche Marketing Channels: Why They're Powerful, and Why Only a Few Can Use Them

We've now covered sixteen other methods of nonviral marketing and learned how they can be merged with viral marketing to make overall growth more rapid. By carefully evaluating how you can use each to promote your product, you'll be in a very good position to win the user-acquisition game.

This includes crunching the following data:

- Cost attributed to using that method
- Estimated number of users you expect to reach with that method
- Likelihood that the channel in question actually works for you

However, the sixteen previous channels we covered are not the only forms of nonviral marketing out there. In fact, many of the channels we've covered didn't even exist just a few short years ago. So there will likely be new channels that exist five years from now that I can't even imagine at this moment.

What's more, there are some additional forms of nonviral marketing that are viable but only in a select few cases, based on your product or the dynamics of your organization. We call these **niche marketing channels**, and they're worth taking a glance at even if they probably won't be the best option for your company, at least not right away.

A Few Examples of Niche Marketing

Say you have a more technical product that's available online. **Open sourcing** part (or all) of your product can be a viable way to speed up the rate at which it spreads. Open sourcing is essentially providing your product, along with the creation method and any improvement of it, to the public. Open-source software is usually free to use. As such, developers all over the world can work on it simultaneously on a volunteer basis.

In a case such as this, it's important to have a business model that can withstand the lack of profit from your open-source product. For starters, you'll probably want a lower-than-average list of expenses. That way, you can make sure quality stays high while you tinker with a high-volume, lower-revenue model that's relatively common.

- WordPress was exclusively an open-source project early on. In fact, WordPress.org is still an open-source project today. Its sister site, WordPress.com, is no longer open source. Instead, it's a hosted solution serving as one of the sources of revenue for its parent company, Automattic.

- Wikipedia runs on an open-source platform constantly being approved by developers everywhere. Its content has also been open sourced and can be accessed and reused anywhere, by anyone (much to the glee of college students everywhere).

These are just two of the more popular forms of niche marketing. If you don't have an online technical product, they more than likely wouldn't be a viable marketing channel. And even then, it requires a special kind of business to keep them running.

How Facebook Used Niche Marketing to Turn Threats into Assets

Another form of niche marketing is to use acquisitions as a source of instantaneous growth. Not user acquisition—I mean your company purchasing another company that's either a competitor with many of the same users or a complementary service you can cross market to.

For example, in 2012, Facebook saw that it was quickly losing market share to Instagram, an up-and-coming photo-sharing application that doubled as its own social network. Instead of competing against Instagram head to head, Facebook bought Instagram for $1 billion. Overnight, Instagram's rapid growth became an asset to Facebook rather than a threat.

Facebook pulled a similar move in 2014 when it decided to invest more time and resources into its increasingly popular Facebook Messenger product. At that time, WhatsApp was the market leader in instant-messaging apps and owned a dominant share of the international market. So Facebook opted to purchase WhatsApp for $16 billion. Today, WhatsApp is still the dominant messaging platform with one billion users. However, Facebook Messenger now has nine hundred million users as well. As both are owned by Facebook, both are huge wins for the company.

You can see why Facebook's attempts to buy the entire world are a special case; while it's incredibly lucrative, the majority of companies aren't in a position to start acquiring other companies.

Niche Marketing Channels: Some You Can Use; Some You Can't

To assess what niche marketing channels you can use that others can't (if any), the first question you need to ask yourself is this:

- *Where do I really stand out?*

What is it about your product or company that's dynamically

different from 99 percent of other cases? Is it your technical prowess? Your access to capital? Your creativity? Something else?

Answering this question will reveal a lot about the future of your nonviral marketing and ultimately show where your brand can really shine.

Viral Fuel: A Quick and Dirty Cheat Sheet of Every Nonviral Marketing Channel

Congratulations! You've made it to the end of our section exploring all the different ways to feed your viral marketing campaigns with nonviral marketing tactics.

Nonviral marketing will inevitably become part of nearly every company's marketing strategy. Even if you have a solid viral loop, the fire you start with virality needs to be fed with fuel. Nonviral marketing is your gasoline.

Let's do a quick recap of these various "**viral feeding**" methods to wrap this section up.

Consider this your own personal clip show.

A Quick Recap of Nonviral Marketing Channels

- **Press and PR**: using niche and large-press outlets to get your product in front of a large audience by creating a story surrounding your product that will be interesting enough to readers of that publication to drive page views.

- **Publicity Stunts**: doing something noteworthy to spark high-arousal emotions in the members of the press, causing them all to want to write about you en masse.

- **Social Media Ads**: placing PPC display ads on social media feeds of prospective customers, leveraging the popularity and massive data-segmentation options social media sites offer.

- **Email Marketing**: acquiring a new list of prospective customers, or striking a deal to cross market your product to the list of another complementary product or service.

- **Content Marketing**: creating unique and valuable content meant to deliver value related to your product and industry that will attract and be shared by prospective customers.

- **Organic Search Optimization**: optimizing your product offering's website or product listing to be more easily and quickly found on search engines and highly searched platforms.

- **Search Engine Marketing (SEM)**: paying to appear at the top of organic-search listings for terms relevant to your product.

- **Engineering as Marketing**: building separate, free, smaller tools to help generate leads you can market your product to.

- **Direct Sales**: reaching out to and contacting prospective customers individually with email, through phone calls, or in person with the goal of having a conversation about your product.

- **Promotional Partnerships**: striking mutually beneficial deals with larger complementary brands, giving them a vested interest in promoting your brand to their prebuilt loyal audience.

- **Affiliate Marketing**: creating a small army of external commission-based sales reps that you give a healthy bounty for each sale or for recruiting other sales reps as affiliates.

- **Niche Search**: optimizing your product's listing for visibility on online marketplaces with the goal of capitalizing on those marketplaces' open viral marketing efforts.

- **Offline Advertising**: what many consider to be "old school" marketing channels, such as radio, TV, and print; these can be lucrative if you're certain of the market who will be seeing them, but they're very difficult to accurately track.

- **Live Events**: creating, sponsoring, or participating in live events such as trade shows, speaking engagements, networking events, or meetups with the goal of exposing new prospects to your product.

- **Community Creation**: a hybrid mishmash of a variety of viral and nonviral channels revolving around building and facilitating a community of people with a common interest in or related to your product.

- **Niche Marketing Channels**: additional marketing sources such as acquisitions and open sourcing that aren't appropriate for every company but are *very* appropriate for a select few.

In Conclusion

Now that you've learned how to build and optimize your viral marketing engine, you should strive to view every nonviral marketing channel through the lens of a viral growth engineer.

To help, ask yourself this: *In the context of my viral marketing engine that I've worked so hard to build, how can I now make it more obvious and valuable for the users I acquire through nonviral methods to bring others back to my site?*

Remember, the more effective your viral marketing engine is, the more of a "discount" you can get on the cost of your nonviral marketing (via your amplification factor). So answer wisely.

But I know you will, because you're basically a viral hero—almost.

What's Next?

You didn't think I was going to end there did you? That would be anticlimactic.

You've the learned the basics. You've created your viral engine. And now you've successfully fueled it. What's left? To take it out for a test drive, of course.

Learning how viral marketing works is one thing. Understanding how to best use nonviral marketing tactics is another. But predicting virality's impact is a whole different beast. That requires the powers of a true viral superhero.

So let's put on our training capes and take a glance into the future to see how viral marketing will help your business.

Every viral engine needs fuel, and the various marketing channels we just covered can be great sources of exactly that. Follow the process I outline in the *Viral Hero* Workbook (available free at viralhero.com/workbook) to discover how you can use them to grow faster.

Part 4: Projecting Your Viral Success

Chapter 13: Saturation and Viral Decay

The Math of Virality: A Basic Viral Growth Formula for Projections over Time

If you've reached this point, you're almost a viral hero already: you've learned what viral marketing is; you've established your own viral marketing engine for your site or app; and you've got it fueled and running with some excellent nonviral marketing techniques. But you didn't think it would be *that* easy, did you?

As a business, what's the main goal you're ultimately building toward—the goal viral marketing is going to help you achieve?

It's growth, isn't it?

In our next few chapters, we're going to work on updating the formulas we've already explored to allow you to make viral marketing projections that are as accurate as possible. But as I've hinted throughout our journey and as you're probably suspecting yourself, there are some other factors we haven't yet covered that can help or hinder your business's success.

We're going to learn about these factors next.

To start, we'll learn how saturation and decay will influence your company's viral growth. But before that, let's take a look at the viral growth projection formula we'll be using moving forward.

A Quick Review

Let's kick off our section on viral marketing projections with a review of our basic formula. As we've already seen, predicting the impact your viral campaigns can have over time can be challenging; but don't worry—I'll continue to break down the math into its simplest forms. By the end of this section, you'll hopefully have a solid understanding of how a peek into the future can help you drive the value of your business.

In previous chapters, I gave you the basic formula for calculating *K*, which is your most basic measure of potential viral magnitude. We learned how to use *K* to calculate your amplification factor and improve your branching factor, and we also discussed how building your product specifically for virality is the one true way to succeed.

We also talked about viral cycle time and how the amount of time necessary to complete your viral loop is the **single biggest factor** in determining your growth over time.

Now that we've gone through some of these more advanced fundamentals, let's explore a basic equation that will allow you to **project the impact of virality** over a fixed period of time as it pertains to your user base.

In other words, I'm about to give you a secret formula for looking into your viral future. But don't go running off to your local bookie quite yet. This won't be the full formula for calculating viral growth over time. **We're building toward that.** Stay with me, and we'll get there.

Our next few sections may seem complex, but if you take a few minutes to understand things step by step and drop the formula I'm about to give you into a spreadsheet, you'll make your life a heck of a lot easier as we move forward.

Are you ready?

Get your math pants on, boys and girls.

A Basic Projection Formula for Viral Growth over Time

Let's start by defining **a few variables**. Some you already know, and some we haven't yet used:

- The fixed period of time you're analyzing: *t*
- Your user growth over that fixed period of time: *u(t)*
- The users you start the process with, or the first users you seed into a new viral engine: *u(0)*
- The number of invites users send out over a fixed period: *i*
- The awareness-to-action conversion rate on the invites users send out: *conv%*
- Your viral factor, or the most basic measure of viral magnitude, calculated by multiplying *i* by *conv%*: *K*
- The amount of time that elapses from the moment a prospective user becomes aware of your product until the moment that user sends the first invite, measured in days as a decimal: *ct*

Here's the formula for projecting viral user growth over a fixed period of time:

$$u(t) = u(0)*(K^\wedge(t/ct + 1) - 1) / (K - 1)$$

This may appear a bit complex at first, but you don't need to commit this formula to memory. You only need to create this formula in a spreadsheet tool or write a function in a programming language so you can simply **drop in your variable values** as measured by your analytics tools. Then you're good to go.

Tap into Your Full Exponential Potential

We talked about this in a prior chapter, but it's important to remember and keep in mind:

- Since *K* is raised to the power of ***t/ct***, reducing *ct* has a *far* more profound effect on viral growth over time than increasing *K* will. In other words, when viral cycle time is shorter, **growth becomes more explosive**.

This is one of the many reasons that companies that pay very little attention to their viral loops find their growth trajectories held hostage by how much exposure they can **buy through nonviral marketing efforts**.

As we discussed, it's also why YouTube exploded at a faster rate than any other company ever before—by creating a service that allowed users to easily stream and share videos without the headache of downloading or sending files, YouTube built virality **deep into the bones of its product offering**; additionally, the cycle time for its product is a little over two minutes on average, which gives each user the mathematical capacity to complete **over 650 viral loops in a single day**. While this would never realistically happen for a single user, with each viral loop that does occur, more and more people are exposed to the product and **send invites of their own**.

I'll save you the obligatory "**focus on cycle time, then optimize *K***" soapbox speech for now. You've heard it before.

Besides, now that you've dropped the basic formula above into a spreadsheet to help you project your own viral growth over time (you *have* dropped this into a spreadsheet already, right?), I don't think you'll forget this advice anytime soon.

Of course, in this section, I only gave you the formula for *viral* growth. We haven't factored in nonviral marketing channels yet, so this still isn't a projection formula for *all* growth.

We'll get there. But first, let's cover saturation and decay and learn how these factors will have a significant impact on your viral growth.

Network Saturation, Viral Decay, and the Peaks and Valleys of Growth

It's probably safe to assume you understood all (or most) of the things we went over in our last section. Maybe you've even already tinkered with the basic formula on your calculator or in a spreadsheet to see the impact virality may have on your company over the course of time.

But as I said at the end of that section, the basic model I've given you so far **is nowhere near complete**. The truth is that it leaves out numerous practical items that will drastically influence user growth over time. Before moving forward, it's important we cover these as we continue building our model.

No Matter Who You Are, You're Going to Lose

The basic formula we've already talked about assumes all your customers will continue to send out invitations during each and every cycle **at the same rate.**

This is ridiculous. Most of the time, there will be **significant variation in virality** over time on a per-user basis. A lot of this has to do with a brand-new stage in the viral customer lifecycle that we're about to learn.

But to better explain what it is, let's first look at an example using an actual contagion.

(If you own a gas mask, this is probably a good time to put it on.)

A Day in the Life of Patient Zero

Let's say Patient Zero has an **incredibly contagious virus** (e.g., $K = 2.5$).

As Patient Zero travels around his normal daily environment, he'll have a high likelihood of infecting most of the people he comes into close contact with. Once he begins interacting with people, **Patient Zero's rate of infection will initially spike.** Nobody in his network has ever been exposed to this virus before, so everybody is susceptible.

However, after a few days, the rate at which Patient Zero infects new people with the virus **will drop dramatically.** Most people who have already interacted with Patient Zero have become infected, have developed some sort of immunity, or had immunity to begin with.

A random new person with a high probability of infection who hasn't yet been exposed might suddenly come into contact with

Patient Zero, but this tends to happen infrequently—that is, unless something out of the ordinary happens that forces Patient Zero to break his normal routine, or the people within his usual network break *their* normal routines.

In summary, once somebody becomes infected with a virus, that person's initial probability of infecting those around him or her spikes but then **quickly drops to a crawl** after most of his or her network has been exposed. Those who can become infected will be, and those who haven't become infected likely won't be.

This same phenomenon takes place in viral marketing (minus the potential for a horrifying and painful disease-ridden death). We call it **network saturation**.

Saturation: Good for the CDC, Bad for Business

Once a user is exposed to a product and sees both the core and viral value, that user's viral infection rate spikes. That person immediately thinks of the people he or she knows who will also see value and sends out invites in quick succession.

However, just like a person with a virus, a user's infection rate is typically limited to **the size of his or her network**. As soon as this network has been fully exposed and has had the opportunity to be infected once or twice, the **infection window** ends. As a result, virality for that infected user drops to a crawl.

This is network saturation in action.

However, note that just because network saturation is beginning to occur doesn't mean viral growth stops. Each newly infected user who is exposed to the product during the original user's infection window typically has at least *some* new people in his or her network to expose to your product.

In addition, as new people enter the original user's network, they too are likely to be exposed. You can also begin changing your viral loop in various ways to act as a sort of "mutation" to your virus (but more on that later).

Also, if you get really lucky (or are very strategic) and you're able to **infect a celebrity**, virality can spike massively. Not only will your product be exposed to a far larger network than average, but the social proof that results from what's basically a product endorsement will send the conversion rate on those invites through the roof.

In other words, **it will become "cool" to be infected**.

So if you and Robert Downey Jr. don't yet follow each other on Twitter, now's the time to somehow make that happen.

Immunity and Decay

Even if you somehow manage to make your product's viral infection become "cool," network saturation will still occur. (No amount of Robert Downey Jr. can stop the laws of viral nature.)

Eventually users *will* expose everyone they have the ability to touch. As such, those new people will either have already been infected or will be temporarily or permanently immune to infection.

This **immunity** can happen for a variety of reasons:

- Maybe some people in the network aren't close enough to the original user to trust that person.

- Maybe they didn't understand the value of the product from the invite.

- Maybe they understand the value but feel it's too complicated or labor intensive for them to really gain that value as quickly as they want it.

- Maybe they heard about a bad experience with the product.

- Maybe they have some sort of negative view of the product or the people who use it.

- Maybe they simply don't want or need what the original user is sharing at all.

Regardless of the reason, those immune to your viral effects won't help you much in further spreading your product.

Factoring In Viral Decay

So based on things like network saturation and immunity, how can we factor in the overall **decay of virality** per user over time?

It's essentially impossible to accurately factor viral decay into a projection equation, but **you can estimate it**—assuming you've managed to establish a solid data collection, calculation, and interpretation strategy, which we'll talk about later.

However, until we're able to realistically build that, let's continue pressing forward. We'll build our formulas by assuming our infected users are simply running out of other people to invite due to all the normal network-saturation factors we've already discussed. Given that assumption, let's use **a simple geometric viral-decay rate**.

We'll say the per-user viral factor is reduced by exactly **50 percent** each month. This means that after a user's viral factor spikes, it will quickly drop by half every month thereafter. While it will never completely stop as long as this person is still a user, it will quickly drop to a very slow crawl.

Our Original Basic Formula Gets an Upgrade

So how does all this apply to our original formula?

If we sum up all these monthly per-user viral factors over time, **we get the lifetime viral factor**, which we will name *K'* (yes, that's *K* with an apostrophe).

As long as we make sure *i* and *conv*% are lifetime factors as well, **our viral equations still apply in the same way**, but we can now sub *K* out for *K'* to get lifetime statistics. Thus, here's our updated formula:

u(t) = u(0)(K'^(t/ct + 1) - 1)/(K' - 1)*

What Can We Do about Immunity and Decay?

Immunity and decay don't have to be the end of the road—at least, not immediately.

We can successfully decrease immunity and prolong virality by changing a user's network to increase susceptibility. How? By mutating the infection (i.e., your awesome product).

Grab your ooze canisters. We're about to transform into the Teenage Mutant Viral Heroes.

Viral Mutation: Implementing Changes to Stave Off Network Saturation

In the last chapter, we started discussing viral decay. To recap, this means that the *K* factor per user will typically spike after the initial viral value is realized and then fall quickly and continue to decline at a slow crawl for the life of each user. We also learned that one of the main reasons for this viral decay is **network saturation**.

In this chapter, I'll give you **a simple mathematical model** for network saturation and a few strategies you can enact to avoid it.

Saturation Revisited

We just learned that just as each person who catches a virus has a network of people he or she typically interacts with every day, each person who begins using a product has a similar network of people he or she could potentially spread that product to.

After the initial exposure occurs, the first wave of "infected" people are no longer candidates for future infection and therefore **cannot be infected again**. If that original user then exposes his or her network to your product again, a few others who didn't become infected the first time may become infected this time, but after a few exposures, most people in a network who are susceptible become infected, and those who don't have likely become **immune**.

As we discussed in our last section, with a real virus, immunity is a friend to all, but when we're talking about spreading your product, **immunity caps your growth**. At that point, the network is considered saturated.

As a network becomes saturated, the infection rate (or *conv%*) decreases **until something changes**. But what needs to change for that original user to infect more people?

Building Mutations to Decrease Immunity

If the original user chooses to continue to expose his or her network to the infection (e.g., your product), one of the following two things must occur:

- The original user **adds new people** to his or her network who have not yet been exposed.
- The "virus" (or product invite messaging) **mutates in your favor** (more specifically, the virus changes into a new form that makes the original user's existing network susceptible to infection through a different way).

This **viral mutation** may be a positive change like a UI or UX revamp, new copywriting or graphics, additional functionality, better incentives, or any number of improvements.

However, **a viral mutation is not always positive**.

For example, if a far superior competitor enters the market and begins activating a viral loop that's more infectious than yours, it's likely that your potential network will become more and more immune to your own viral infection. You may even experience **churn** (which we'll discuss and factor into our model later).

A Simple Model for Network Saturation

To understand the dynamics of immunity through network saturation, let's cover a few stages of exposure for a product with **an initial *conv%* of 10 percent**:

- If you infect **0 percent** of an overall network, then your natural *conv%* remains **10 percent.**

- If you infect **50 percent** of that same network, then your *conv%* decreases by 50 percent to **5 percent.**

- If you infect **99 percent** of the same network, then your *conv%* decreases by 99 percent to **0.1 percent.**

One thing to note is that the decaying percentages in the bullets above don't factor in the percentage of users who are immune to infection, meaning they've been invited before but haven't become users. For example, if somebody hates your product and doesn't want to use it, that person is about as likely to become newly infected as somebody who has already been infected before (i.e., not likely at all).

This model also doesn't factor in how these numbers change when you introduce a viral mutation, thereby reducing the immunity of some of those uninfected users.

So how does **a viral mutation alter our formula**?

Updating the Equation

While *conv%* as we know it so far is a static measurement, this is not totally realistic, because it doesn't factor in the saturation of a network or of the market as a whole (i.e., immunity). Therefore, we're going to need an **adjusted conversion rate**, or *Aconv%*.

$$Aconv\% = conv\% * (1 - saturation\%)$$

(*Note:* conv% *and* saturation% *should be in decimal form.*)

Now all we must do is substitute *Aconv%* for *conv%* in each equation we've been working with so far, and we'll have a more accurate measure of the current state of virality for your product.

The Harsh Reality of Saturation

As simple as this sounds in theory, it's all just another animal to implement. After all, how can you *truly* measure *saturation%*? To my knowledge, it can't accurately be done.

However, *saturation%* is a bit more measurable during nonviral marketing efforts. (For example, by understanding audience size and impression data for various modes of PPC marketing, you can estimate foot traffic per day past an offline ad.) Given this, depending on your product, you *may* be able to loosely estimate network size and *saturation%* for your viral campaigns using similar strategies, such as quantifying network or market sizes using third-party tools and comparing those numbers to exposure estimates.

This might sound tricky, but the important thing to keep in mind is that most viral marketing campaigns—even the ones driving insanely viral products—are only truly viral for a short time. The subsequent **plateau and inevitable decline** they reach is often the result of network saturation.

Over time, users can get less viral for various reasons. Your job is to prevent this from happening as long as you can. The process I outline in the Viral Hero Workbook (available free at viralhero.com/workbook) can help you identify how to do that in your business.

Chapter 14: Factoring In Churn

Churn: The Savior of Humanity and the Silent Killer of Viral Growth

Now that we've formed a strong foundation for understanding viral growth projections over time, let's find out if there's anything we can do to speed up the process. (Hint: there is.)

It's one thing to be able to look into the future; it's something entirely different to be able to shape it.

What Happens When a Virus Spreads?

In the world of virology, mass infection is one of the most terrifying possibilities. Men and women at the CDC and various disease-control-and-prevention organizations around the world make it their top priority to keep outbreaks from occurring. If and when one does, they shift their top priority to controlling the outbreak to ensure it doesn't become an epidemic.

However, outbreaks and epidemics and zombie apocalypses will sometimes happen. As such, people will get infected by viruses. Depending on the virus, **four things will normally happen**:

- Some people who are exposed will get infected and will **remain** infected.

- Some people who are exposed will not get infected because they're **immune**.

- Some people who are exposed and get infected **will then churn** and become uninfected.

- Everyone else simply won't be exposed at all.

(*The man, the myth, the legend, and the doctor who cured polio—Dr. Jonas Salk.*)

With a disease, the more often churn occurs—that is, people get better and no longer exhibit symptoms or risk infecting others—the better off the entire population is. This usually happens because of modern medicine working with the natural power of the human immune system.

Churn: Good for Health, Bad for Business

When a product spreads virally, **the same four things will occur**:

- Some people who are exposed to your product will become users and will **remain** users.
- Some people who are exposed will *not* become users because they don't need your product or don't see enough **value** in it.
- Some people who are exposed will become users, **then churn** and become uninfected.
- Everyone else simply won't be exposed to your product at all.

Unlike when a disease spreads, when we're talking about growing your business, number three is, as the kids say, bad news bears.

The Inevitability of Churn

No matter how incredibly fantastically awesome you make your product, every month a certain percentage of your users will **churn**—meaning they'll transition from user to nonuser. This will even happen for users who were previously exhibiting viral tendencies and could be called "infected."

Churn may happen for a variety of reasons, such as the following:

- The user's ongoing experience of the product didn't live up to his or her expectations.
- A competitor with a superior product or price entered the market.
- The user simply lost the need to use the product.
- The user received the value he or she desired from the product and no longer has use for it.
- The user thought he or she understood the product but didn't and decided not to learn.
- The user lost the ability to use the product.

In other words, you can decrease churn to a degree, but many factors will be outside of your control (i.e., a user dying, which we'll discuss in the next chapter), so **churn will *always* exist**.

The Impact Churn Has on Virality

Since you'll often lose converted customers at different intervals and because those churned users previously contributed to your viral growth, this loss will have a varying impact on your ***i* value** and, by association, your ***K* factor**.

Churn is typically measured as an average percentage, and that percentage represents the fixed probability of losing a user in each defined time period.

Here are two examples of fixed time periods:

- **Month-one churn** is the percentage of users who stop using your product within the first month.

- **Day-one churn** is the percentage of users who stop using your product within the first day.

Here's an example of a monthly cohort analysis on churn rate:

	Months after starting use						
Cohort	1	2	3	4	5	6	7
Jan	85%	75%	65%	62%	69%	58%	55%
Feb	87%	78%	70%	67%	63%	59%	
Mar	88%	84%	79%	75%	71%		
Apr	92%	89%	86%	82%			
May	93%	89%	85%				
Jun	94%	90%					
Jul	96%						

Churn will affect your viral growth even more dramatically if most of your users churn before the point at which your remaining users are the most viral. Therefore, your goal should be to identify **the point of maximum virality** on average and focus all your churn-reduction efforts on the periods of time both **before** and **during** that viral window.

For most products, most of the churn will occur over the first few days or weeks and will inevitably level out. Your job is to craft the process by which users gain **repeated value** from your product so that it's as easy and intuitive as possible, while also taking users' hands and **teaching** them how that process works.

As a side note, know what has a really low churn rate? Herpes.

Learning from Herpes

We don't exactly know when herpes first appeared, but there are written accounts of herpes spreading as early as the time of ancient Greece. It's still common today, and it's estimated that one out of every six people age fourteen to forty-nine in the United States alone has a form of herpes.

Herpes spreads through contact, usually with saliva or other bodily fluids from an infected area (more often than not, this involves sexual contact of some type), and it can be passed on even if the infected person isn't experiencing an outbreak. However, the most relevant aspect of the herpes virus to our purposes is that there is currently no cure. Once you have herpes, you have it forever.

There are several other viruses with no known cure, but the important part here is that herpes is not fatal—which means infected people have a longer-lasting window during which to infect others (meaning their *i* value is likely much higher).

So what can we learn from herpes?

1. First and foremost, before we really try to crank up our growth efforts, we should strive to reduce churn as much as possible. We can do this by increasing the value we offer users, growing their awareness of how frequently they're getting value, and creating the perception that by leaving our product, they'd be leaving behind serious value as well.

2. Then, we should ensure the infection window is not limited to the beginning of a user's time with our product. If users

continue to have both reasons and opportunities to expose our product to others, this will have an impact on our continued viral growth.

3. Lastly, and possibly most interestingly, we should examine how pleasurable it is for existing users to expose new users to our product. For example, in contrast to how many viruses spread (being around sick people, getting bitten by an animal or mosquito, etc.), a unique aspect of herpes is that it's most often spread during sexual contact, which can be . . . well . . . fun (in most cases anyway). So how can we make the act of being exposed to our product a more fun and enjoyable experience, rather than a dry, academic sales pitch?

Carrying Capacity: Understanding Where User Growth Goes to Die

It's important to note that churn isn't the only thing that will affect viral growth. If your user growth stays static, your product will eventually hit a growth threshold called your **carrying capacity**. At this point, all growth stops completely *unless* either churn decreases or acquisition velocity increases.

Carrying capacity is basically a growth engineer's worst nightmare. So let's figure out how to avoid it at all costs.

Carrying Capacity: A Growth Engineer's Worst Enemy

Most people assume that the clear path to getting more users starts and ends with getting more and more people to sign up and become users. After all, it seems completely logical to assume that if you could just get more people to *become* users, the more users you'll *have*, right?

Not necessarily.

Let's say your nonviral user-acquisition efforts (e.g., through PPC) bring you **four hundred new visitors** per day. Out of those four hundred visitors, you convert **fifty** into users.

This is a **12.5 percent** conversion rate, which is pretty strong in most cases.

Along with this conversion rate, let's assume you have a **1 percent daily churn** rate, which means each day you'll lose 1 percent of your total user base. Users may leave, they may cancel, their payment information may stop working, they may never update, they may discover a superior competitor, they may die—the list goes on. There are any number of reasons a user may churn.

Regardless, if this data holds true, when you reach **five thousand total users**, your growth will level off. You simply won't be able to acquire any more users, as you'll be churning exactly as many as you're acquiring on average.

This is your **carrying capacity**.

Uh oh . . . we're going to need a bigger bowl.

You're Not Locked into Zero Growth Forever

Carrying capacity is the point at which **your average daily number of acquired users equals your average daily number of churned users.**

To put it simply, **carrying capacity is the point at which growth stops.**

Don't panic. When you reach your carrying capacity, you just need to make a change.

Let's say you increase your ad spend by 50 percent and attract **six hundred** new visitors each day as a result. If you maintain your existing conversion rate, you'll be converting **seventy-five** of those visitors into users. With your same 1 percent daily churn rate, your growth will level off again at **7,500** users.

You may be seeing a trend here. Your carrying capacity is dictated largely by the total number of users you already have, the new users you're acquiring on top of those users, and your churn rate.

Let's label our carrying capacity variable ***CC***.

CC = avg. daily users acquired / avg. daily churn rate

So when we plug in our numbers, here's what it looks like:

CC = 75 / .01

CC = 7,500

Carrying capacity becomes a much harder nut to crack without viral growth. With zero viral growth, your only options to increase growth are your traditional **fixed** nonviral acquisition channels. Couple that with the fact that you have a fixed average churn rate, and your user growth will predictably stop (and sometimes even **decline**) until something changes.

The Key to Reducing Churn and Overcoming Carrying Capacity
At the end of the day, **success always starts and ends with the perceived value you provide**.

> How do you **reduce churn**? Try doing some of these suggestions:

- Listen to your users and make the improvements they suggest.
- Fix critical bugs that ruin key parts of your experience.
- Create reactivation flows to bring users back when they're at risk of churning.
- Provide stellar onboarding documentation to get users to the moment of value faster.
- Add more value to your product, content, or service.

- Focus marketing on more well-targeted users who need your product more.
- Offer incredible customer support to help users through issues.
- Engineer your product to encourage habitual use.

The list goes on.

To sum things up, if your churn sucks, you can't grow—no matter how awesome your viral and nonviral acquisition channels are.

Address the **quality of your product** and the methods by which you're delivering **clear and obvious value**. Successfully do that, and all this time and effort you're putting into learning how to grow virally will pay off in spades.

When A Meets G: Where Viral Marketing, Carrying Capacity, and Advertising Collide

Let's keep this road show churning, shall we? (See what I did there?)

Since most marketers out there probably never consider carrying capacity, consider yourself ahead of the game. But knowing and doing are two entirely different things.

So while I just indicated how you could strategize to overcome carrying capacity, that was only a teaser. Now, let's find out how you can stave off stagnation by injecting your business with a welcome dose of virality.

As we just learned, **if you're only using nonviral channels, you have two choices if you want to continue growing**:

- Increase your marketing spend or improve conversions to acquire more users.

- Decrease churn to keep more users.

However, engineering a few viral loops will not only provide a **dynamically different source of traffic** but will also most likely **decrease churn**. This is because users acquired through viral means have been shown to stick around longer than users acquired through ads or nonviral channels. My theory for this is that the social proof of being invited by somebody we know and trust *and* the knowledge that those we know are also using the product cause us to feel more pressure to continue using a product longer than we otherwise would.

How Carrying Capacity Changes with Virality

As you've probably guessed, injecting virality into a boring, normal marketing machine really throws a monkey wrench in the dollars-in, dollars-out math most marketers are used to. And while most marketers have no clue what carrying capacity is to begin with, the few who do likely haven't factored the effect of viral marketing into the traditional carrying-capacity equation.

> Remember, the traditional carrying-capacity equation is this:
>
> $$CC = g / c$$
>
> I'll break this down for you a bit further:

- *CC* signifies *carrying capacity.*
- *g* is your average daily nonviral customer-acquisition rate.
- *c* is your average daily churn rate.

This is a static measurement using nonviral acquisition channels only. Let's now kick it up a notch by factoring virality into the equation, which is quantified most easily using our viral amplification factor.

Amplification factor is represented by the variable *A*. Do you remember the formula for how it's calculated? If not, **here it is again**:

$$A = 1/(1 - K)$$

And remember, ***K* is your viral factor.** (*If you forgot the formula for finding* K, *revisit our section on how to calculate your viral factor.*)

We apply *A* directly to our nonviral customer-acquisition rate (*g*) to discover how our growth rate changes when virality is factored in. This is most helpful for the 99.99 percent of companies that will never achieve $K > 1.0$.

Thankfully, we're using many of the same variables in our various formulas. So rather than creating a totally new equation, we can just multiply *A* right into our carrying-capacity equation:

$$CC = ((1 / (1 - K)) * g) / c$$

$$CC = g / (c * (1 - K))$$

$$CC = g / (c - cK)$$

Remember, churn (*c*) cannot equal zero in this equation (though I can't think of an example of when it ever would in practice). Also, since we're using *A*, your *K* **factor must be less than one.**

Putting Our Equation to the Test

Here's a quick **example with real numbers:**

- Let's assume your product is growing by two thousand new users per day through nonviral channels, so g **= 2,000.**

- Let's also assume you lose an average of 15 percent of your total users each day, so c **= 15%.**

Given these assumptions, **what's our carrying capacity *without* virality factored in?**

$$CC = g / c = 2{,}000 / 0.15 = \mathbf{13{,}333}$$

Okay, so with only nonviral channels, this means that at just over thirteen thousand users, our growth levels off. And it will stay that way until something changes with either our acquisition rate or our churn rate.

Now let's add some virality.

- Let's say that for every five users we recruit through nonviral means, one of them will recruit a friend, meaning we have a

$K = 0.2.$

So what's our carrying capacity **with virality factored in**?

First, let's find *A*:

$$A = 1/(1-0.2) = 1/(0.8) = 1.25$$

Next, let's add *A* into our carrying-capacity equation:

$$CC = (A^*g) / c = (1.25^*2,000) / (0.15) = \mathbf{16,667}$$

With these numbers, as soon as we hit a total user count of 16,667 users, our growth will level off until something changes.

How are you doing so far? Keeping up?

We're not done yet. Are you ready for the best part?

Virality to the Rescue

Did you check the percent increase in viral carrying capacity versus nonviral carrying capacity?

If you didn't, our viral carrying capacity of 16,667 is right around 1.25 times our nonviral carrying capacity of 13,333. And oddly enough, **our *A* was 1.25**.

Some of you math wizards out there probably already figured this out by glancing at the equation, but for everyone else, this hopefully makes things click just a bit more.

So why was this the case?

Remember how I said that your carrying capacity would stay the same unless something changed? **Something did**—your customer-acquisition rate is now 1.25 times higher thanks to your viral loop, so your carrying capacity rose by the same amount.

In hindsight, not too difficult after all, right?

Churn Rate: How a Leaky Bucket Can Sabotage Your Customer-Acquisition Efforts

Unfortunately, no matter how hard we try, we'll never be able to completely stop the leaking bucket that is churn rate. That's just a cold hard fact all growth engineers must accept.

However, there is good news. By knowing this, we can better predict it. And by predicting it, we can better prepare for it.

See where I'm heading? Not yet? Just stick with me.

As we've learned, churn is another word for user loss, and your **churn rate** is the average number of users you can expect to lose during a predefined time period.

The inverse of churn is called retention, which is the percentage of users you can expect will stick around during the same predefined time period.

Just as churn is your bitter enemy, **retention is the foundation of all growth**.

Think of your growth as a bucket of water. You're currently working very hard to fill it up (with user acquisition). But then you notice there's a hole in your bucket that's leaking water (i.e., your churn rate). You try to plug it completely, but no matter what you do, **this hole will always be there.**

Churn Rate: A Slowly Leaking Bucket

As your bucket of water leaks, **three scenarios may happen**:

1. If your bucket's hole leaks water faster than you can fill the bucket, you'll quickly have an empty bucket—which means you're screwed.

2. If your bucket's hole leaks water as quickly as you fill the bucket, your bucket will hold water, but it won't fill up any higher.

3. If you work hard and learn everything there is to know about your users and your product, you can reduce the size of that hole so that it leaks more slowly. Then you can add water to the bucket until it's full.

Okay, I'm obviously working toward the third scenario. But at this point, you're probably asking yourself one question: *What does my churn rate have to do with virality?*

Well, let me tell you.

Churn Rate and Virality

First and foremost, we want virality because we want growth. Growth only happens when **two things take place**:

- You acquire new users.
- Those users stick around and remain users.

As you saw in the section about carrying capacity, without a solid retention rate, **all growth will stop**. It doesn't matter how crafty or creative you are with your acquisition efforts or how revolutionary you believe your product is, growth is a very simple if/then statement: *if* your acquisition rate is greater than your churn rate, *then* growth occurs.

Based on this, **virality and churn are related in a few ways**:

- Decreasing churn improves virality, as users stick around longer to send more invites.
- Virally acquired users churn less frequently because of factors like higher social proof and social pressure.
- Building a viral engine increases your acquisition rate without increasing your marketing spend (aside from the cost of any viral incentives).

Churn: The Silent Killer of Growth

In previous chapters, we learned how viral cycle time is the most important viral KPI and saw how much of an impact cycle time can have on your growth. We then discussed how impactful knowing your viral factor (K) can be once you've optimized *ct*.

While these are all strong examples of viral KPIs, they rely on **the king of *all* growth KPIs**, which is your **churn rate**.

A stellar cycle time and K factor may result in incredible growth for a while, but very quickly it'll level off. So to give yourself the best chance of continuing to grow over a longer period of time, you should focus your energy on decreasing your churn rate (remember my suggestions for how to do this in an earlier section?).

Predict Churn to Prevent Churn

Churn is typically measured using cohort analysis to showcase the number of users who have churned **over set time intervals** relative to the time they were acquired.

For example, say your churn rate over a set period of time is 50 percent. If you start with three thousand users, when that predefined period is over, you will be left with fifteen hundred users.

	Months after starting use						
Cohort	1	2	3	4	5	6	7
Jan	85%	75%	65%	62%	69%	58%	55%
Feb	87%	78%	70%	67%	63%	59%	
Mar	88%	84%	79%	75%	71%		
Apr	92%	89%	86%	82%			
May	93%	89%	85%				
Jun	94%	90%					
Jul	96%						

If you're not nearing saturation and you haven't yet approached your carrying capacity, many of these lost users will be replenished with new traffic and new users. But when you *do* hit saturation and carrying capacity, adding users at the same rate will no longer help plug the leaking bucket.

On the other hand, if your churn rate is very low, you *will* still see a user-base decline when you hit saturation. It just won't be nearly as pronounced, and because of this, you should have time to scramble and compensate to continue to grow.

The takeaway is that if you get up to speed with your carrying capacity as frequently as possible, you shouldn't have to scramble, as you'll know *exactly* when to increase acquisition velocity.

Reverse Growth: How Badly Can Churn Rate Harm Your Growth?

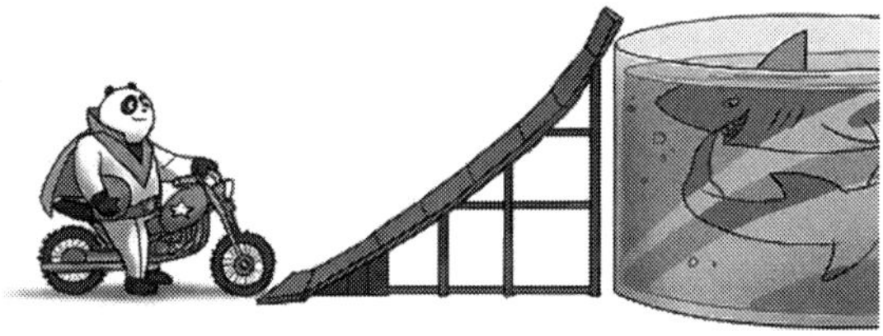

What happens when all the water leaks out of your bucket? Take it from me—it's not good.

However, knowing what the worst-case scenario looks like is often the best way to avoid it. So let's take a look at the perfect storm of awfulness known as **reverse growth**.

Happy Days?

Back in the midseventies, *Happy Days* was the coolest show on television. Every week, viewers tuned in to watch Richie Cunningham (played by Ron Howard) and his rough-around-the-edges leather-jacketed friend Fonzie (played by Henry Winkler) get into trouble and then somehow find their way out of it by the end of the episode.

However, after four seasons, the writers were running out of ideas, **and the viewers knew it**. The show's viewership started to level off, and in an act of desperation, the writers decided to get "creative."

Your Happy Days Are Over, Fonzie

In the season five premiere, the writers decided to create an incredibly odd situation that ended with Fonzie on water skis jumping over shark-infested waters.

While the scene did briefly capture the attention of viewers, it was clearly a one-off gimmick that was a far cry from what the show had been known for—and a blatant last-ditch effort to maintain the popularity the show had enjoyed in years prior.

Although *Happy Days* continued to air for a few more seasons, fans noted that after the moment Fonzie "jumped the shark," the show declined in quality and was never the same again.

To sum up, the idiom "jump the shark" refers to **the turning point** at which a once-popular and high-quality TV show **starts to decline** and never returns to its former glory.

(*Note: It has come to my attention that there are, as ridiculous as it may sound, arguments on whether the "jump the shark" moment was the true moment when* Happy Days *began its decline. However, this book is not about debating the viewership stats of seventies TV shows. It's about viral marketing. So let's all agree to say this is the origin of the idiom, shall we?*)

Okay, so what's the million-dollar question now?

How the Hell Does This Relate to Viral Marketing?
Ayyyy, I'm glad you asked.

We're going to borrow the "jump the shark" idiom to describe our turning point at which user growth begins to decline.

In growth engineering, "jumping the shark" refers to **the perfect storm of awfulness** that occurs when a company

- has a high churn rate,
- hits its carrying capacity, and
- reaches network saturation

all at the same time.

If any of these were to happen by themselves, it would suck and also take time and effort to overcome. If two happen at once, you better have an incredible team ready to solve a big problem. **But if all three happen at once, you're sunk.**

Why does this happen? Let's take a closer look.

How to Jump the Shark of Virality

Let's say you have **five thousand** users, and your churn rate is **10 percent** per week. This means each week, **five hundred** users become nonusers.

We'll also say you're adding **five hundred** users per week. Once you reach **five thousand** users, you've got a customer-acquisition rate that equals your churn rate—meaning you've hit your carrying capacity—and all growth stops until something changes (i.e., acquisition rate increases or churn rate decreases).

Network saturation then smacks you in the face. You've overexposed your marketing channel to your product, and fewer and fewer people are buying. Because suddenly your ability to acquire users is decreasing more every day, **you now *lose* users faster than you can acquire them.**

In other words, you've achieved **reverse growth.** You are now officially shrinking.

What's Next?

The more you can educate yourself on the mathematics of growth and virality, the more carefully you can plan, and the more advanced warning you'll have to stave off the negative factors we covered above—including reverse growth.

To give you a push in the right direction, in the next chapter I'll share a useful equation to prevent your company from pulling a Fonzie and embarrassingly "jumping the shark."

As much as you might hate to admit it, you're going to lose users. If you're only losing a few, a great viral loop can skyrocket your success. If you're losing a lot, a great viral loop can kill your chances of success. With great power comes great responsibility, as they say. The *Viral Hero* Workbook (available free at viralhero.com/workbook) can help ensure you can reduce churn, and grow faster.

Chapter 15: Users

Growth Projections: Using Simple Math to Prevent Your Company from Tanking

In the last few chapters, we analyzed all the horrible things that can happen to your growth over time. From experiencing churn to hitting your carrying capacity, things can get ugly fast if you aren't prepared. But the point is not to scare you into giving up viral marketing altogether; it's to give you the lay of the land so you can better navigate it.

In this chapter, we'll explore one of the most essential factors that will affect your company's success—user acquisition. But first, a word of caution.

Most startups these days use some form of analytics. They install a little tracking snippet on each page of their site or app, they add in various events, and they start to get visualizations of what's happening as it's happening. They then (mistakenly) assume that these analytics can serve as growth projections.

Event-based analytics are **historic**. They tell you what has *already* happened. This is pretty cool, but companies don't succeed because they can tell others what happened in the past. They succeed because they plan effectively with the future in mind and then expertly adapt to ensure nothing holds back their growth.

The Past Is the Past

Leading indicators are metrics for events that have happened. They act as predictors of **lagging indicators** (other metrics that are difficult to predict otherwise). By using a leading indicator like customer complaints, a good data-driven business can infer what its customer churn rate will be in the near future. If complaints are up, churn rate soon will be as well. If they're down, a churn-rate improvement is likely in store.

However, even if a company uses leading indicators, **most growth projections are just wishful thinking in disguise**. They're often used to hype up new employees, investors, or partners but have no basis in reality.

Even when done with sound data science, predictive analytics aren't 100 percent accurate; however, they *can* be incredibly helpful nonetheless.

Modeling User Acquisition over Time

Now that we've learned a bit about viral marketing, growth, churn, and carrying capacity, the logical next step is to tie them all together to help you derive some business value from your knowledge.

The goal here isn't to teach you how to make predictions with 100 percent accuracy (which isn't possible); it's to give you a useful tool that may help you avoid the disaster of hitting your carrying capacity.

To get started, **let's set up a scenario**:

- $i = 4$
- $conv\% = 10\%$
- Given these two, $K = 0.4$
- $ct = 1.0$
- $t = 20.0$
- $u(0) = 10{,}000$

Next, now that we've been discussing it in so much detail for so long, let's finally introduce a new variable into the mix: **nonviral marketing**. We'll name our new variable ***nm*** and use ***nm(t)*** to signify the number of users our nonviral marketing efforts will yield within a specified number of days.

Let's say our nonviral marketing efforts yield **two hundred users per day** for our new app. Since our t value is already set as 20.0, we'll use that here:

$$nm(20) = 200*20 = 4{,}000$$

Now let's try to **predict growth over time** using the following equation:

$$u(t) = \{u(0)*[K\hat{}(t/ct + 1) - 1] / (K - 1)\} + nm(t)$$

This essentially adds the number of nonviral users acquired into our basic equation for projecting viral growth over time that we covered back in chapter 14.

$$u(t) = \{10{,}000*[0.4\hat{}(20/1.0 + 1) - 1] / (0.4 - 1)\} + 4{,}000$$

$$u(t) = \{10{,}000*[0.4\hat{}(21) - 1] / (0.4 - 1)\} + 4{,}000$$

Okay, so using the above variables, after twenty days, we should have right around 20,667 users. Given that we gained approximately 4,000 users from our nonviral marketing efforts, this means we acquired 6,667 users from our viral loops.

Not bad, right?

Well, it wouldn't be bad at all *if* **the projection equation were correct**.

Can you spot the issue?

$$u(t) = 20{,}667$$

Fine Tuning Our Equation

With most viral engines, whenever nonviral users are acquired, those new users seed your viral loops similarly to the way users who joined via a virally acquired user would. Right now, **our equation simply bolts them onto the end**. But in fact, all of these users will result in individual virality themselves.

To correctly account for this, your equation will change in two ways:

- You can *only* run this equation when $t = ct$.

- At the end of each predefined *ct* interval, you'll need to rerun the equation again while **updating your *u(0)* value to your previous *u(t)* value.**

So let's try this again. For simplicity's sake, let's keep *ct* at 1.0. And remember, *nm(1)* = 200.

$$u(t) = \{10{,}000*[0.4\verb|^|(1.0/1.0 + 1) - 1] / (0.4 - 1)\} + 200$$

$$\mathbf{u(t) = 14{,}200}$$

After a single day, we've grown from 10,000 users to 14,200 users. *Wow! That's incredible!*

But don't go throwing a viral party quite yet, because this technically isn't growth. **It's user acquisition.**

The Difference between Growth and User Acquisition

Let me clarify something most amateurs masquerading as experts and thought leaders don't tell you. **Growth does *not* equal user acquisition.** User acquisition is only a piece of the overall pie chart of growth.

Once we acquire users, we still need to keep them. If we don't keep more than we lose, **we won't grow.**

Of course, we know all too well by now that you *will* lose a percentage of the users you've acquired every single day. This is your **churn rate.** If you're not carefully tracking your churn rate in comparison to your growth rate, you'll risk hitting your carrying capacity, or the point at which your growth rate equals your churn rate.

As we've learned, **your carrying capacity is the mathematical moment at which your growth plateaus.**

In Summary

Most novice (and even many seasoned) founders and growth engineers assume that they can always find a way to acquire more users faster to stave off their carrying capacity. As such, they choose to believe that their carrying capacity is unlimited given enough money and resources.

This couldn't be farther from the truth.

In fact, we just talked about the creeping surprise of network saturation, new competition, and the various other factors that may affect your ability to acquire new users in your existing channels at the rate you're used to.

The most prudent thing to do is place your best people and your most powerful resources on the issue of continually **retaining users** and **reducing churn**. Then and only then is continued growth more of a sure thing.

User Experience versus Viral Marketing—Why They Should Never Compete

We've established mathematically that one of the most important things you can do for your company is reduce your users' churn rate—in other words, make them want to remain users—but what are some ways you can actually do that?

Let's first look at how your product's user experience can affect your product's viral success.

As I've begun to write and speak more about viral growth mechanics, I've often heard one surprisingly common question, even from seasoned, successful entrepreneurs: "How much should I be willing to compromise my user experience in favor of viral marketing?" Most of these people have come across sites in the past that they **believe have a high viral factor**. To the layman, this may simply be a site with a ton of sharing buttons.

Don't judge a book by its cover. Sites like these have compromised user experience for what they're hoping will result in a bit of a viral boost. (Hint: it doesn't.) In the minds of these sites' developers, if they shove enough sharing buttons down a users' throats, users will share.

This brings us to the first of two myths about virality versus user experience.

Myth 1: Great User Experience Must Be Visually Appealing

Sites like Reddit and Amazon offer user experiences that are historically the absolute farthest from aesthetically pleasing. In reality, a great user experience is built with behavioral analytics, qualitative feedback, and ample testing rather than artistic design.

Sites like Reddit and Craigslist have fairly antivisual design, but they still provide a good experience for users. This disproves the thesis that great UX must be visually appealing.

Myth 2: Focusing on Virality Makes for Worse UX

Bolting on low-value sharing buttons, poorly crafted referral programs, weak viral calls to action, and more black- and gray-hat viral "hacks" definitely compromises a user's experience—which, as you probably guessed, will probably increase your users' churn rate. However, it doesn't have to be this way.

If you asked me, I would reiterate what we've been talking about since page 1 and tell you to shrug off your preconceived notions of what viral marketing is. Great viral marketing does *not* happen *despite* your user experience; it *adds* to it.

Remember these simple rules:

- Visitors become users because they want the value you're offering.
- Great viral marketing is driven by the **inherent desire** of your user to unlock *more* of that value in exchange for sharing or inviting others.

In other words, they're not doing you a favor. They actually *want* to share or invite others because of the value unlocked by doing so.

As we've learned, for a viral engine to become successful, the following things need to be absurdly obvious:

- **Core value** the user gets from using your product
- **Additional value** the user gets from exposing your product to others
- The process of **understanding *and* acting on** both forms of value

The point is, viral marketing doesn't work if it's obligatory or if it doesn't make total sense. If people don't *want* to spread your product, shoving it down their throats is a terrible idea and will most likely result in a higher churn rate.

Again, it's not about you; it's about your users.

Habit Creation: How Getting Users Hooked Results in More Viral Growth

As we continue to cover some of the methods you can use to side-step falling into stagnation or, worse, reverse growth, we can head in a more positive direction. A really, really positive direction.

As you know by now, the goal of any good growth engineer is to hook users. How do we do that? By getting them addicted to your product, of course.

We've talked about viral hook point in the past, but now we're going to focus on it to engineer that sweet spot at which user action meets user desire, to the benefit of your viral engine.

We've created a pretty awesome model to project viral growth over time so far. We've factored in things like viral magnitude, cycle time, churn, and network saturation. Pretty slick, right? But while we've talked about how virality can decay over time due to things like network saturation, we haven't yet touched on how some of our other KPIs may change over time. For example, our churn equation is relatively static, which isn't the way churn is measured.

As we discussed in a prior chapter, churn is typically measured using **cohort analysis**. This is essentially a visualization of the percentage of users who churn throughout intervals of time relative to their first exposures to the product. Thus far, our model hasn't factored this in yet because we haven't yet covered things like **habit creation**.

How Long Does It Take to Create a New Habit?

Typically, as time passes, users will be less likely to churn.

As you dig into your analytics, your churn cohort analysis visualization will show that just as a user's ***i* value** changes over time, that same user's likelihood of churning will also change. Usually you'll then be able to pinpoint an **exact moment** in the user journey **where all churn stops.**

Nine times out of ten, users will exhibit a retention curve in a descending hyperbolic fashion—meaning, the curve will start with a sharp down slope and then quickly level off. How dramatic that downslope is, when it happens, and when it levels off depends on three key factors:

- The type and quality of the product
- The value in contrast to the price
- How well you target your marketing channels to attract users

In addition, the retention curve also depends on how effectively you create a "**habit path.**"

Factoring Habits into the Retention Curve

In his book *Hooked* (which I love), author Nir Eyal describes a data-driven framework you can work through to identify the exact moment users adopt the use of your product as a new habit, thereby **bringing churn to a complete halt.**

While you won't be able to get every user to this point, it's critical to know exactly where it's located. In other words, you need to determine what needs to happen over the course of your user journey for a user to get hooked on your product, and precisely at what moment this occurs.

- If your product is a game, maybe this moment occurs once

a user opens the app four times, casts twenty-two spells, and gets to level three.

- If it's a fitness app, maybe this moment occurs once a user completes twelve workouts, posts two photos, and logs a 2.24 percent reduction in body-fat percentage.

- If it's a social network, maybe this moment occurs once a user follows ten other users and uploads a profile photo.

The last example above actually comes from Twitter. You may notice now that when creating a new Twitter account, users are essentially forced (or at least very strongly encouraged) to follow a specific number of users before their accounts are fully set up. This is because **Twitter identified its habit path** and built it into its new-user-onboarding process.

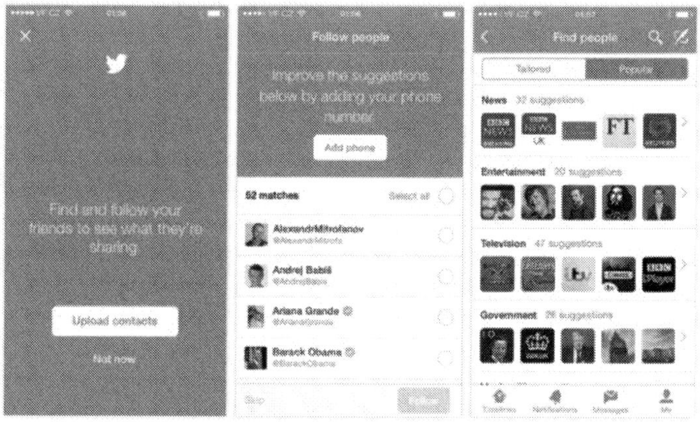

To sum things up, your retention curve is important because, so far, we've assumed users will only invite others in the first month. However, as retention improves, you should see an overall increase in viral growth, since your product will more frequently be on users' minds and they'll have more time to send invites and will simply be more satisfied overall.

In short, **as retention improves, so does *K'* (i.e., your lifetime viral factor).**

Your New-User Funnel: Where Your Finish Line Should Be

Last section, we discussed the "how" of viral addiction, specifically *how* users form habits when using your product. Now that that's settled, I'd like to talk about *where* those habits form.

It's a mythical place where magical, wondrous things happen for your viral growth. And it's found somewhere in your **new-user funnel**—you just have to know where to look.

The New-User Funnel: The Map to the Holy Grail

Before you get too excited about your new-user funnel, let's pump the brakes and get one thing straight: **you're (probably) *not* Indiana Jones.** Also, I'm not going tell you where a mythological artifact that will grant you everlasting life is. Sorry to burst your bubble; there are just some things I need to keep to myself.

However, I do want to talk about the next-best thing: creating **the roadmap to user immortality**!

[*Cue thunderclap from above.*]

Fedora hats and overdramatizations aside, an incredibly common mistake I see in growth and optimization occurs during the pretty basic step of mapping out your new-user funnel. This funnel can seem like your best friend, but if you set it up wrong or use it incorrectly, it can just as easily be your worst enemy.

Making Enemies out of Your User Funnel

Here are a few (possibly surprising) ways your funnel could become **your worst enemy**:

- If you didn't run the proper QA on your analytics and you're experiencing a reporting error, you're likely making decisions based on bad data. This results in bad decisions.

- If you set up your new-user-funnel analytics correctly but never actually use them to run or prioritize experiments, you've now got "vanity analytics" (i.e., analytics with the sole purpose of saying you have analytics to all your friends).

  But arguably the **sneakiest mistake of them all** is this:

- Ending your new-user funnel at a user signup or a sale

But wait! Isn't our user funnel supposed to be a signup funnel or a sales funnel? *Shouldn't* it end at the signup or the sale?

Yes, this is exactly what it should do . . . ***if*** **you want to** ***fail*** **or perpetually be mediocre.**

Not All Users Are Created Equal

Maybe I'm being a little harsh. I don't want to entirely discount the pros of a signup (or sales) user funnel. These funnels do tell you two very important things—namely, how many unique signups or sales you have.

However, long-term repeat users and customers are the heart of your business's success. So to judge them solely on when they first became users or made purchases ignores all the great stuff they might continue to do afterward. We've talked time and again about the fact that **retention is the foundation of all growth**, so this shouldn't be a surprise.

The critical question most people get wrong is **where the new-user funnel should end**. They simply assume it's when somebody becomes a user. However, people who poke their heads in and leave are relatively worthless; those who instead decide to stick around are valuable. So your funnel should end at the typical point in the journey at which users hit the **"Aha!" moment** and then never leave.

To decipher this (which is likely one of the biggest puzzles you'll face as a growth engineer), you'll need to collect enough data to answer two key questions:

- What, on average, does a user have to do, or not do, to get "hooked" on your product?
- What, on average, does a user have to do, or not do, to "die" (i.e., churn without the possibility of reactivation)?

Sound confusing? **Let's simplify a bit.**

Where Your Funnel *Should* End

Let's say a user starts using your product and takes his or her **first** action. What happens next?

A large percentage of users will take this action, and then a large chunk of those users will "die" at some point afterward, many without ever taking a **second** action.

Now let's say a different user takes his or her **100th** action. Nearly all such users are almost 100 percent certain to take the **101st** action afterward.

This is because, over time, these users have **created a habit** of using your product. We in the growth biz like to call this "product addiction." Once this product addiction is identified, our goal is to work backward to identify the exact moment this addiction happened for all users on average, which we call the hook point.

That hook-point moment is where your user funnel should end.

The entire purpose of your activation experience is to bring as many users as possible to that exact moment.

This, my friend, is your **finish line**.

(*Note: A shortcut to pinpointing the exact moment of addiction is to look for the moment where the "drop-off point" is 5 percent. In other words, find the moment where 95 percent of people who get there* will *return.*)

The AARRR Model versus Your Viral Loop

In the famous "pirate metrics" acronym (of which I'm not the biggest fan, but we'll use it here for simplicity), here's what the letters

AARRR stand for:

- Acquisition
- Activation
- Retention
- Referral
- Revenue

Notice the placement of the words. Each is a phase of your user journey that ends at the **exact moment that the next phase begins.** For example, consider the second and third words—*activation* and *retention*; this means that activation ends as soon as retention begins.

This fixed order is actually why I'm not the biggest fan of the AARRR concept, and it's all because of the second *R* (referral).

In a user's journey toward virality, the phases of a viral loop are a bit different. We've seen them before, but let's sum them up again:

1. **Prospect** (*nonvirally acquired*) or **Friend** (*virally acquired*): people exposed to your product.
2. **Lead:** prospects or friends checking out and learning more about your product and therefore entering your activation process.
3. **User:** leads who have decided to use your product by taking the early steps in your activation process.

4. **Acolyte**: users who have completed your activation process, have reached an "Aha!" moment, and now love your product.

5. **Advocate**: acolytes who have reached a second "Aha!" moment and now see the value of exposing friends to your product.

Your activation experience should **begin** when prospects and friends turn into leads and **end** as soon as users turn into acolytes.

Now let's zoom out.

How Activation Efficiency Fuels Virality

You might have noticed that the activation process above is only comprised of three of the five steps in your viral loop. What about the other two? Shouldn't these steps be added to the activation funnel as well?

I know what you're thinking: *Travis, shouldn't it be our job to get all prospects and friends to become leads, all leads to become users, all users to become acolytes, and all acolytes to become advocates?*

My answer to that is no.

The reason is because of the fluidity of the last phase in the loop: the advocate phase.

- The jump from a user to an acolyte (i.e., a retained user) is a very specific "Aha!" moment. It cannot be reached unless somebody goes through **the prior three steps first**. These must happen in order, or retention will not be achieved.

- In contrast, the jump to becoming an advocate (i.e., a viral user) is a totally different "Aha!" moment at which users become aware of your product's viral value. In many cases, people do *not* have to hit the prior four steps in order; they can enter the advocate phase at any point after the second step.

For example, a product like Skype requires the advocate phase to occur as the third step in the process, right after a prospect or friend becomes a lead. Because Skype uses inherent virality, a user can't become an acolyte without first becoming an advocate. For Skype, retention could *never* occur without virality happening first because the advocate phase is **a requirement for addiction**. Inviting friends is built right into its activation funnel.

This won't apply to most products.

By now, it shouldn't surprise you that the addiction process is different for every single product, and without good data science and analysis, you won't know where your advocate phase should happen for your product.

Connecting the Viral Loop and the Retention Funnel

Since we've established that our viral loop and our retention funnel are not the same thing and must be measured separately in most cases, we need a way to connect the two in order to derive maximum business value from both.

To do this, we need to boil down our activation process (i.e., the process of getting users to hit the moment of addiction) and turn it into one metric that we can weigh against all the other viral data we've learned up to this point.

So let's set three variables:

- **Total Activated Users (*Au*)**, which we'll set as 1,000;
- **Total Prospects and Friends Acquired (*Nu*)**, which we'll set as 1,500;
- **Addiction Factor (*Af*)**, which is what we'll solve for.

This is our equation:

$$Af = Au / Nu$$

$$Af = 1000 / 1500$$

$$Af = .67$$

This example equation is somewhat ridiculous because **an *Af* of 67 percent is insane**. But having this data point makes it much easier to create visualizations around virality and retention for your specific product and in turn understand what both mean for your business.

For example, if your product is a B2B SaaS company that requires users to become acolytes before they can become advocates, knowing that you have to **optimize *Af* to elevate *K* and *ct*** is helpful.

If you're instead like Skype and you want leads to become advocates before they can become users, let alone acolytes, you'll then know that **you need to do the opposite** and optimize *K* and *ct* first.

User Death: How to Know When Users Are Beyond Saving

You now have a step-by-step process of all the actions users must take to go from awareness to addiction. But sadly, there's a far more somber event that mirrors this journey. That's right—we're talking about "user death."

As hard as it might be to believe, some users just won't take the awesome path you've laid out for them and get hooked on your amazing product. Some of these users you may be able to resuscitate; others will be beyond saving.

To be able to predict when the latter might occur—and hopefully prevent it from happening—we must learn "the Formula for Death."

User Death: Ashes to Ashes

Just like your hook point, there's a series of actions users either do or do not take that create a path that, if followed, basically guarantees they leave and never come back. At some point along this journey, there's an exact moment at which users transition from being able to be reactivated (i.e., sick but not dead) to beyond saving (i.e., dead).

This is **the moment of "user death."**

Identifying this moment, just like with your hook point, is a critical task.

The Path to User Death

Knowing what drives user death in your user funnel ensures you can do everything in your power to keep your users alive and on the path to the advocate phase. These retention efforts can include anything from strategically crafting your required onboarding process to implementing messaging and outreach campaigns or simply saying, "Pretty please don't leave."

Here's an **example of a pathway to user death**:

- User experiences a bug.
- User submits a support ticket.
- Ticket is not marked as "resolved" within twenty-four hours.
- User does not open the app for seven days.
- User unsubscribes from your email list.

This is an oversimplified example, but you can likely see why this user should be considered "dead" and not just dormant. After having a bad experience that doesn't get resolved, this user takes an action that likely means he or she has deleted your app and unsubscribes from your mailing list. Not only does this person dislike his or her experience with you, but you now have no way of communicating with him or her. This user is dead and buried. There's nothing you can do except **move on and do better next time**.

The Formula for Death

MUAHAHAHAHAHA!

Thanks to the last section, we already know that our viral loop and our retention funnel need to be measured separately. We also know that we must boil activation down into one core number that we can weigh against our viral data.

So we need to do **the same thing for user death.** Here are our variables:

- **Total Dead Users (*Du*)**, which we'll set as 300;
- **Total Prospects and Friends Acquired (*Nu*)**, which we'll set as 1,500;
- **Death Factor (*Df*)**, which is what we'll solve for.

And here's our equation:

$$Df = Du / Nu$$

$$Df = 300 / 1500$$

$$Df = .2$$

(*Note: This example is crazy high and not indicative of the actual death factor you should see in your business.*)

Thanks to our formula, we've figured out that the death factor is 0.2 (20 percent). Now I bet you're wondering what we do with this piece of morbid information.

This **death factor metric** allows you to do the following:

- Identify where your business's death factor is today;
- Visualize improvement over time as you make the required changes to prevent death from happening;
- Compare your changes in death factor with your changes in virality over time.

What's Next?
Well done, sir or madam—you're nearly at the end of our journey.

We've come a long way through navigating all the ups and downs of virality. We laughed, we cried, we did some math, we watched some users die, we snagged a lot more new users, we saw YouTube punch a competitor in the face, and we watched a bunch of rabbits reproduce. Good times.

You're now ready to be caped an official **viral hero**.

But first, there's just one teensy-weensy little thing left to do: ***show you the money!***

I love a good zombie movie as much as the next guy, but bringing people back from the dead isn't the topic of this book. However - bringing your users back from the dead…or at least reactivating them after they've churned, can work wonders for your company's growth. Explore how you can do this in the *Viral Hero* Workbook - available free at viralhero.com/workbook.

Chapter 16: Growth

Revenue Growth: Building a Bridge between Virality and Profits

Remember when we learned that user acquisition isn't technically growth? That's still true at this point in our journey—having more users isn't going to financially help your business unless you can transform your user growth into revenue. Now that we've spent all this time learning about viral marketing and building a thriving viral marketing engine for your product, it's time to learn how virality relates to business success.

Being Viral Doesn't Always Lead to Revenue Growth

Every time the "next big thing" app appears and takes the internet by storm, our first assumption is usually that the app's creators are now phenomenally wealthy. After all, millions of people are using their app, so obviously a good chunk of them are buying too, right?

Wrong.

More often than not, the new apps that take off like rocket ships actually do pretty poorly from a monetary perspective. At least for a little while.

While they may have nailed their viral loops early on, most product creators have a *lot* to learn about these details:

- Who their customers are
- How these customers interact with the product
- What keeps them around
- What makes them buy, buy more, and buy more often

The list goes on.

The important thing to remember here is that most financially successful companies are *not* viral at all. On the flipside, many absurdly viral products are *not* financially successful. **One doesn't equal the other.**

However, if you take the smart path and inject great optimization processes into your product to help you to become a thriving business, you can make these factors **feed each other**.

Viral Loops Are Good for One Thing and One Thing Only

And that's bringing in traffic.

Once you've got traffic, here's what you need to do:

- Convert the traffic into users, acolytes, and finally, advocates.
- Monetize all of these roles by transforming them into customers.
- Transform customers into repeat customers.
- Proactively maintain the relationship with your long-term repeat customers.

In other words, your traffic is worthless unless you can **build a bridge between growth and revenue.**

We've already talked about the key transition from activation to retention. Similarly, there's another key transition from retention to monetization. And like its predecessor, it's important that this transition be mapped in detail and optimized diligently.

How Virality Can Hurt Your Bottom Line

If you're not careful, you can optimize your product for virality without building business value and monetization into your strategy. Why might this happen? Because truly great viral loops often give advocates a sense of completion after finishing the loop, and as a result, many of these users will then leave immediately—which means you've missed out on an opportunity to monetize loyal users.

Many absurdly viral products that sweep the internet like wildfire are just plain old viral loops. They contain no retention or monetization strategies. This is the growth engineer's version of the "if you build it, they will come" mentality—**which kills most products.**

Real viral marketing "nirvana" occurs when you successfully blend your viral loop with your retention funnel and monetization funnel.

Achieving Viral Marketing Bliss

So how can you obtain **viral marketing nirvana**?

Here are two success examples we've already discussed:

The best retention and monetization methods for your product may not be obvious, but put your thinking cap on, and you'll get there. And remember that you're engineering a viral product in order to create a self-driving growth engine for your business—emphasis on "for your **business.**"

- Hotmail (now part of Outlook.com) leveraged viral communication marketing to continually fuel viral growth through the day-to-day use of its product. As users communicated with others who were using other email services, Hotmail exposed more and more people to its brand-new free web-based email application.

- PayPal leveraged viral incentive marketing to drive monetization. The primary use of its product involved PayPal taking small fees from transactions digitally sent and received online. Early on, PayPal offered a "bounty" of twenty dollars per referral when friends signed up. This then led to those friends sending and receiving money from others, which further led to more transactions, more fees incurred, more referrals, and so on.

The best retention and monetization methods for your product may not be obvious, but put your thinking cap on, and you'll get there. And remember that you're engineering a viral product in order to create a self-driving growth engine for your business—emphasis on "for your business."

So the (hopefully obvious) question you need to ask yourself is, in year one, which of the following would you rather have?

- Ten million signups that result in ten thousand retained users after thirty days (1 percent retention)

- One hundred thousand signups that result in five thousand retained users after thirty days (5 percent retention)

If you answered something like "ten million signups because I'd have more overall retained users after thirty days," then you should probably rethink your priorities.

The *correct* answer is the second choice, for the following reasons:

- Your five-times-*higher* thirty-day retention rate means more users stick around, which means you're creating more value for the customers who sign up.

- Your one-hundred-times-*lower* signup total means you haven't already saturated the market with a product you clearly haven't optimized for value or retention.

- Since you haven't totally saturated your market, you'll have far higher growth potential going into year two.

- Your issue now is simply **finding traffic**. Of all the problems to solve, this is by far the easiest.

So while it's true that the more efficiently you can bridge the gap of growth and virality using retention and monetization, the more successful your business will be, it's important to not confuse growing fast with growing successfully. To emphasize this fact, let's look at a real-world example of a company that made this mistake.

The Hot or Not Viral Sensation: How Accidental Virality Is More Common than You Think

In 2000, James Hong and Jim Young befriended one another while studying electrical engineering at UC Berkeley. Like many red-blooded male college students, they'd often pause their conversations to ogle at passing coeds. On one such occasion, they found themselves in a ridiculous disagreement about the "hotness" of a woman on a scale of one to ten.

Hong and Young knew that others had similar arguments all the time. So they decided to settle the subjective "physical-appearance rating" argument once and for all.

Thus **Hot or Not was born.**

The two students set up a website where people could submit photographs of people so others could then take polls to rate those people's physical appearances on a scale of one to ten. The cumulative average of the rankings would then categorize those people as "hot" or "not."

Within a week of launching, the site had reached almost two million page views per day. However, here's where we can learn a valuable lesson from Hot or Not's viral explosion.

Virality can often make and then very quickly break an entire company.

Here's how this happened to Hot or Not.

The Story of the Hot or Not Viral Sensation

It was stupidly simple. With one click, you rated the person in the photo.

Hot or Not became a viral sensation virtually overnight.

While there were no invite mechanics to speak of early on, the controversial nature of the site (fueled by curiosity, vanity, and the competitive nature of its users) created the perfect emotional cocktail to drive ample online and offline word of mouth.

Almost immediately after the site launched, users began uploading their photos to see how they ranked. If they found they ranked well, they bragged about it to friends. If they ranked poorly, they often uploaded different photos in attempts to rank higher and potentially salvage their self-esteem, asking their friends to vote to drive up their average rankings.

A high rating was a badge of honor. A low rating often made people hate the site. Both cases got people talking about Hot or Not, which was a win for the company any way you look at it.

But it wasn't all good times. Hot or Not made one fatal error in its rise to the top.

The Slow Death of Hot or Not

To clarify, Hot or Not never faded into oblivion. However, for a site that was one of the top five most trafficked sites within a few weeks of launch, its slow fade into mediocrity was predictable.

Why? Was it because Hong and Young mismanaged? Did they run out of money? Did a superior competitor immediately enter the market and take over?

Nope—it's because **Hot or Not grew too fast.**

Despite Hot or Not's viral beastliness, Hong and Young were unable to implement a successful revenue model for quite some time. They tried monetizing by tacking ads onto the site, but it was only marginally successful and ruined the clean user experience.

It wasn't until Hot or Not morphed into a dating experience that they started to actually add value. This helped because that value was tailored to work with the site's viral engine—the ratings game. It was an obvious bridge. When one person gives another person a good rating, it stands to reason that that person might want to send a message as well.

However, by the time Hong and Young discovered this, Hot or Not had already saturated most of its market with the old experience. Former Hot or Not users—millions and millions of people—only remembered the old ratings experience they'd been exposed to and didn't know that the product had since become a dating site. As such, they had no reason to return to the site—especially since no retention strategies had been established early on, which was when most of the traffic had originally funneled through the site.

That said, the world was watching. As I mentioned several chapters back, YouTube initially began as a video version of Hot or Not before it realized that the video upload, embed, search, and view process on its own was far more valuable. Tons of other dating sites have since gone viral using some of the same early mechanics as Hot or Not. Tinder is the perfect example. It's basically a Hot or Not clone for mobile. But Tinder had a chance to inject retention and monetization into the app prior to release, which helped spur its continued popularity increase and longevity.

In the pantheons of viral history, Hot or Not was a raging fire for a moment back in the early 2000s. As quickly as that flame rose, however, it just as quickly began to die. This led to an exit of $20 million a few short years later. While this is no small chunk of change, that payout was nowhere near the nine figures the company should have gotten. The owners would likely have earned much more if they'd either opted to sell at the height of the site's popularity or quickly injected retention tools into the site and reengaged users that they could have later better monetized.

Critical Mass: Why You're Using This Term Wrong, and How to Use It Correctly

So what's the takeaway from Hot or Not's rise and subsequent fall?

In the survival of your company, virality and good business practice are not mutually exclusive. If you want to make money and prolong your product's upward viral trajectory, you need to implement sound business models around retention and monetization to work alongside your viral marketing efforts, and you need to do this early on.

This is why knowing your "critical mass" can come in handy, so let's cover that next.

"We'll Worry about That Once We Hit Critical Mass"

This is an asinine thing to say when making a decision connected to your product. It's vague, and nobody really knows when it's been officially reached.

So what is critical mass?

This is the official definition: *the smallest mass of a fissionable material that will sustain a nuclear chain reaction at a constant level.* However, most people use this term to mean, "Later on . . . when we get bigger." This is incredibly ambiguous and just a smarter-sounding way of procrastinating.

So if you're using this term because your goal is to do as little as possible while giving the impression you're doing as much as possible, kudos! You're on the right track. But for everyone else who's trying to successfully bridge the gap between viral marketing and business right from the start, there's a far better use for this term.

When Critical Mass Makes Sense

In some cases, there actually is some validity to the use of the term *critical mass*—namely, when it refers to a situation in which the dynamics or issues facing a new product **will change after a certain base number of users is reached**.

For example, if you're a user-generated-content site with no users, you'll therefore have no content. If you're an online forum with no users, you'll have no activity or forum topics with discussion. If you're a closed-system communication tool (like the telephone) and you have no other users using that system, your tool has no value.

Imagine you're the only person in the world with a telephone. What a sad thought, right? Not to mention that phone is completely useless.

This example describes a phenomenon called **Metcalfe's law**. I briefly mentioned Metcalfe's law way back in chapter 2, but we'll cover it a bit more thoroughly now, because understanding this concept can really help you understand your business strategy.

Metcalfe's Law Explained

Metcalfe's law states that the value of a telecom network is proportional to the square of the number of the connected users of the system. It applies to telephones, the internet, and everything in between. For our viral purposes, we'll concentrate on how it works for users in an online network.

In short, for closed-system networks where value is driven by user interactions with each other, **the system with few users is worthless.** Here's why:

- It's worthless in terms of **the monetary value of the owners.**
- It's worthless for any new users to begin using it, as they won't be connected to many others and therefore **won't be able to derive any core value from the product.**

In these situations, critical mass can be a helpful indicator of the moment at which the core value for new users is **high enough** to transform the main problem of "why would a new user join?" into "where can we find new users who haven't already begun using the product?"

But how will you know when critical mass happens? And when it happens for one user in one place, will it automatically happen for everyone everywhere?

Probably not, and this is an important realization to make.

Overcoming Too Few Users

For products that are subject to Metcalfe's law, the hardest days will be the early days. This is when you'll need to brute force your way through some tough times by **doing things that don't scale.**

Here are some examples from existing companies:

- **Reddit** initially created hundreds of fake user accounts and conversations to make the site appear more active (and therefore more valuable) than it actually was.

- **Skype** spent considerable time and resources making the product and the new-user-invite process stupid simple. They eventually got creative by targeting their marketing efforts for Skype's free worldwide VOIP service to countries that were subjected by monopolistic long-distance telecom carriers that charged crazy-high rates. This led to a significant increase in virality in those regions.

- **WhatsApp** took a similar approach to Skype but focused on using the internet to mirror SMS and MMS messaging without the fees carriers used to get away with charging—all by simply replicating the routine experience of text messaging, adding in better features (like video messaging and group texting), and rapidly offering service to virtually every cell carrier. Because of the company's dramatically lower cost and zero-ad approach, international and third-world traction became key drivers.

In the cases above, critical mass is reached **when more than 75 percent of users** in a market have enough friends already using the product that they don't need to invite others to derive ongoing core value. This is the point at which these three sites will have to change something in order to keep growing.

Identifying a Key Moment

Let's see if you can identify a critical-mass moment in a few examples.

As we've learned, a critical-mass moment for a product will typically occur when that product reaches the minimum required size for the site or application to work and be valuable without a user first having to recruit others to use the product.

For example, **which of the following products would you say has reached a moment of critical mass**?

Scenario 1:

- An online forum acquires five hundred users in Des Moines, Iowa, who actively engage with each other on a regular basis about disc golf. This discussion includes where they plan to play that week, what techniques are superior, and what outings and events are upcoming for forum members.

Scenario 2:

- An online forum with space to discuss fifty different topics acquires five hundred thousand users evenly distributed across one hundred countries. The average user is interested in one or two topics of the fifty.

So which forum has obtained critical mass? If you said the latter, you're sadly mistaken. Don't let big numbers fool you.

In the first scenario, the disc-golf forum is driving specific value for a specific audience. It's doing its job, and users are sticking around. In all likelihood, there aren't many additional hardcore disc golfers in Des Moines who'd be so interested in the sport that they'd socialize around it online; thus, this forum has **reached critical mass.**

Because of this, the people running that forum will need to change their growth strategy. They'll either need to expand the forum topics to one or more related topics to acquire a broader audience in Des Moines, or they'll need to expand their focus to other geographic locations.

In the second scenario, the forum will contain an average of five hundred users per country. Of those five hundred users, only about fifteen will be interested in the same topic. So the value users gain from interacting with so few people in this forum is dwarfed by the value users gain in scenario 1. But since there are likely still many other people in each country who are not in the forum but would be interested in those topics, this forum's growth strategy won't need to change to reach them.

Granted, the second scenario isn't a completely realistic example, since it's next to impossible that user distribution would be even roughly equal across each country. However, we can still see why the product in the second scenario is likely to fail, specifically because of **the ultrafragmentation of the audience and the value they desire**. This forum's strategy spreads the focus of the team running it so thin that no audience will receive much catered attention.

The takeaway is to not get ahead of yourself and act bigger than you are before you can get there.

For example, take Facebook. It might now seem like a brand whose product caters to virtually everyone, but don't forget that it started out targeting a specific audience in a single location: college students at Harvard University.

If you try to please everyone before you're able to, **you'll end up pleasing no one**.

Reaching Your "Critical Mass"

You can do your best to estimate the moment of critical mass for your product, but a blanket approach will be tough. Most likely, you'll find that while pockets in each geographic area and user segment hit critical mass, others will basically remain untouched. Identifying the point at which this happens will be helpful as your business moves forward. (For example, this might be the point at which your user base reaches a large-enough size that when a user joins, that user already has eight friends using the product and therefore doesn't have to invite a single additional friend and has a 90 percent chance of remaining a user after thirty days.) When you reach this point, **you typically need to make a change in marketing strategy**, shifting your main efforts away from your specific market to target less saturated segments.

When this takes place, the activity of some of your users will also drive the reactivation and retention of others who would have gone dormant otherwise. These user-driven retention efforts ensure your product never uses retention tactics that feel spammy.

In other words, critical mass can help you determine **when and where is the best time to grow**. Hopefully figuring this out prevents you from dumping time, resources, and money into areas that won't provide the most bang for your buck.

Being at Scale: How to Ensure It Doesn't Eat Your Company Alive

Let's move from one vague phrase to another and talk about a concept that's used incorrectly even more often and to a greater detriment than *critical mass*—because while critical mass is misused so often when discussing growth and business strategy that it should be made illegal, not properly understanding this next term could outright kill your company.

So what did we learn is wrong with the term *critical mass*? It lacks specificity. Critical mass doesn't happen all at once, and when it happens for one group of people somewhere, it doesn't happen everywhere for everyone. It's simply a milestone in a product's growth journey that, when reached, causes the growth strategy to change.

Now, in this section, we're going to address another equally vague buzzword: **scale**.

Being at Scale Doesn't Refer to Fish Skin

If you run in circles with people who like to talk about business or startups or growth strategies, you've likely heard the word *scale* used in sentences like the following (in fact, you've probably heard me say it several times in this book):

- "We're prepping to scale."
- "You have to do things that don't scale."
- "When we're at scale, we'll need to figure that out."
- "That strategy can't scale."

The dangerous thing about it is we *think* we know what it means, and we *think* we'll know when it happens. But if I forced you to tell me **what metrics officially demonstrate being "at scale,"** what would you say?

Attaching Viable Meaning to "Scale"

As we learned in the last section, when a product reaches critical mass, this means that product has reached the minimum size required for it to work and be valuable without a user first having to recruit others to use the product. Of course, this will happen at different times for different product types, but it will be delayed if you and your team build product features that don't match your audience or, worse, don't provide value for the users you're acquiring.

Now let's see if we can nail down an understanding of scale.

A product reaches scale when it attains a size that requires **internal processes to change** in order to continue to maintain the high level of service customers have enjoyed up to that point. It's often measured in the total number of customers served.

For example, when you start a new T-shirt company, you'll likely be shipping out all new orders yourself. You package your orders, label them, drive to the post office, and drop them off.

As things start to pick up (let's say you reach one hundred sales per day), you find that you're spending so much time packaging and shipping orders that other things you need to focus on, such as customer service or ad optimization, are not receiving the attention they deserve. You decide you need to hire a new employee to focus on order fulfillment so that you can focus more on other areas.

This was a moment in your company's journey that you hit a certain scale. Your internal strategy needed to change: to maintain a high level of service, you had to hire a specialized employee for a time-consuming task.

See where I'm going with this?

To Scale or Not to Scale

Now let's go back to those two scenarios we discussed in the last section. I'll give them to you again, and this time, try to figure out which you think **has hit one or more moments of scale**.

Scenario 1:

- An online forum acquires five hundred users in Des Moines, Iowa, who actively engage with each other on a regular basis about disc golf. This discussion includes where they plan to play that week, what techniques are superior, and what outings and events are upcoming for forum members.

Scenario 2:

- An online forum with space to discuss fifty different topics acquires five hundred thousand users evenly distributed across one hundred countries. The average user is interested in one or two topics of the fifty.

This time, **the second scenario wins**.

The forum in the first scenario delivers great value for a core audience, but the overall audience size is small. Even if every user submits support requests to admins every few weeks, the overall magnitude of those requests would still likely be so small that one person could handle the volume while still spending adequate time improving the experience on the site.

However, the forum in the second scenario has five hundred thousand users. If those users interacted with support at a similar frequency, a single support person would get pummeled, and one-to-one interactions would suffer tremendously. In all likelihood, this forum would require multiple support agents to keep up with this sort of communication volume.

This means forum number two has a big problem.

How Scale Can Kill Your Company

As we've already determined, the company in the first scenario above has already hit a moment of critical mass. Because it's delivering enough value for enough of a core audience in a specific location, it has saturated the market. As a result, the company's growth strategy needs to change. However, its user volume is still pretty low. It hasn't reached a moment of scale yet, so it can still function with a smaller staff and manual processes.

The company in the second scenario has *not* hit a moment of critical mass. Its value is fragmented across one hundred different countries and fifty different topics. The market is still far from saturated, and the growth strategy doesn't need to change to compensate for that saturation. However, user volume is extremely high at five hundred thousand users, and it likely has already reached at least one or two moments of scale.

Which company do you think is about to go up in flames?

(Spoiler alert: **it's the second one.**)

Many novice (or ignorant) founders and growth engineers think that the goal of their company is to achieve a certain scale and that this will signify their success. These are what we call **vanity metrics**. They're cool to tell your mom about, but that's about all they're good for.

What most don't realize is that without reaching one (or hopefully a few) moments of critical mass *first*, **scale will eat their company alive**.

When You Should Scale

Retention is our foundational metric. It ensures that when we add "water" to our "bucket," the bucket doesn't leak. Retention comes from value, and you offer value by building a product that serves the needs of a very specific subset of users.

By first focusing on *them* and ensuring you make them happy, you can then expand bit by bit.

So **only scale** when your company can boast real growth metrics.

Eighty/Twenty Viral Marketing: Why the Growth You Get May Not Be the Growth You Need

Okay, so now we know when to scale our company and when to expand our business. But before we can achieve sustainable, healthy growth and continue to earn more money in the long run, we have to consider one last important concept.

This is it—the last step in our process before you can officially cape yourself a viral hero. Are you ready? Let's do this!

Eighty/Twenty Viral Marketing: Not All Growth Is Created Equal

When newbie growth engineers start building their viral loops, they often mistakenly set their primary KPI as something like "total users acquired" or "total unique visitors." They believe these KPIs will indicate the overall growth and health of their company. They're wrong.

In such cases, it's important to remember **the Pareto principle** (also called the eighty/twenty rule). This rule states that 80 percent of results come from 20 percent of causes. If we apply this concept to virality, we can infer that 80 percent of your business value comes from 20 percent of your users.

It's more valuable to **define a primary KPI as something like these:**

- Total ideal users acquired
- Total unique customers
- Total retained users after thirty days
- Total profitable users

These metrics imply that you're not only acquiring new users for your product but also measuring the acquisition of users who will actually drive business value and profitability.

This is the essence of **eighty/twenty viral marketing**.

When you've identified the top 20 percent of users or customers driving 80 percent of your results, you'll need to learn what makes these users so valuable—more specifically, you'll need to search for patterns, find out how they're alike, and determine the cause of those patterns to figure out why users behave the way they do.

Once you have this information, your nonviral acquisition efforts will be far more powerful. You'll now be able to better craft the context and language driving those users into your viral loop and guiding them toward inviting specific friends who fit the same pattern.

As an example, let's say you launch a restaurant reservations app in the App Store and focus first on a certain local market (say, Chicago). While your app is downloadable for users nationwide, there's very little value for users outside Chicago at this point.

It is obvious that your nonviral marketing efforts will be targeted to users within Chicago who frequently visit restaurants requiring reservations. However, what may *not* be as obvious is the best way to craft the language of your viral loop.

Encouraging Correct Targeting for Virality

In the situation above, rather than simply asking users to invite friends after they see both the core and viral value your application may offer, you'll be far better off doing the following:

- Build your viral loop so that invites are rarely sent to users who are **not ideal or who are out of market**. In the context of the above example, you might try prompting users to invite those they plan to dine with so either one of them may change the reservation if needed.

- Craft the language of your invite calls to action to **encourage more specificity**. For example, rather than saying something like, "Invite a friend, and get a five-dollar discount off your next meal for each friend who signs up," you might write, "Got dining buddies in Chicago? Get a five-dollar discount off a meal for each Chicago-based friend you invite who signs up!" This better encourages your users to invite in-market friends rather than just random people in their address books.

If your viral acquisition strategies aren't carefully built to bring you users who actually drive value for your business (i.e., eighty/twenty viral marketing), the growth you get may not be the growth you want—or need—to achieve success as an organization.

What's Next?
High five!

You've reached the end of your epic journey toward viral awesomeness. **I now cape thee a viral hero!**

What's that? You don't feel any different? That's not surprising. You can't expect virality to happen if you just sit there reading this book. You now have to get up off that chair (or better yet, fly off it!) and start putting what you've learned into practice. But don't worry—you don't have to go it alone.

To help, I've compiled a list of all the key things you'll need to remember as you're building and growing your business more effectively.

Okay, so at this point if you haven't gotten your free copy of the *Viral Hero* Workbook from viralhero.com/workbook, you're probably not going to do it. But…hang on a second. Why are you here if not to implement what you've learned? So if you're not following along, c'mon. Go make it happen! I wrote this book so you - yes, YOU - can make your company more viral. And I want to hear exactly how you're using it. So while you're at it, head over to viralhero.com/contact and drop me and my team a line.

Part 5: Viral Marketing Cheat Sheet

Chapter 17: Thirty-Five Things to Remember

1. **Viral marketing** refers to the process of a product's users "exposing" others they encounter to that product for the first time, thereby "infecting" a percentage of those new people and making them users as well. (See the introduction.)

2. **Viral engineering** is the act of strategically building a product to use virality as a significant growth lever. (*See chapter 1.*)

3. **Inherent viral marketing** is a viral engine in which a product offers *no* value unless users use it with others. A company that uses this engine well is Skype. (*See chapter 2.*)

4. **Viral communication marketing** is a viral engine in which users use the product to communicate with nonusers and by doing so expose the product to those nonusers. A company that uses this engine well is Hotmail. (*See chapter 2.*)

5. **Viral collaboration marketing** is a viral engine in which users work together using the product to achieve a common goal. A company that uses this engine well is Dropbox. (*See chapter 2.*)

6. **Open viral marketing** is a viral engine in which users distribute their products through another product (often a marketplace), driving their own users there and by doing so exposing those users to the marketplace. A company that uses this engine well is Apple. (*See chapter 2.*)

7. **Viral incentive marketing** is a viral engine in which users unlock even more value—positioned as a "payment" of sorts—from a product by inviting others to use the product as well. A company that uses this engine well is PayPal. (*See chapter 3.*)

8. **Embeddable viral marketing** is a viral engine in which users embed a product into their own products to add value for their users and by doing so expose the embedded product to their users. A company that uses this engine well is YouTube. (*See chapter 3.*)

9. **Viral signature marketing** is a viral engine in which users route the users of their own product to a completely different product as an augmentation of their own service, thereby exposing their users to that product as a result. A company that uses this engine well is Zendesk. (*See chapter 3.*)

10. **Viral transaction marketing** is a viral engine in which users share (often on social media) achievements or value they gained through use of a product, exposing their audience to that product as a vessel for that value. A company that uses this engine well is MapMyRun. (*See chapter 3.*)

11. **Viral credibility marketing** is a viral engine in which the use of a product adds to the user's credibility. Likewise, the fact that the user uses the product adds to the product's credibility. A company that uses this engine well is RED. (*See chapter 4.*)

12. **Online viral word-of-mouth marketing** is what most people assume all of viral marketing is. It results when companies strategically trigger high-arousal emotions in users to inspire and encourage "sharing," often through content creation. A company that uses this engine well is BuzzFeed. (*See chapter 4.*)

13. **Offline viral word-of-mouth marketing** is the most common viral engine and involves companies attempting to create unique, memorable, and conversation-worthy experiences that users spread through offline interactions. A company that uses this engine well is Cards Against Humanity. (*See chapter 4.*)

14. **Viral satisfaction marketing** is a "cherry on top" viral engine in which companies attempt to create over-the-top, best-in-class touch points with their users (usually via support interactions) that are so good they drive online and offline recommendations from users. A company that uses this engine well is Zappos. (*See chapter 4.*)

15. **Conversion rate optimization** is *not* just used in your sales funnel. The exact same tactics and strategies can and should be applied to all steps in your viral loop to help engineer your product for virality. (*See chapter 5*.)

16. **The foundation of all growth is value.** There are two forms of value you must pay close attention to. *Core value* is what users truly want when they purchase something, and it's what makes them stick around and purchase more often over time. *Viral value* is similar, but rather than compelling purchasing, it's what drives invite behavior (i.e., it makes users invite others, follow up on those invites, and proactively spread your product throughout their networks). (*See chapter 5*.)

17. **Your viral loop** encompasses every step in your user journey from awareness to invite action. One full loop is achieved when all steps are completed. When new users are exposed to the product, whether through invites or nonviral methods like advertising, a new loop begins. (*See chapter 6*.)

18. **Your viral carrier** is the method by which invites are sent. If your carrier is not the most obvious, intuitive, and logical way of sending invites, users will not complete viral loops as frequently. (*See chapter 6*.)

19. **Your viral branching factor** is the average number of invites a user sends for every individual invite action he or she takes, or how many others that user touches during a single viral loop. If one invite action is the trunk of a tree and each branch on that tree reaches another person, your branching factor is the average number of branches on each tree you plant. (*See chapter 6*.)

20. Your product's **hook point** is the "Aha!" moment when users realize your product's value, after which they're far more likely to be retained. Your **viral hook point** is another "Aha!" moment, when your users realize your product's *viral* value is something they want. (*See chapter 6.*)

21. The Fogg Behavioral Model (**Behavior = Motivation + Ability + Trigger**) is a great rule of thumb to structure the process of both sending and accepting invites. Users must have a clear motivation to take action, you must give them a simple and frictionless path for doing so, and you must create some sort of signal that tells them that now is the time to take that action. (*See chapter 6.*)

22. A **viral invite** is a user's act of sending an individual invite to a friend to expose your product or service to that friend after the user has reached a viral hook point. This moment signifies **the end of a viral loop**. (*See chapter 7.*)

23. **Your viral message** is the default message you prompt users to send as a viral invite. While some loops allow for customization of this message, others are curated by the company and can't be changed. (*See chapter 7.*)

24. **Your viral media** is typically a piece of content that offers a use case or demo of your product and thereby exposes others to your product when shared by a user. An example of viral media is a video shared via YouTube. While many people assume that the video is what spreads virally, it's actually YouTube itself that's experiencing viral growth. The video, or the media, simply allows the company to spread its player to prospects or to dormant users to

reactivate them. (*See chapter 7.*)

25. **Viral conversion** describes the act of accepting an invite that has been sent. In other words, if User A sends an invite to User B, the viral conversion does not take place unless User B actually accepts that invite and signs up (i.e., becomes a lead) to seek more information. (*See chapter 7.*)

26. **Your viral marketing funnel** is a more familiar way of visualizing your viral loop. It represents your viral loop in a linear fashion and is similar to a sales funnel. Visualizing your viral loop in this way can make it easier to adopt third-party tools for optimization reasons. (*See chapter 8.*)

27. **Your viral factor**, commonly referred to as *K*, is a measure of potential viral magnitude. While it's an essential viral metric, it can't project viral growth over time by itself as it does not factor time into its calculation. (*See chapter 8.*)

28. **Your viral amplification factor**, often referred to as *A*, is a more common and practical KPI than *K*. It indicates the total users you can expect to acquire for every user you acquire from nonviral means after viral marketing does its job. Ninety-nine percent of companies should use *A* instead of *K* as it will be far more practical. (*See chapter 8.*)

29. **Viral cycle time** is the granddaddy of all viral metrics and is the exponent in the viral-growth-projection equation. The optimization of this metric will drive far more growth than the optimization of any other viral KPI. (*See chapter 8.*)

30. **Retention is the foundation of all growth**, viral or otherwise. No matter how quickly you fill your "bucket," the amount of "water" it holds will not increase if the holes in your bucket leak as much or more water than you're pouring in. (*See chapter 14.*)

31. **All acquisition methods are network dependent**, meaning your addressable market is not infinite and will often change rapidly due to factors both in and out of your control. Don't assume the growth rate you have today can always be increased through a simple marketing spend or will even remain available at its current rate if you maintain the budget you currently have. (*See chapter 14.*)

32. Without continually addressing your churn rate, you *will* reach a point at which your growth rate equals your churn rate. This is called **your carrying capacity** and is the moment at which your growth levels off. (*See chapter 14.*)

33. If you neglect retention efforts and instead hit your carrying capacity and **network saturation** (the reduction of availability of new leads into your funnel), you'll experience reverse growth. This can be fatal for your company. (*See chapter 14.*)

34. Just as there's a moment in your user journey called a **hook point** after which users will remain users forever, there's also a moment in the same journey called **user death**. If reached, this is the point at which users leave and never return. It's your job as a growth engineer to identify both moments, then build your product to encourage the first while avoiding the second. (*See chapter 15.*)

35. Viral growth, no matter how profound, is next to worthless without the ability to **connect virality to profitability**. At the end of the day, you're running a business, and your viral loop is simply a tool with which you can grow that business faster and more cost effectively. (*See chapter 16.*)

I encourage you to review this viral marketing cheat sheet periodically to ensure that your business is on the right track and that you've thought through everything you're doing to build and grow more effectively.

A Final Message

Thanks for taking this journey with me. I hope you now have a better understanding of viral marketing as a whole.

Of course, this isn't the end of your adventure; in fact, it's just the beginning. As you move forward and apply what you've learned here, be sure to come back and reread pertinent chapters to brush up on your skills. In no time, you'll be well on your way to achieving viral success.

Until then, good luck and viral speed.

Glossary of Acronyms and Mathematical Variables

A	The variable representing the amplification factor, which is used instead of *K* when a product or service does not have a *K* factor above 1
AARRR	Acquisition, activation, retention, referral, and revenue
A/B	A form of testing that pits an *A* version against a *B* version to find the top-performing version
Aconv%	A conversion rate that factors in network saturation, making it a more accurate variable for predicting the impact of a viral loop over time
Af	The variable representing addiction factor

AMA	A community event called "ask me anything," usually involving a notable figure or expert in a field
Au	The variable representing the total number of activated users
B2B	Business-to-business, or a business that sells products or services to other businesses
B2C	Business-to-customer, or a business that sells products or services directly to consumers
C4R	Cash for rewards
c	The variable representing the average daily churn rate

CC	Carrying capacity
CDC	Centers for Disease Control and Prevention
conv%	The variable representing the conversion rate of invited friends becoming users
ct	The variable representing cycle time, or the time between the moment a prospect receives an invite to the moment that person sends his or her own invite
CTA	Call to action
CTR	Click-through rate
Df	The variable representing "death" factor

Du	The variable representing the total number of "dead" users
g	The variable representing the average daily non-viral-customer-acquisition rate
i	The variable representing the average number of invites each user sends to friends
K	The variable representing viral factor
K'	The variable representing "lifetime" viral factor, or the average virality you can expect from a single user over his or her "life" with you
KPI	Key performance indicator

micro-KPI A smaller key performance indicator that, together with other micro-KPIs, makes up a full KPI

nm The variable representing nonviral marketing

nm(t) The variable representing the number of users that nonviral marketing will yield within a certain number of days (represented by *t*)

Nu The variable representing the total number of new users acquired (both nonvirally and virally)

PPC Pay-per-click

QA Quality assurance

ROI Return on investment

SaaS	Software as a service, or a type of business that uses software to automate a service previously done by a human workforce
SEM	Search engine marketing
SEO	Search engine optimization
u(0)	The variable representing the number of users at the beginning of a specific period of time
UI	User interface
u(t)	The variable representing the number of users after a certain number of days (represented by *t*)

UX	User experience
VC	Venture capitalist

Bibliography

Chen, A. "Facebook Viral Marketing: When and Why Do Apps "Jump the Shark"?" AndrewChen.co. 2011. http://andrewchen.co/facebook-viral-marketing-when-and-why-do-apps-jump-the-shark/.

———. "What's Your Viral Loop? Understanding the Engine of Adoption." AndrewChen.co. 2011. http://andrewchen.co/whats-your-viral-loop-understanding-the-engine-of-adoption/.

Conversion Rate Experts (blog). Conversion-rate-experts.com. https://conversion-rate-experts.com/articles/.

ConversionXL (blog). Conversionxl.com. https://conversionxl.com/blog/.

Ellis, Sean. "Using Survey.io." Startup-marketing.com. http://www.startup-marketing.com/using-survey-io/#.

Eyal, Nir. *Hooked: How to Build Habit-Forming Products*. New York: Portfolio, 2014.

Godin, Seth. *Purple Cow*. New ed. New York: Portfolio, 2009.

Greenland, Sander, Timothy L. Lash, and Kenneth J. Rothman. *Modern Epidemiology*. Third ed. Philadelphia: Lippincott Williams & Wilkins, 2008.

Krempels, Dana, PhD. "*Why* Spay or Neuter My Rabbit? Some Scary Numbers . . ." H.A.R.E., University of Miami. 2006. http://www.bio.miami.edu/hare/scary.html.

Lawler, K. "A Virality Formula." KevinLawler.com. December 29, 2011. https://kevinlawler.com/viral.

Mares, Justin, and Gabriel Weinberg. *Traction: How Any Startup Can Achieve Explosive Customer Growth.* New York: Portfolio, 2015.

Masters, Blake, and Peter Thiel. *Zero to One: Notes on Startups, or How to Build the Future.* New York: Crown Business, 2014.

Nash, A. "User Acquisition: Viral Factor Basics." AdamNash.blog. April 4, 2012. https://adamnash.blog/2012/04/04/user-acquisition-viral-factor-basics/.

Ries, Eric. *The Lean Startup.* New York: Crown Business, 2011.

Rothman, Kenneth J. *Epidemiology: An Introduction.* New York: Oxford University Press, Inc., 2012.

Schmilovici, U. "Eight Ways to Go Viral." TechCrunch. December 27, 2011. https://techcrunch.com/2011/12/26/eight-ways-go-viral/.

Silver, Nate. *The Signal and the Noise: Why So Many Predictions Fail—but Some Don't.* New York: Penguin Books, 2015.

Skok, D. "Lessons Learned—Viral Marketing." ForEntrepreneurs. 2017. https://www.forentrepreneurs.com/lessons-learnt-viral-marketing/.

———. "The Science behind Viral Marketing." ForEntrepreneurs. 2011. https://www.forentrepreneurs.com/the-science-behind-viral-marketing/.

Unbounce (blog). Unbounce.com. https://unbounce.com/blog/.

Vohra, R. "How to Model Viral Growth." LinkedIn. October 12, 2012. https://www.linkedin.com/pulse/20121002124206-18876785-how-to-model-viral-growth-the-hybrid-model/.

Wilson, R. "The Six Simple Principles of Viral Marketing." PracticalEcommerce. May 5, 2018. https://www.practicalecommerce.com/viral-principles.

Made in the USA
Columbia, SC
04 August 2020

15584425R00235